POLITICAL IDEOLOGIES

Second Edition

D0809215

POLITICAL IDEOLOGIES

An Australian Introduction
Second Edition

Robert Leach
Queensland University of Technology

M

First published 1988
This edition published 1993
MACMILLAN EDUCATION AUSTRALIA PTY LTD
107 Moray Street, South Melbourne 3205
6 Clarke Street, Crows Nest 2065

Associated companies and representatives
throughout the world

National Library of Australia
cataloguing in publication data

Leach, Robert, 1940–
    Political ideologies.

    2nd ed.
    Includes bibliographies and index.
    ISBN 0 7329 2002 7.
    ISBN 0 7329 2001 9 (pbk.).

    1. Political science. 2. Ideology. I. Title.

320.5

Cover design by Richard Pieremont
Set in 10/11 pt Palatino by Typeset Gallery Sdn. Bhd. Malaysia
Printed in Hong Kong

Contents

INTRODUCTION   1
Political Spectrum Model   1
Criticisms of the Model   2
Approaches to Politics   4
The Normative Role of Political Ideologies   4
The Changing Nature of the Ideological Response to the Political
   Problem   7
Outline of the Structure of this Book   13

1. FASCISM/NAZISM   16
Origins of Fascism   16
Italian Fascism   23
German Fascism: Nazism   27
Contemporary Fascist Trends   33
Fascism in Australia   39

2. CONSERVATISM   46
Origins   50
European Conservatism   54
Contemporary Trends: The New Right   56
Contemporary Conservatism in Australia: The New Right   67

3. LIBERALISM   78
Origins   83
Classic Liberalism   84
State Liberalism   87
Contemporary Liberalism: The Liberal Welfare State and
   Left/Right Critiques   93
The Keynesian Economic Revolution   94
Critiques of Liberalism   98
Liberalism in Australia   101

4. DEMOCRATIC SOCIALISM   114
Origins   115
The Utopian State of Socialism: 1800–48   117
Marxist Ideological Domination: 1848–90   119
The Triumph of Revisionism: the Rejection of Marx:
   1890–1954   121
The Welfare State Ideology: Liberal/Social Democratic
   Consensus, 1945–80   124
Contemporary Social Democracy   127
Social Democratic Inheritances   127
Major Contemporary Political Designs Emerging Within a Social
   Democracy   130
Social Democracy in Australia   137
External Dependency and the Role of the State in Internal
   Change   139
A Summary of Social Democracy   147

5. COMMUNISM   153
What is Communism?   154
Marx and Engels   157
A Summary of Communist Theory   168
Contemporary Communism   168
Communism in Power: The Problem of the Party   174
Australian Communism   182

6. ANARCHISM   195
Origins   199
Anarcho-Syndicalism   204
Contemporary Anarchism   205
Anarchism in Australia   207

7. CROSS-SPECTRUM IDEOLOGIES   214
Imperialism   214
Racism   225
Feminism   229
The Green Movement   234

Index   244

Introduction

This book is an introduction to political ideologies. It is meant to provide a basic theoretical understanding of the origins, basic tenets and values of the major modern political ideologies. Some orientation towards the contemporary ideological scene and the Australian context will be given for the beginner at secondary and tertiary levels.

The text will aim at familiarising the reader with contemporary political concepts and the importance of the Left/Centre/Right model of political ideologies underlying much media usage and public political debate.

Political Spectrum Model

The underlying model for the text is the classic 'political spectrum':

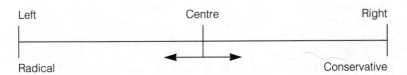

This model has been used as a basic tool of politics since the French Revolution of 1789. Its underlying assumptions are:

1 There is constant social or political progress initiated by the Left and opposed by the Right, even if this is often marked by temporary reversals.
2 This progress is marked by the increasing material betterment of the masses of the people.
3 The centre moderates the desire for change of the radical and the opposition to change of the conservative.
4 Industrialism is a good thing as it provides the material basis for this progress.
5 Politics is mainly about the struggle for an increasing share of this material base and/or the increasing freedom of the individual.
6 This Left/Right struggle is translated into a power relationship which has both an individualistic and a collective face.

The model always assumes a dynamism implicit in these ideologies which can stir people into action. The spectrum is constantly in flux, so that today's radical position may be tomorrow's conservative one.

Ideologies are thus defined as tools which give first, 'a set of comprehensive explanations and principles about the world'. Second, 'they provide a program of political and social action presented in general terms'. Third, there is 'an idea of struggle in carrying out the program'. Last, there is 'a sense of commitment by its adherents'.[1]

Criticisms of the Model

Many criticisms of this model have emerged since the 'end of ideology' arguments of the 1950s.[2] These include:

1 *Industrialisation underlies the ideology of movements of both the Left and Right.* This has produced a similar dominant group of managers, or a technocracy, wedded to growth and 'efficiency' rather than the traditional slogans of the Left or Right. The Left/Right spectrum is meaningless in the face of such technocracy. These managers are interchangeable.

2 *The Left/Right duality has produced a false split in the political and social order.*[3] The Left pursues collectivism, or the good of the many, while the Right pursues *individualism*, or the freedom of each person. But this duality is misleading. 'Left' and 'Right' are abstractions with no true existence. They stem from the dualism of Greek Platonic thought dividing all nature into opposites such as 'night/day' or 'vice/virtue'. But all mankind is one.

This 'Left/Right' duality is unsound[4] as it encourages violence to overcome what seem mutually exclusive poles.

3 *The Left/Right duality is of European cultural origin.* It stresses European modes of looking at the world and the underlying European approval of industrialisation and conquering the earth, rather than living in harmony with it. The political spectrum is all about 'growth'. Political ideologies are measured as successes if a rise in the standard of living is achieved.

For increasing numbers, this spectrum traps mankind into one mode of approach to the earth which is ultimately disastrous, even for Marxist societies which supposedly offer an alternative:

> I do not believe that capitalism itself is really responsible for the situation in which [American Indians] have been

declared a national sacrifice. No it is the European tradition. European culture is itself responsible. Marxism is just the latest continuation of this tradition not a solution to it. There is another way ... it is the way that knows that humans do not have the right to degrade the Mother Earth; that there are forces beyond anything the European mind has conceived; that humans must be in harmony with all relations or the relations will eventually eliminate the disharmony. All European tradition, Marxism included, has conspired to defy the natural order of things ... Mother Earth will retaliate, the whole environment will retaliate and the abusers will be eliminated. Things come full circle. Back to where it started. That's revolution.[5]

4 *The Left/Right spectrum reflects the Judaic/Christian European heritage of the Children of Light versus the Children of Darkness.* Hidden under this political spectrum is a parallel ontological (common assumptions for all participants) tradition of dividing the world into moral villains versus the enlightened. This struggle, in Western religious or moral terms, is eternal. Politics, when affected by this underlying religious outlook, becomes the abode of righteousness and fanaticism.

This, however, lends a dynamism to Western politics. Each epoch has its own battle of ideas concerning the superior path to development. (This 'path' can be called an ideology.) This domination gives temporary hegemony to the reigning ideology. The Left/Right spectrum simply represents a psychological divergence amongst people of Western culture which is unavoidable given the religious and cultural demands for 'either/or' solutions to problems of existence.

These criticisms will not, however, affect the usage of the political spectrum model in this book. The model reflects the common usage given in the media and everyday speech to the terms Left and Right. In an introductory text, it is essential to outline such common usage.

The book will therefore follow this common usage through chapters explaining the *Right* (fascism, conservatism and liberalism) and subsequent chapters explaining the *Left* (democratic socialism, communism and anarchism). Students will be given basic knowledge of these ideologies and their historical origins. Subsequently, questions of ecology, the impact of imperialism, racism and feminism will be examined, in a concluding chapter on cross-spectrum ideologies. This name has been chosen to indicate that these ideologies are in the process of affecting and re-aligning much of the traditional Left/Right spectrum, even if people are still largely locked into the basic belief that the

Left/Right spectrum is simply a confrontation between capitalism and communism as economic systems. New questions created by these cross-spectrum ideologies, such as the role of women, are constantly arising.

Approaches to Politics

Why choose political ideologies, or 'the science of political ideas' as an area of study? As Banks points out,[6] there are four ways to study politics. We can take a *normative* approach which focuses on the ideas or principles (norms) emanating from great philosophers such as Locke or Marx. We can take a *legal-institutional* approach which focuses on constitutions and structures of government. We can study how political actors operate using a *behaviourist* approach, where we study the role and actions of politicians and others involved in influencing opinions and individual decision making. Lastly, we can study *systems*, an approach which focuses on organised political behaviour, such as what occurs in political parties or social movements, and assesses their effectiveness.

Ideologies stem largely from the normative approach although they have to adapt to the realities of the system and its structural imperatives. This book studies ideologies on the basis that theory and practice are a unity, and that all four approaches are valid. But in order to understand politics, the student must first come to grips with modern ideologies in their normative role.

The Normative Role of Political Ideologies

Most ideologies have a common normative theme in that they believe politics are the key to social change. Since the Enlightenment of the seventeenth century and the Industrial Revolution which began in eighteenth century Britain, political ideologies have competed with religion, while drawing on elements of it, such as its ethical framework, in order to provide an interpretation of 'how' and 'why' the world works.

Such ideologies have defined how the world 'ought' to be for their believers. This acts as a measurement against how the world 'is'. They therefore provide a constant critique of individual and social action.

The possession of such ideologies acts as a spur to action for change or counter-action to retain the status quo. Mass movements possessing such ideologies have been driving forces for change or reaction to such change since the American and

French Revolutions. In a sense, political ideologies are a secular religion or 'form of ethical life'. All political ideologies thus contain:

1 a set of comprehensive explanations and principles dealing with the world, man and experience;
2 a program of political and social action presented in general terms;
3 an idea of struggle to carry out the program;
4 a sense of commitment by its adherents.[7]

Many political ideologies may exist side by side in the same national culture. For a society to be cohesive, however, and to avoid possible polarisation which could lead to violence between contending ideological views of the world, a dominant view tends to be held, consciously or unconsciously, by the majority of citizens. This is the middle ground so avidly pursued by political parties in, (for example) Western parliamentary-type democracies, such as Britain or Australia. Initially, however, this political ideology may have been imposed by force by a dominant group which captured the state in a revolutionary situation, as in the American Revolution. Presented to society in the form of charters, ideas and institutions, the new ideology slowly becomes acceptable to succeeding generations.

Even so, there may exist different groups within society which do not totally or partially accept the dominant ideology. Such groups may represent residual ideological thinking from previous ruling ideologies, or they may represent emerging ideas about the course or nature of society. In Western parliamentary democracies these groups can be represented on the extremes of the Left/Right spectrum model. This assumes that a range of ideologies exist in society, especially liberal democratic pluralist societies where many ideas, movements or parties may compete for popular support. These ideologies range from Right (conservative) views on the questions of the universal political problem to Left (radical) ones. The model also assumes an implicit dynamic: today's radicalism may be tomorrow's conservatism.

The Political Problem

All societies have to provide answers both in theory and practice to the political problem. This problem poses the questions of what resources will be divided up; how decision making might be undertaken; who will share in the decision making, and who will be excluded. Will the problem be best solved by giving the power of decision making to a single person (dictatorship) or king (monarchy), to a small group of ruling families or people (oligarchy) or the rich (plutocracy), or to a priesthood (theocracy)? Will it be solved best by letting all the people share in political decision making (democracy) or by allowing a small élite of experts (technocracy) or the more intelligent (meritocracy) to rule for them?

Endless variations of government structures have evolved to answer the political problem, particularly as it involves (amongst others) questions of justice, equality, liberty, rights and duties, and power and morality. Most such government structures therefore have to resort to ideologies with their norms and long-term aims in order to rationalise their existence. Some examples of this link with ideology are as follows:

Ideology and Justice

Ideology must rationalise the distribution of wealth and power to the few or the many. It must justify the exclusive or inclusive nature of the regime, e.g. are people to be excluded by virtue of race, sex, class or wealth?

Ideology and Morality

Ideology must rationalise its stand on morality by outlining a basic perspective on human nature. This justifies a coercive or personal mode of morality and the role of the state in the area of morality. The whole question of humankind being formed by *nature* (personality is formed at birth) or by *nurture* (personality is formed by society) underlies this.

Ideology and Liberty

Ideology must incorporate answers to the limits of individual versus collective liberty. The tension between collectivity and individuality as well as the abstract notion of citizenship is the basis of the code of individual rights and duties and the limits of the state, particularly in liberal democracies.

Various countries will answer the questions of the political problem from alternative perspectives. This will be due to differences of historical development; the economic system in power; the pre-eminent social values; the concentration of internal power; and the world power position of the country involved.

While these factors are not spread evenly from country to country, nevertheless the questions that ideologies must answer are universal.

The Changing Nature of the Ideological Response to the Political Problem

The political question applies to every society and each generation. Questions reach from the world situation down to that of the basic level of human organisation, the family. Power distribution, institutional values and negotiation over power exist in small groups as well as at more complex levels of human political organisation, such as the nation.

The period of ideological response to the questions of the political problem really begins with the Industrial Revolution in Europe in the eighteenth century. This revolution, along with its governing values and ethic, has spread to the ends of the earth. As Immanuel Wallerstein[8] argues, we have now one world system, an outgrowth of the spread of European economics and ideas in the sixteenth century.

As mentioned, the development/industrial ethic lies at the basis of most European-derived contemporary ideologies. Almost all countries throughout the world argue in terms of these adopted and adapted ideologies. The developmental/industrial ethic is not questioned in most ideologies, except perhaps for anarchism and the recently emergent Green/environmentalist, anti-industrial thought. The real argument is over distribution of the spoils of growth.

Progress is universally thought to be an outcome of economic growth. Government is thought to be fundamentally involved in this process, negatively or positively. The state has a mission. Rather than simply regulating human activities, as in pre-industrial society, the state has to direct and aim human activities onto a clear and dynamic path. Growth is 'good'.

Ideologies outline and light this clear and dynamic path. But how did human society come to be obsessed with the notion of material growth?

Pre-seventeenth century ideologies covering the role of politics, the state and society stress a harmonious world, as in Plato's *Republic* and More's *Utopia*, where the prince is a strong ruler, 'the foundation of the walls protecting his people' (see Machiavelli's *The Prince*). The basic emphasis of pre-industrial ideologies was on order, civic virtue and security, on institutional permanency (such as monarchy) and organic harmony, rather than change. The order of the universe was represented in the person of great sovereigns. Hierarchy, power and obedience were central to these themes. True political ideologies emphasising change, justice, liberty and equality began with the Age of the Common Man and industrialism: the eighteenth century.

The arrival of democracy allied to the industrial ethic has been the driving power behind the formation of modern ideologies. To understand this process requires a short outline of Western development.

Pre-Industrial Society: The Ancient World

The great empires of the ancient world were wealthy but static societies. The three great empires, Egypt, Greece and Rome, were basically peasant agricultural economies. Surplus production was minimal in these pre-technical societies. Land was the basic source of wealth. Cities were largely commercial rather than industrial centres. What industry did exist was in the form of easily transportable consumer goods. Due to the limits of transport, trade often became regionalised, especially in the later stages of the Roman Empire.

The emphasis of political culture was always upon the unity of the state, society and the citizen. While freedom did exist in certain forms for the citizens of Greece and Rome, the political mode in Egypt was always towards the God-King sovereign. Such trends also emerged in Rome and Greece.

While the age of Greek and Roman democracy was constantly held up as a 'Golden Age', the actual political movement within the ancient world by the time of the empires was always towards the loss of rights and a God-King command economy in a militarised society. Kautsky[9] argues that this was due to the slave economy of such societies. The free peasant and worker became superfluous to them due to the use of slaves who cost less. But while the free peasants and workers were superfluous to the economy, they were not superfluous to politics. In Rome, the rich vied for their free citizens' civic favour through massive expenditures in the pursuit of the republican myth of Roman democracy. These expenditures were not derived from growth, but from tributes extorted from the Roman provinces.

Eventually, these tributes, along with massive militarisation, land concentration and civic alienation due to the arbitrariness of tyrants, led to the impoverishment of the Empire. Rome declined before it fell. It looked backward politically. The notion of 'progress' did not exist.

The eternal political questions that arise here are: Can an excluded and alienated citizenry be called to carry out collective duties if they lack individual shares in wealth? Can a 'republic' succeed without growth? (This is a particularly important contemporary question, with the emergence of dual labour economies of well-paid and low-paid workers, and future ecological demands for a slow-down in growth.) Other questions include:

Who will bear the cuts in shares of growth? Who will be excluded?

Feudal Europe

The transition of the late Roman *latifundia* (or large land-holdings) system into the feudal one was a natural step for an empire in decline. The power of the landowners had already been underscored by the movement of political power in a slave economy to rich commercial city families and large provincial landholders. The late Roman Empire shifted more and more political responsibility to such groups, especially the landowners, as the bankruptcy of the towns, the decline of population and the invasion of barbarian tribes became problems.

Social and economic life revolved more and more around the manor. Political reality was soon to follow, attended by political ideology. Peasant farmers, whether small landholders or land-less labourers, placed themselves under manorial protection. An ideology of mutual obligation grew up, 'reaching up to the King'. The political objective of such a society was order and security. The major ideological emphasis of the political values of feudalism was security and hierarchy.

The feudal world was a dark place made worse by ignorance. Plague and dynastic wars were constant, but at least the world was simply defined and understood. The natural order of things was hierarchical, something the mediaeval church reinforced. The rebel was the darkest criminal, identified with Lucifer, who had attempted to overturn the natural order. A good monarch who attained domestic prosperity and peace and foreign respect was the sun for his people.

The Middle Ages were, however, the birthplace of the utopian pursuit. The Christian message outlined a great moral path for man which could be achieved by an act of will, through pursuing a moral path in secular life. From Augustine and his 'City of God' begins the ideological notion of what 'ought' to be as a measure of what 'is'. What 'ought' to be is the moral measure-ment all men should use to guide their actions in secular life.

While it is true that pre-Christian groups such as Spartacus and Hesiod also stressed a Golden Age, theirs was a nostalgic belief, looking backwards to a 'City of the Sun', from which they had fallen. Christianity pointed the way forward.

Mediaeval Christianity created a dual order of political culture, the struggle of Popes and Kings ending in a truce. The notion of 'two swords' emerged — a dual universe of the secular and religious world. The world of unified power and order, inherited from Rome, was rent by this revolutionary notion. Later rebels, heretics and ideologies were able to argue for their position quite logically by appealing to a higher set of values than the ones they were challenging in the practice of the state. They could appeal to God's 'natural' law.

Implicitly, this duality, in the tradition of the Children of Light versus the Children of Darkness, proclaimed that man had a duty, if not a right, to speak out against an immoral system, one that was against God's moral order.

It would not be long, of course, before such judgements on a secular world would require an outline of how such a world 'ought' to be. If an individual could not exist uncontaminated in an evil world, it was his duty to change that world for the 'better'. The age of Ideology was about to be born.

The Age of the Common Man and Industrial Society

The end of feudalism and the rule of monarchs was a long-drawn-out process. Many factors caused their decline.

Initially, the power of monarchs increased through a class alliance of monarch and merchants against the power of the landed aristocracy. This process varied across Europe but the general trend was towards the breakdown of manorial *political* power, the rise of urban *commercial* power and the increasing fluidity of internal trade, labour and the price of land. The market system began to dominate the European economy. This meant a decline in hereditary rights and traditional modes of thought.

No system declines without a rearguard action. Classes and groups in decline will always mount a defence of privilege or advantage under the guise of some ideological set of values.

Europe was wracked, therefore, by the great religious wars of the sixteenth and seventeenth centuries. The emerging ideas of the Enlightenment and the Reformation were locked in battle with the ideals of the Catholic Counter-Reformation. The increasing secularisation and fluidity of life meant an alternative emphasis upon the common man. The humanism of the Enlightenment fell upon increasingly responsive ears as men searched for means to articulate their protests against privilege, and the obstacles to their advancement.

The state, particularly in Protestant countries, quickly learnt to remove itself from the realm of individual conscience. Increasingly, the monarchs of such states found their compensation in the aggrandisement of their secular power through the partnership of state and commerce. The system of mercantilism, the united effort of state and commerce in building the nation's wealth and hence political power, flourished. In such countries as England this meant the ordering of national goals towards the increase of secular power. Such power was no longer dynastic, since such a form had no link with the notion of growth. The new mercantile growth was measured by external colonies and captive markets. Internally, it meant the increase of industry and the demolition of the old barriers of class, privilege and attendant political power. The lords declined, or joined for survival with the merchants. The commercial classes approached the throne of political power by the electoral system or through influence. From the time of Adam Smith (see *The Wealth of Nations*) onwards, political power and the notion of growth are intertwined.

Political ideologies, drawing from humanism, Christianity and notions of the free market were soon to make their appearance. English *liberalism* spoke of the role of the state and society in terms of the market (see Locke's *The Social Contract*). A contract broken was the end of the deal between citizens and the state. Implicit equality was assumed between state and citizen. If the state broke the contract, natural rights upon which individual liberty rested would allow the citizen the right to rebel.

Liberalism everywhere followed a similar path. It destroyed hereditary right or adapted it. It produced social mobility and an ideology of society based upon rationality and scientific development. Unlike the Roman age, the new liberal democratic order did not look back to a golden one, but forward to an age of increasing plenty and common wealth. It looked forward to growth.

The ideology of liberalism was the first to outline in some detail the rationale for its economic existence. It also was the first to use slogans such as 'equality' and 'liberty' to rouse its defenders. In its conflict with kings, this meant that it also aroused its opponents to follow suit. Conservatism as an ideology was created in response to the challenge of liberalism throughout the eighteenth and nineteenth centuries.

Increasingly, too, liberalism was to call for support from the individual workers and urban poor that its own commercial and manufacturing system had created. These new groups were seen as democratic allies by the merchant liberals in a world-wide struggle against the forces of conservatism.

Throughout the nineteenth century, the appeal of liberalism as an ideology to such working groups grew less and less. Working class interests obviously differed. A working class must have its own ideology. By the end of the nineteenth century *socialism* had emerged, as a world-wide ideology, with a differing rationale and national characteristics.

The Twentieth Century

The impact of these ideologies upon various national societies was necessarily uneven. The political problem was always approached through a filter of nationalism. The new power grouping of the state, capital and labour focused ideological thinking according to the uneven social and class development of the nation. For instance, German liberalism was weak, as it was drawn into a state dominated by aristocratic hierarchy, militarism and conservative romantic nationalism, full of notions of race.

American liberalism was strong. It fought the Revolution of 1776. It struck a bargain with the landed conservatives via its constitution. In this document and in American institutions, liberalism became the dominant ideology, setting the parameters for discussion. In such a dominant ideological system, socialist thought and action had to adapt to liberalism or die.

By the middle of the twentieth century, the world was divided between two contesting major ideologies, liberalism and socialism. These differed ideologically on the political problem, and were shaped by local nationalism and authoritarianism. Both shared, however, the ideological aims of progress, via growth, towards a future of plenty. The industrial ethos was unquestioned. The argument was over which class — the merchants and their allies or the workers and their allies — would remake the world.

The late twentieth century, however, has seen the emergence of ideologies questioning the very basis of these industrial ideologies and also the crisis and collapse of European communism as an industrialising rival to capitalism.

Such issues as the atom bomb, the environmental effects of rampant industrial growth, and the questioning of seemingly meaningless consumption, for example, have seen the rise of *Green ideologies*, particularly in European settings. Growth has become a question of 'growth for what'?[10]

The Enlightenment stress upon individual worth and equality has not been lost upon those concerned with the politics of gender. The rise of *feminism* in the latter half of the twentieth century is a natural outcome of the path of liberalism. Gender politics is one of the most important ideologies of post-industrial society. Whether, however, it stands alone or as an adjunct to liberal, socialist or conservative ideology is increasingly a focus for contemporary ideological debate.

Lastly, the impact of *democracy*, unleashed particularly by the French Revolution, has not gone unnoticed. The ideological belief that democracy must be applied to all situations of group political power, has re-emerged, particularly in Eastern Europe with consequent problems for those wishing to re-introduce capitalism in the former Soviet bloc. The belief increasingly grows in such countries that the industrial ethos, and the struggle of capitalism and socialism, has resulted in a loss to both capitalist and worker. The capitalist has been overthrown to be replaced, more perniciously, by the bureaucrat. The new middle class public service technocrat has inherited the earth. The state has swallowed society.[11]

Anarchist and anarcho/syndicalist ideas of workers' power democracy based upon occupations and workers' councils[12] have re-emerged in Eastern European and Latin American societies. The 'end of ideology', as prophesied by Bell and so many political scientists in the post-war period,[13] is nowhere in sight.

Outline of the Structure of this Book

This book will aim at a short outline of several contemporary ideologies. These will be discussed in terms of their origins, basic theories and beliefs, and contemporary trends. The outline will begin from the so-called far Right ideologies, will move through the moderate liberal and socialist centrist ideologies (as depicted in relation to the political spectrum model), to a discussion of so-called far Left ideologies such as communism and anarchism.

In conclusion, there will be short sections dealing with imperialism, racism, feminism, and environmentalism or Green politics. They will be included but given no specific position on the political spectrum outlined below, as they are cross-spectrum ideologies.

Political Spectrum Model with Ideologies according to Chapter

Left			Centre		Right
6	5	4	3	2	1
Anarchism	Communism	Democratic Socialism	Liberalism	Conservatism	Fascism

Notes

1. 'Ideologies', Brief 20, *The Economist*. London, 1970, p. 5.
2. Bell, D. *The End of Ideology*. UK, Collier Books, 1970.
3. Hoey, I. 'The Assumptions made in Articles on "Radical Culture"' *Social Alternatives* 5 (2) 1986, pp. 6–8.
4. Hoey, p. 8.
5. Means, Russell, Excerpt from an address given in 1980 at Black Hills Alliance Survival Gathering, as quoted in Rankin, W. and Croall, S. *Ecology for Beginners*. NY, Pantheon Books, 1981.
6. Banks, J.A. *Teaching Strategies for the Social Studies*. Addison-Wesley, USA, 1977, pp. 331–37.
7. Brief 20, *The Economist*.
8. Wallerstein, Immanuel *The Modern World System*, NY, Academic Press, 1974.
9. Kautsky, K 'Slave Society in Imperial Rome', from *Foundations of Christianity*. Sydney, Current Book Distributors, 1938.
10. Bahro, R. *The Alternative in Eastern Europe*. UK, New Left Books, 1979.
11. Kuron, J. 'An Open Letter to the Party' *New Politics* 5 (2) 1965.
12. Heller, A 'The Great Republic', *Praxis*, August 1985.
13. Bell, D. *The End of Ideology*. UK, Collier Books, 1970.

References

Bahro, R. *The Alternative in Eastern Europe*. UK, New Left Books, 1979.
Banks, J.A. *Teaching Strategies for the Social Studies* Second Edition. USA, Addison-Wesley, 1977.
Barratt Brown, M. *Models in Political Economy*, UK, Penguin, 1984.
Bell, D. *The End of Ideology*. UK, Collier Books, 1970.
Cohen, G. *Karl Marx's Theory of History: A Defense*. UK, Oxford University Press, 1979.
Gamble, A. An *Introduction to Modern Social and Political Thought*. UK, Macmillan, 1981.
Hall, S. 'The Problems of Ideology' in Matthews, B. (ed.) *Marx: A Hundred Years On*. UK, Lawrence and Wishart, 1983.
Heller, A. 'The Great Republic' *Praxis* 5 (1) April 1985, pp. 23–25.
Hoey, I. 'The Assumptions made in articles on "Radical Culture"' *Social Alternatives* 5 (2) 1986.
'Ideologies', Brief 20, *The Economist*. London, 1970.
Kautsky K. 'Slave Society in Imperial Rome' *Foundations of Christianity*. Sydney, Current Book Distributors, 1938.
Kuron, J. 'An Open Letter to the Party' *New Politics*, 5 (2) NY, 1965.
Nettl, J. 'Ideas, Intellectuals and Structures of Dissent' in P. Rieff (Ed.) *On Intellectuals*, Doubledry Anchor, New York, 1970.
Preston, N.S. *Politics, Economics and Power: Ideology and Practice under Capitalism, Socialism and Fascism*. London, Macmillan, 1967.
Sargent, L.T. *Contemporary Political Ideologies*. Illinois, Dorsey Press, 1969.
Shklar, J. (ed.) *Political Theory and Ideology*. Macmillan, NY, 1966.
Wallerstein, I. *The Modern World System*. NY, Academic Press, 1974.
Weale, A. *Political Theory and Social Policy*. Macmillan, UK, 1983.

Recommended Reading

Bell, D. *The End of Ideology*. UK, Collier Books, 1970.

Preston, N. *Politics, Economics and Power: Ideology and Practice Under Capitalism, Socialism and Fascism*. London, Macmillan, 1967.

'Ideologies', Brief 20, *The Economist*. London, 1970.

Gamble, A. *An Introduction to Modern Social and Political Thought*. UK, Macmillan, 1981.

Matthews, B. (ed.) *Marx: A Hundred Years On*, UK, Lawrence and Wishart, 1983.

1

Fascism/Nazism

... Fascism is fundamentally a revolt against [the] view of man as an economic unit, a view which both capitalism and socialism held in common. Instead Fascism turns from 'Economic man' to 'Heroic man' and appeals to man's non-economic values — values of heroism, self-sacrifice, discipline and comradeship ... [such values] were to provide non-economic returns for the working class. Similarly, [Fascism] offered the capitalist classes the non-economic values of nationalism and cultural or racial supremacy. Heroic man was the ideal throughout.

(Drucker, *The End of Economic Man*, Heinemann, 1939)[1]

Origins of Fascism

The quote above reflects a major ideological attraction of fascism. There were others.

On the one hand, the Fascism of the 1930s offered *law and order* and *secure prosperity for those who obeyed*. On the other hand, it offered a *clean revolutionary sweep* of the rotten old world of decadent democracies, over-cultured and effete upper classes and greedy politicians.

Fascism thus appealed to both the conservative and radical in its supporters. It emphasised change yet stability. Change would come about by the cleansing of the nation of racial and political deviants and agitators who had allegedly corrupted the unity of society. Once it was cleansed, the state would show the way, led by the theory of dynamic romantic nationalism into an adventurous yet secure and prosperous *new order*. The natural selection of the fittest in this struggle would create an élite who could demand from the masses

Credere! (Believe) *Obbedire*! (Obey) *Combattere*! (Fight)

(Italian Fascist slogan, 1939)

Nature had ordained biological struggle. Struggle was dynamic. Political struggle, too, was ordained. But it was a dynamism caused by an act of will, not by the workings of economic history and class warfare.

Definition

Fascism is a form of radical conservative ideology and world view drawn from ideas of race and Social Darwinist competition between men, groups and nations. It usually centres on the lower middle class, landowners[2] and status-conscious groups who fear their traditional position and power is being crushed between big business and big unions.

Fascism seems to prosper where there is a strong tradition of irrational, romantic nationalism stressing the role of the state; capitalist insecurity, and a threat to conservative social values and morality by a strong Left-wing challenge.

Fascism is *socially defensive* in that it preserves the interests of the existing property order but it is *revolutionary* in that it turns social discontent into *scapegoatism* (Jews, dissidents, etc.) or into external *military aggression*.

Fascism emerged first in the twentieth century in post-World War I European society, particularly in Italy. It saw itself as a true third path, between the discredited liberal democratic capitalism which had led to the holocaust of World War I and the looming class war of Communism.

Fascism offered the classes Marx forgot (those lying between capital and labour) a peculiar synthesis of conservatism and radicalism. It did not lay hands on the social order and transform it, but it did transform the state into a radical instrument of power to direct and control capital and labour in a totalitarian system.

State power in order to control capital and labour needed, it was believed:

(a) a highly centralised autocratic regime
(b) charismatic leadership
(c) totalitarian links between state and individual citizen, bypassing or controlling the *local* community groups which in democracy arise among the citizens themselves
(d) a one party structure to ensure transmission of élite orders, and obedience
(e) a mystical sense of unity between the leader and the masses (Sorel's populism: see later) usually based upon ideas of blood, race and nationalism

The word 'Fascism' itself is derived from the Italian word '*fascio*' meaning a bundle of 'rods'. In the Roman Empire, such a bundle with an insert of an axe was the sign of the ultimate magistrate's authority — to beat and behead. Fascism thus stressed obedience and authority.

Ideology

The ideology of Fascism is both vague and complex, due to its different national cultural sources. Nevertheless, Fascist regimes put similar stress on certain aspects of society and state. Authoritarian oligarchies or military governments or movements of the radical right such as the American 'Klu Klux Klan' may exhibit some elements of the ideology of Fascism. But they should not be confused with true fascist dictatorships, such as those of Italy and Nazi Germany.

True fascist regimes have ideological foundations based on:

(a) aggressive nationalism idolising force
(b) a theory of unified, organic society devoid of class antagonism
(c) a theory of a dynamic totalitarian state with a mystical link between charismatic leader and masses
(d) theories of economics and history defined by race and struggle

Italian Fascism (1922–43) was the prototype of this ideology. But in varying degrees, fascism became the ideology for several other governments in the post-World War I period, such as Germany, Portugal, Spain and Hungary. Quasi-fascist political movements also appeared in many other countries, including Australia.

Governments recognisable as fascist continue today, even if such an ideological name is not stressed because of the tragic memories of the genocide of World War II. The difference between European fascisms of the 1930s and modern fascisms seems to be both political and cultural. Politically, European fascisms were an alliance between national capitalist firms, the lower middle class, especially small business people, landowners and the army.

Modern fascism, especially in Latin America, seems to be an alliance of foreign capital and its local agents; an oligarchy of landowners and rich families; the army/police; and small privileged enclaves of workers and farmers.

From this it can be seen that fascism is basically a political rather than an economic model. However, fascist cultural origins cannot be overlooked in the formation of its political ideology. This is particularly so with European fascism.

General European Foundations of Fascism

Winston Churchill once described fascism as an 'anti-Western belch'. The great British politician was no doubt making reference to statements such as those of Alfred Rosenberg, the Nazi ideologue. Rosenberg rejected not just the idea of Western intellectual rationalism, but the very principle of rationalism itself. He attacked the heritage of the Greek philosophers who insisted that arguments could be solved by reason and debate, not force.

Fascism, nevertheless, belongs in the mainstream of Western culture, along with liberalism and communism. All three ideologies represent a notion of dynamic secular life, goals of destiny and faith, and outline an ideal community.

Fascism was both a critic and synthesiser of the ideas of liberalism and socialism. First, it denied the idea of the eighteenth-century Enlightenment 'rational man' that history represented inevitable improvement. It denied the message of the French Revolution that democracy and equality were not only inevitable, but generally desired.

Liberal ideas had been the dominant ones of confident, expanding, nineteenth-century Europe, when European society dominated the world. The intellectual climate stressed humanism, science, positivism and industrialism. Above all, the concept of 'rational men' sank deep into prevailing beliefs. Reason was the basis of life and development in bourgeois liberal society.

Marxism opposed this society. But it used the same tools of 'rational' man and 'scientific' analysis for its criticism of capitalist society.

By the end of the nineteenth century, the two ideologies of liberalism and socialism filled most of the ideological arena. The classes Marx forgot — the middle classes; the self-employed; the prosperous farmers; socially conservative workers — felt excluded from the impending struggle so often trumpeted as inevitable.

Other intellectual forces, were also abroad in the nineteenth century. These denied the Marxist/socialist analysis of capitalist society and drew vastly different conclusions about equality and class struggle. Some of these European intellectual forces were represented in the writings of:

(a) *Hegel*: The German philosopher, Hegel, produced the notion of the state being superior to the individual: 'species-wisdom'. The state demands necessary obedience from 'species life' (or society) as it is superior, being a repository of accumulated values and the vehicle of the world spirit working itself out. The notion of *Fuehrer Prinzip* or leader principle is allied to this concept.

However, the leader principle is also buttressed by the works of Nietzsche.

(b) *Nietzsche* contributed to Fascism the notions of the 'supermen' and the 'master/slave' morality, which are closely linked. In real life, there emerge two types of person — those who struggle by any means to achieve success and greatness, and those who accept given cultural values and rules. Christianity has contributed to this world in that it has given a set of values which have dominated our cultural system since the fourth century AD. These values, according to Nietzsche, are those suitable for slaves and women, stressing meekness and non-aggression. As such they have suborned the true desire and destiny of races to conflict with, and dominate, each other. Christianity is thus to Nietzsche a 'slave' morality.

However, Nietzsche argues that history shows that Christian values have become mere 'practical' ideology. They are simply useful for social control. The leaders of society — kings, soldiers, dictators, successful business-men, etc. — who have risen to the top, have done so by struggle and ruthless action. They may give lip service to Christian values but, in effect, do not — indeed, could not — practice them if they were to survive. This is the 'master' morality. Nietzsche argues that these master values (those of élites who possess leadership) should become the real values of society. The Hegelian state should not foster values which are lies. 'World spirit' (in so far as Nietzsche can be adapted to Hegel) is not 'working itself out' by conforming to Christian values, but to struggle and conflict. Certain races, such as the Nordic race, have shown themselves historically to be more receptive of struggle and the need to dominate, or 'the Will to Power'. The state should foster this principle to be at one with the 'true' principles of human nature. A race of supermen will thus emerge, one not weakened by slave attitudes.

(c) *Arthur de Gobineau, Herbert Spencer and H.S. Chamberlain*: All these nineteenth century gentlemen were apologists for imperialism and racial differences. They developed the notion of the superiority of the white race as a natural concomitant of the 'survival of the fittest' in a world of cultural clash. Imperialism, with the white man at the top was a *natural* outcome of their mental, physical and cultural achievements. This system of thought became widely known as Social Darwinism. Its tenets were adopted by politics, racial law, poetry, literature and art.

It was an essential factor in the rise of racism, which is intolerant of both racial and sexual differences from the norm. It curled back upon Europe, underwriting the racial differences between Celt/Briton, Teuton/Slav etc., and their endless struggle.

(d) *Gaetano Mosca, Robert Michels and Vilfredo Pareto*: All three of these intellectuals contributed to nineteenth century thought concerning the inevitability of rule by an élite over the ignorant or easily swayed masses. Michels, in particular, stressed the 'Iron Law of Oligarchy'. His study of socialist parties proved, at least to his satisfaction, that even with an egalitarian ideology, an inner élite was inevitable in such parties.

Fascist thought reflected the notion of inevitable élites as reality. Socialist notions of the 'state withering away' and all men becoming autonomous were regarded as dangerous nonsense. They fostered disorder and alienation and particularly dehumanisation of the masses to the lowest common denominator of crude ignorance. Democracy and the media would, it was alleged, pander to such low tastes in order to stay in power. Élite rule meant the preservation of higher values and culture.

(e) *Georges Sorel*: Sorel stressed the role of 'direct action'. He dismissed the idea of operating through institutions such as parliament and via delegates. In particular, even though Sorel was a Left syndicalist, he stressed suspicion of socialist intellectuals. These people simply twisted and shaped the emotions of the masses to their own liking, he said. Sorel stressed populist notions in his notion that the masses' emotions should link directly and intuitively with a charismatic leader and bypass the intelligentsia and other civic leaders. Intuition, emotion and irrationalism were stronger bonds between leader and led than rational discourse. The power of a 'myth' such as the Marxist utopia or the Jewish threat was far more important to spur the masses to action than the rational discussion of ideology. Sorel stressed the need in mass politics for charismatic leadership; social myth (even if lies); anti-intellectualism and irrationality. He stressed romanticism and élitism as essential characteristics of the new mass politics. Fascist politics (particularly Hitler's and Mussolini's) were to emphasise Sorelian ideas, e.g.:

Vehemence, passion, fanaticism — these are the great magnetic forces which alone attract great masses.

(A. Hitler, *Mein Kampf*)

(f) *Ortega y Gassett and Oswald Spengler*: Both of these thinkers stressed the fact that the rise to power of the dehumanised masses must end in demagoguery and totalitarian government. Ortega y Gassett in his book *Revolt of the Masses* regretted the passing of élite rule, but regarded demagogic populism as inevitable. Spengler argued in *The Decline of the West* that the transition from simple village and 'racial' culture to urban, formless and dehumanising industrial 'civilisation' was destroying the very heart of decent humanity. Mankind was becoming an animal and being reduced to the lowest emotions by this industrial process. Only charismatic leadership, which used and turned this dehumanised regressive mass emotion onto scapegoates or outwards, could avoid internal decline and chaos.

Fascism was to stress the notion of regaining 'folk' culture and 'racial soul' as well as openly recognising the drive to aggression. The state should stress the irrational, cultural soul of the nation via the 'people's state'.

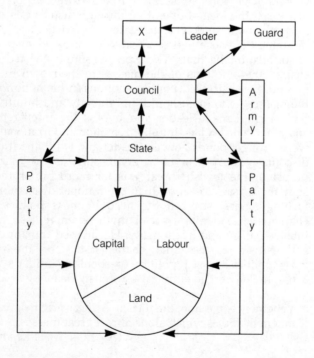

World War I

World War I was the turning point for nineteenth-century Europe. To the socialist, it meant the beginning of the end for capitalism with the birth of the Soviet Union. To the liberal, it was a triumph for liberal democracy over militarism and autocracy. The rational world order was expected to emerge from the League of Nations.

But to those who would become Fascists, the war endorsed the reality of brute primitive force and notions of struggle that the Enlightenment hypocritically rejected. In addition, the war had endorsed romantic nationalism and the spiritual values of bravery and will. Patriotism had united all groups and proved the existence of a higher mystical spirit that could surmount mere class struggle.

It was obvious that the irrational force of patriotism could be the source of a third ideological path beyond liberalism and socialism. In the face of adventure, with an ideal leader and a sense of sacrifice, a people would act in ways that denied both liberal rationality and the socialist dream of equality. Beginning in Italy in 1919, the third way of Fascism groped for ideological expression.

Italian Fascism

The ideology of Italian Fascism was never as seriously detailed as that of Nazism. Mussolini had received parliamentary endorsement as leader of the government after his march on Rome in 1922. He was in fact a 'legitimate' autocrat. He had achieved a legal dictatorship to maintain law and order in the manner of an ancient Caesar. He was endorsed primarily as a guardian of law and order by groups interested in his firmness, not his ideology.

Italian Fascism was initially interested in the 'state' elements of law, order and discipline. Unlike Nazism, Italian Fascism did not possess a strong enough *social* ideology to attempt to sweep away the old culture and forge new social beliefs.

This was a mistake that Mussolini himself recognised and attempted to rectify. He published many of his ideas in the *Encyclopaedia Italiana*.[3] But Italian Fascism never touched the national soul as deeply as German Nazism.

Italian Fascist ideology emerged piecemeal around its three stages of development[4] — 'the activist/nationalist stage; its semi-military stage; and its regime stage'.

Italian Fascism established a state before it defined its philosophy and its links with society. This was essential in rationalising its totalitarian style. Italian Fascism built upon the vague idea of the Third Force[5] between capitalism and socialism for the first time. In so doing, it laid out some fundamentals of Fascism:

Aggressive Nationalism

Nationalism was the keystone of Fascism. Italian Fascism built upon the earlier nationalist ideas of men such as Mazzini[6] who had stressed the pre-eminence of nation over individual. Unlike Mazzini, however, Italian Fascism stressed competition between nations, not co-operation. Nations, it was believed, should prepare constantly for war.

War was the ultimate mystical experience. It brought all classes together in a higher purpose — survival of the whole. Romantic nationalism rationalised the sacrifice of war.

Essentially, Fascism endorsed Hobbes' idea of the two states of man's society — 'the state of nature' and the 'state of law'. In the 'state of nature' (lawless society) every man's hand was raised against every other's. This was overcome by imposing 'a state of law' upon society in order to tame men's brutish natures. To the Fascist, such 'a state of law' which did not take man's aggressive nature into account, was a false path. Aggression did not occur due to the lack of rational thought via education. Nor did it exist due to class war or the domination of a ruling class. It simply was part of man's nature. But it should be allowed to emerge; to be exalted in a doctrine of action and heroic virtue and organised and disciplined by the state.

Inevitably, therefore, the philosophy of violence and struggle permeating Fascist thought plus its military style of organisation would lead to the totalitarian state.

Theory of the State

The Italian Fascist state took several years to emerge fully in its structural and ideological form.

First, the Fascist state endorsed the notion of an élite leadership. This élite was self-selected by their vigour and ability to fight their way to the top via the Fascist Party and militia.

The class struggle was outlawed as an obsolete concept. All political actions had to be for the good of the nation and would be judged in that light.

Pluralist democracy, with different parties serving the separate interests of the peasantry, labour, business or the church, was banned. To the Fascists, they tended to produce only self-serving politicians who had a vested interest in maintaining these differences as well as subsidiary groups of farmers, labour and business, who had a distorted and narrow perspective of national interest.

The solution was one 'total' party where all interests would be represented. The Fascist Party would parallel all levels of the state to ensure all demands would be met. Finally the state and party would blend in the person of the Leader.

Theory of Society

While essentially obsessed with statist doctrine[7] and the occupation and use of the state framework, Italian Fascism had to develop elements of a theory of society to ratify its quest for state control over both capital and labour. It was also necessary in order to ratify its vision of nationalism and human purpose.

The constant stress upon 'nation', 'war' and 'vigour' gave all Fascisms certain themes:

(a) *Anti-Pacifism*: War alone brought out the nobility in man. Pacifism was not only ignoble but a lie. Life was struggle. This attitude would bring Fascism into conflict with much Christian thought, if not necessarily the major churches.

(b) *Sex Stereotyping*: The constant stress upon so-called male virtues of 'aggression' 'competition' and 'violence', and the glorification of the warrior, meant a permeation of sex stereotyping in Fascist law and attitudes towards women. Conventional family roles for women were reinforced by propaganda and underlined by family law. Women's lives were largely defined by 'Kitchen, Church, Children'. Feminism was regarded as a radical offshoot of Marxism or liberalism, and in conflict with the laws of nature.

(c) *Scapegoatism*: The decline of the organic purity of the nation was due to conspiracies of malcontents, not of classes. In the Italian case, these conspiracies were largely liberal or Marxist. Exile or prison was the usual outcome. To German Fascism, however, these agitators — Marxists, Jews, homosexuals, feminists ect. — were much more important to the fascist theory of society than in Italy. This was especially true of the Jews, who were the central scapegoats of the Nazi world view.

All fascisms, however, agreed that certain exconsensus groups existed which offended political or social morality, e.g. Marxists or homosexuals. These ex-consensus groups gave false example, distorted morality, and attacked the basis of decency and law and order — the family. So they should be punished, cast out or forced to re-educate themselves. They were at the centre of the world conspiracy against decency.

Theories of History and Economics

Throughout fascist theories of history and economics are echoes of the nineteenth-century Carlylist emphasis upon the role of heroes in history and the Victorian liberal capitalist stress upon the self-made man.

To Marxists, the history of civilisation was the history of class struggle and changes in the ownership of the means of production. Fascism, however, stressed not 'economics' but the pursuit of 'ideals' in history. The motor of changes in history was the spiritual movements like the Crusades, led by 'supermen'. Unlike capitalist individualists, these 'supermen' were not motivated by mere greed and selfishness, but by ideals.

Such people struck out existentially into unknown areas of thought, war or industry for instance. They had no guides but their own self confidence. For such people to be controlled by the mass of insecure, sheep-like people via democracy was thought ludicrous. The inequality of mankind was obvious, unchangeable and actually desirable. Liberal democracy was simply a smokescreen for the reality of capitalist power concentrated in a few hands or families.

To the fascist, such hidden capitalist power, in economics and history, should be recognised. While it represented correct spirit i.e. the ability to survive and struggle, such power was motivated by the wrong spurs — greed and self-interest. The state had a duty to protect the worker from such selfcentredness. This was especially so if they were of the *Volk* (race) or the nation. The state had to link capitalism to a higher motivation — the good of the nation and of the race, and capitalism had to be disciplined in some form. In fascist economies, this took the form of the corporate state.

The Italian corporate state[8] proclaimed the end of conflict between workers and employers. It stressed tripartite partnership in the economy. Business and labour would unite in corporations based upon function (e.g. transport) or product (e.g. the meat industry). These corporations would be supervised by the state to ensure no capitalist exploitation or union misuse of power. Each region would elect a committee that would then elect members to a National Chamber of Corporations (set up 1933). Finally, in 1939, a Chamber of Fasci and Corporations replaced the old Parliament.

Italian Fascism borrowed the idea of the corporate state from syndicalist socialism and elements of Catholic social doctrine.

However, to the idea of the corporate parliament of workers and producers, the Fascists added the state as enforcer and co-ordinator. The Fascist party and the Leader dominated the corporate Parliament. Eventually, the intrusion of Party and Leader emasculated it, and it was reduced to a rubber stamp organisation.

This was partly due to hidden deals such as the Vidoni Pact of 1925 where economic power was left in employers' hands by a secret deal between the Fascist Party and employer organisations. Strikes were banned and labour was further disciplined by laws and by stacking workers' committees in factories with Fascist sympathisers. The state, as an instrument of the Fascist Party, thus combined with capital against labour.

The practical outcome of Fascist ideology was not the dream of the neutral state, adjudicating the law and enforcing order on capital and labour. It was a temporary and imposed solution to class conflict for the ultimate benefit of business.

Eventually, early enthusiasm for the Fascist regime declined, partly due to the bias of the state. Fascism attempted to rekindle this enthusiasm by overseas adventures of conquest, but finally these attempts to maintain itself by military gambles led to its own destruction.

German Fascism: Nazism

German Fascism was built upon the doctrine of National Socialism or Nazism. This purported to be a synthesis of nationalism and socialism but in effect its major tenet was racism.

Racism provided a deep and satisfying social ideology that bound all German classes together against outside forces. It immediately provided a unifying national factor transcending social contradictions. A race-conscious nation was homogeneous. Race consciousness dispensed with class consciousness and the inevitable revolution that Marxism said preceded a homogeneous society. Nazism thus began with the masses, their culture and their deepest prejudices. It welled up from the bottom of German society. Italian Fascism, on the other hand, was Caesarism. It aimed first at conquering state power, and then fumbled to define a unifying social ideology that all classes could support.

Nazism almost achieved the second aim of ideological fascism — to get rid of 'culture', particularly what was seen as the 'effete' democratic political culture based upon Judaeo/ Christian ethics. In its place, it fostered an ideology of race.

The Nineteenth Century Background

Nazism, and its success in gaining mass support, is usually explained by reference to immediate events between 1919-33, particularly the defeat of 1918, the harsh Versailles Treaty, and the Depression with its destructive impact upon the institutions of government and power.

This liberal historian's view of immediate events is matched by the Marxist historian's one of the role of economics and class in the rise of Nazism. To the Marxist interpreter, Nazism was the last stage of desperate German capitalism. In the face of the disintegration of the liberal state, the Weimar Republic had lost the respect of all classes due to its weakness. Monopoly capital turned increasingly to classes threatened by the rise of worker's power. These included the landowners, small business men, and the socially conservative worker, which rallied behind the Third Path to smash socialism.

Why this happened in Germany needs to be examined for deeper cultural reasons. Specifically, what existed in Germany compared with other countries, was a tradition of authoritarian culture as opposed to one of liberal ideology. This was the key to the rise of Nazism.

Politically, the German state had stressed authoritarianism rather than democracy throughout most of its existence. The heritage of the Prussian state, and previously the various kingdoms and fiefs of the Holy Roman Empire had all stressed loyalty and obedience to the prince. The emphasis of most German Protestantism upon obedience to lawful princes after the great Peasants' Revolt of 1524–25, plus the traumas of the Thirty Years War (1618–48), and the Napoleonic invasions of the nineteenth century, all effected German nationalism. In Germany, this stressed order, obedience and unity in the face of dreadful external threats from east and west. Survival lay in unity.

Even earlier notions of the superiority of German *Kultur* (culture) affected social attitudes. German history of the nineteenth and early twentieth centuries constantly stressed the historic German mission in the *drang nach osten* (drive to the east). Men like Duke Henry the Fowler of Bavaria who pushed back the Slavs and Hungarians and settled the conquered eastern marches with Germans in the early Middle Ages were the focus for a heroic national history.

The mediaeval Teutonic Knights of the Baltic coast were an early example of German thoroughness in gaining *Lebensraum* to the East. The Knights' spartan lifestyle, their dedication to Western Christian civilisation, and their military victory over the 'sub-human' Pole, Lithuanian and Russian were an example to the later SS and 'Special Action' groups.

The nineteenth century was the period of the formation of German unity and nationalism. Under Bismarck's Junker tradition, German nationalism leaned towards the élitist, aristocratic national state. Such a state rejected the European liberal tradition of equality, liberty and natural law, and pursued a model of the 'closed' state stressing power, uniqueness, imperialism and discipline (although it is true that elements of this closed nationalism existed in all states in the imperialist, late nineteenth century).

Added to this style of state was the deep effect of Romanticism upon German culture. Romanticism in Germany in the late nineteenth century became a philosophy of law, the nature of man, society and the state. Intellectuals such as Herder created the mystical notion of 'folk spirit' (*Volkgeist*) or the biological drive to greatness of a people unified in culture and state. Treitschke emphasised the German destiny to unite all Nordics in to one racial state whether they lived in or out of Germany. *Volksdeutsch* were always German by virtue of blood.

1919-33

Nazism could thus draw upon some of the deepest elements in German culture. But it was much slower coming to power (in 1933) than Mussolini's Fascists (in 1922). The first reason for this was the premature attempt by Hitler and his National Socialist German Worker's Party to seize power by force, in Bavaria in 1923. Hitler was to realise his mistake and thus depict his party to the respectable German middle class as just another gang of street thugs. Fascism, it was realised, must claim power legally, or at least in the name of law and order.

The second reason for Hitler's late access to power was the revival of the German economy which lasted until the Depression of 1929. There was also the problem that a truly ideological party has in gaining adherents in stable times. Pragmatism, careerism, opportunism or even love of adventure may be a stronger motive for conversion to a party than a belief in ideology. As Goering said, 'I joined the Party because it was revolutionary, not because of the ideological stuff.'[9]

Good economic times and poor party prospects do not attract the opportunist. By 1932, however, due largely to the impact of the world Depression on the German economy, Hitler had gathered a wide following and support in Germany. Staying assiduously with the policy of 'legal power', he was offered the leadership (Chancellorship) of the Republic by President Hindenburg in 1933.

Hitler came to power in coalition with a number of conservative parties. Like Mussolini, he drew his support largely from the lower middle class, the prosperous peasantry and conservative workers.

Hitler, like Mussolini, used his talents as a demagogue to press home his message of the Third Way of Nazism. He stressed both nationalism and socialism and pointed to the need to control both capital and labour. Like Mussolini, Hitler wooed the industrialists and the military. He made secret agreements concerning the future limitation of his movement's socialism and paramilitary nature in return for their support.[10] He also used private armies to capture the streets for 'law and order'.

In most aspects, therefore, the characteristics of the Nazi takeover were similar to those of the Italian Fascist conquest of power. The major outstanding difference was the ideology of race.

To be a Nazi was to be in possession of a nihilist ideology which explained man and his history, the aim of the state and the world mission of the 'Master Race'. Nazism, through its ideology of race, was a world ideology.[11] Italian Fascism was, by comparison, chauvinist nationalism.

The Characteristics of Nazi Ideology: the Theory of Race

The central tenet, connecting all elements of Nazi ideology, was race. Throughout *Mein Kampf* (My Struggle) written by Adolf Hitler in Landsberg prison in 1923–24, runs a core of anti-Semitism.

The purpose of this racist core is to draw together all the theses of struggle: German nationalism; the nature of the state; power and 'folk' culture. The Jew was cited as a common enemy to all these theses. Thus, all the various class elements and the mutually contradictory social groups that made up the Nazi political movement had a convenient scapegoat. Anti-Semitism was necessary as ideological cement to bind up a basically irrational political force and to blueprint a New World Order under the German Master Race.

The 'Master Race' idea had emerged from a variety of intellectual sources of the eighteenth and nineteenth centuries. These stemmed from the European conservative reaction to the French Revolution and general European rationale for the age of imperialism. The discovery by linguistics that most European languages descended from an original Indo-European source made possible the claim of the existence of an original foundation race, called 'Aryans' for convenience.[12]

Beginning with the Comte de Gobineau, a theory of Aryanism to explain European civilization was created. Europe owed her pre-eminence to the original conquest of the darker races by the (invariably) blue-eyed, blond Aryan. Where this race was pre-eminent, either through all classes, as in Nordic countries, or as a ruling class, as in France or North Italy, civilisation prospered and advanced. An Aryan nation committed race suicide by intermarrying with non-Aryan migrants or subjects, it was alleged. Therefore, civilisation could only be saved by a strict process of racial purification and intermarriage laws.

The purpose of the Nazi party was to carry out this historic mission.

The 'Master Race' theory was a Sorelian myth. But it buttressed the idea of European imperialism. It was widely believed that Europe had come to rule the colonial world through its inherent racial superiority, not its technical prowess or through the expansion of capital. The 'Master Race' concept fitted closely with the prevailing Social Darwinism of imperialism. Social Darwinism rationalised empire under H. Spencer's doctrine of the 'survival of the fittest' in the nation/race struggle.

Anti-Semitism formed the other main plank of the Nazi theory of race. Christian Europe had intermittently persecuted the Jewish race throughout the Christian era. 'Pogroms' (or massacres of Jews) were still part of Russian government policy under the Czars and during the Russian Civil War (1917–21). Religious persecution had, however, faded in Western Europe by the late nineteenth century. In its place grew the 'conspiracy' theory, with Jewish bankers and Bolsheviks cast as the villains. Anti-Semites argued that both capitalism and Bolshevism were controlled by a world-wide secret Brotherhood of Jewry. Jews were alleged to despise Christians, meaning to destroy their culture, their economy and their race by capitalist interest rates or Bolshevik revolution.

Documents such as 'The Protocols of the Elders of Zion' (later exposed as a forgery of the Czarist secret police) purported to outline this plot.

Anti-Semitism was thus, it was concluded, a sacred mission to protect Western civilisation.

The Theory of Nationalism

Originally, Nazism stressed both socialism and nationalism. But by 1934, Hitler was playing down the socialist aspects of the doctrine to meet his working arrangements with German business and the army. In 1934, he purged the organisation of the SA, who were calling for a second (this time) socialist revolution. Henceforth, Nazism stressed an all-class nationalism.

This was the 'closed' nationalism of Herder's Romantic *Volksgeist* or folk spirit. Intolerance and purification of the race was necessary to achieve such a mystical biological utopia. Germany would become a society of 'supermen' served by conquered races. Her national hegemony in Europe would be serviced by a *Volkstaat*, a people's state which would maintain this hegemony by reordering Europe to serve racial, not national, needs.

The Theory of the State: Society and Economics

Like Italian Fascism, Nazism dispensed with a parliamentary system. This was done by the simple expedient of passing an Enabling Act in 1936 which Hitler as Chancellor would legally use to construct his own state.

A corporate state with Nazi Party supervision was set up, with the Party and the state meeting in the person of the Leader (*Fuehrer*). The concept of *Fuehrer Prinzip* endorsed the hierarchical structure of Party and state, and this rested on the ideological notion of struggle and Social Darwinism. Fate selected out those who had the 'will' to be leaders. Obedience and loyalty to such men of destiny was an act of sense. Rebellion and deviancy from such natural selection was an act against the Hegelian state and its destiny.

However, as M. Geyer[13] points out, instead of the traditional notion of the well-oiled Hegelian state with each part efficiently and loyally co-operating for the good of the mystical spirit of the nation, Nazi ideology produced a peculiar hybrid. The Nazi state was composed of political fiefs competing with each other, under the control of various individuals or organisations such as the SS, and increasingly dependent on plunder rather than production.

The loyalty of the ordinary German citizen was guaranteed in this process. As long as he was a member of the *Volk*, he had access to the privileges of racial superiority and minor plunder.

The social contract between the elements of the *Herrenvolk* (the 'Master Race') depended on the literal implementation of the ideology of superiority, and the extraction of plunder from the 'subhuman' races.

> It was thus a peculiarly perverted system of participation; for while the Germans were not allowed to govern themselves, they were encouraged to dominate others. This was the Nazi 'social contract' on which the state rested.[14]

The Nazi state, with its plunder economy and its racist social contract,[15] came to its climax in 1942. 'The Nazi utopian racist state was always posited upon victory in war. In 1942, such a state seemed possible.' There was emerging a Europe cleansed of

Bolshevism and the Jews. The 'Master Race' was fed by industry and agriculture thriving upon plunder from subject nations. 'The SS guarded ihe race within and the *Wehrmacht* (armed forces) without.'

By 1945, the German Fascist state had disappeared with its wartime collapse. But the power of ideology in the mobilisation of society and the use of the state had never been so powerfully exhibited. And Fascism as an ideology has not disappeared. While 'pure' forms (such as Nazism) do not exist today, recognisable fascist regimes and ideologies have appeared in contemporary times, as well as 'radical Right' movements exhibiting elements of fascist thought and organisation. The next section will deal with some of these contemporary trends.

Contemporary Fascist Trends

The number of movements and ideologies selected in this section on neo-fascism is limited. Two have been chosen for their recent notoriety, political interest and semblance of some mass support.

Most neo-Fascist movements in liberal democracies are fringe groupings operating under the general political tag of the 'radical Right'.

Movements grouped under this name tend to possess some elements of fascist-style, 'exclusionist' ideology. They should be differentiated, however, from groups reaching back to an idealised traditional society lost by moral decay, and those whose targets are more pragmatic. These latter groups aim at the resurrection of a new-style capitalism, and will be dealt with under the 'New Right' section of the Conservatism chapter. All radical Right groups try to influence, infiltrate and persuade existing conservative parties, those that stand closest to them on the ideological spectrum.

Radical Right groups tend to be motivated by three elements — a desperate sense of threatening moral decay which they must combat; a fear of some element in society (such as another race) which is seen as threatening the organic unity of that society; or a sense of mission to restore the capitalist economic system or preserve it from interference by malignant forces.

In the political field, therefore, contemporary radical Right groups tend to coincide on several similar ideological points. These are drawn from a social anxiety based on the confrontations of the Cold War since 1945, and the deeper clash between humanism and religious fundamentalism.

The ideology of the radical Right tends to emphasise:

(a) *The conspiracy theory*: All Communist successes are due to the weakness of the West. Not only are there traitors[16] and secret Communists/Jews in Western governments, but liberals themselves are 'soft on Communism'.

(b) *Anti-Communism must be anti-liberal*: The crusade against communism will be a long one. Any weakness due to humanist Christian or liberal sentiment is treason. A plural, tolerant liberal state is inherently decadent.

(c) *Morality*: 'Pure' morality can exist only in a society freed from liberalism, socialism and humanism. Earlier moral society has been corrupted by secular education, feminism and hedonism.

(d) *Populism*: Populism is a term denoting the unity of the organic society, (or the ruler with the ruled), which can be achieved if false notions such as 'the class war', interest group society etc., can be dispensed with. Populism denies the existence of social division and political pluralism based on differing prespectives. Instead it postulates a mystical unity of the masses with their leaders. This unity has been betrayed by selfserving élites: political agitators and racial out-groups such as Jews. Populist movements thus stress *mass movements* which are extra-parliamentary and which promote *direct action*. Such movements are seen as crusading bodies and instruments of the *people's will*, given that they can see the issue clearly without their vision being clouded by liberal, humanist and socialist teachings.

(e) *Race*: Many radical right groups use race as the central cement in their many-faceted approach to ideology. The target of racism may vary from Jewish/capitalist/Marxist scapegoat, to the 'Yellow Peril' and race pollution theme.

The National Security State

One important element in recent Latin American military dictatorships has been the ideology of the 'National Security State'. National Security doctrine emanating originally from the Brazilian[17] War College from 1948 onwards. It has revealed ideological similarities with European fascism although its social basis tends to differ.

The National Security State ideology stresses:

(a) *The military have an ideological mission*: They are the guardians of the nation's soul against internal ideological enemies and external aggressive enemies. The armed forces are not neutral as in liberal democratic doctrine.

(b) *The state is too important to be left to democracy*: National Security doctrine stresses the Hegelian notion of the universal state. It is the centre and soul of the nation. It works for all, not just for some political faction that captures the state by election. All rights flow from it. Nothing exists outside of it.

(c) *The state today is at war even in times of peace*: There is a total war underway between capitalism and communism. The military and its allies should hold the reins via state power until the enemy threat of class war within dissipates, with the rise of a middle class wedded to the good of the nation.

(d) *Repression is necessary*: Society must be cleansed by the state controlled by the military and their technocratic allies. Until the desired middle class arises, the doctrine asserts, the state is at war. All war is without morality.

The use of terror and fear is prophylactic. It paralyses opposition. Consequently, the use of Nazi-style techniques of control evolved during the occupation of Europe are underwritten—torture houses; arrest without warrant; disappearances (as in Argentina, from 1976–81); concentration camps; secret executions; death squads.

Repression is also non-selective. Like the radical Right exponents, the National Security doctrine regards liberalism as a cloak for communism. Any liberal or Christian action, no matter how petty, can be judged as pro-Marxist. The major aim is the suppression of the 'class war' psychology. This is an internationalist idea and therefore treasonous.

Proponents of the National Security doctrine argue that they have three enemies: *the developed nations* who exploit their Third World economies. This North/South division of the world can be overcome two ways: by national autarchy or by a 'blind growth' model. Most National Security states, especially Chile, (1976–90) and Brazil (1964–81) have opted for the latter model.

Wages are held down by force. Protection of internal industry and agriculture is dropped. Safety and environment controls are scrapped. The government usually endorses full 'market' economies. The regimes tend towards co-operation with multinational capitalism.

The second enemy is *internal injustice*. National Security states stress in their ideology that the distortion between wealth and poverty inside their countries is due to past foreign control and the greed of political power groupings. They stress that to overcome this, only *growth* is the answer, not *redistribution* of wealth. In effect, this policy has usually meant the smashing of union power, the decline of worker income and a rise in wealth of the powerful financial élite.

The third enemy is *Marxism/Socialism*. This is seen as a disease of society, destroying national unity. It introduces a psycho/social ideological attitude poisonous to the social unity necessary for endurance of the period of restructuring of society.

The proponents of National Security are proud of the 'scientific' nature of their ideology.[18] They stress 'geopolitics' as one of its bases: i.e. each nation is important in the Cold War because of its geographical position in the world. This can be used in trade with the super powers.

They are proud of the 'scientific' nature of their regimes, based on the tripartite foundations of military, technocracy and some elements of the churches. This is part of the classic Fascist pattern of government (with, perhaps, the absence of church in non-Latin countries). However the similarity of these regimes with classic Italian and German Fascism seems to end there.

European fascisms were basically an alliance of national capital, the state and the middle class. They could even claim a form of egalitarianism under the ideology of Aryanism or nationalism. In Latin American National Security states, by contrast, the alliance has come to rest upon foreign capital, the state, cooperating local capital and a dual labour system. (In the dual labour system, workers in special areas or enclaves, e.g. mining, may get special wages and conditions. Those outside these areas get what they can.) No German in the 'Master Race' period would have been so excluded.

The basic system of the National Security State is very well established in Latin America. Perhaps the best known original state was that of Mexican dictator Porfirio Diaz (1876–1910). His regime rested on an alliance of strong dictatorial state, techno-crats with a development model (*Cientificos*)[19] and foreign capital linked to a small national élite. His regime was also in a hurry to build a middle class, but it ended instead in the bloody Mexican Revolution (1910-1921) led by liberals allied to the marginalised peasant/worker.

National Security State ideology seems to be in many ways the result of an analysis of the fall of such Latin American regimes like that of Diaz and the methods needed to avoid such a fall.

The National Front

During the period 1964–80, a new phenomenon emerged in British politics. This was the racist ideology of the National

Front. Similar groups soon emerged in Australia and New Zealand. The United States already possessed the century-old Klu Klux Klan as a racist radical Right movement.

What was new about the National Front in Britain was the substantial electoral success it achieved in the period 1964–80, and the rise of an electorally successful racist ideology in a Britain which had always been proud of its supposedly dominant liberal-democratic political culture.

The political culture of Britain has always been dominated by the myth of 'tolerance'. British society is a parliamentary one with a traditional generosity to all ideologies and ideologues prepared to obey the law.

But no society escapes a period of being an imperial power without some elements of 'domination' becoming part of the national psychology. As in Germany, Social Darwinism was an element of nineteenth-century British nationalism and imperialism. The nineteenth century concept of 'survival of the fittest', with its racist overtones, filtered into British attitudes[20] as it did in the case of most European nations and the United States. The National Front in Britain represents a political recrudescence of extreme Right-wing politics and Social Darwinism. But an explanation for its emergence in 1964-80 as a political movement can be found if we sketch a short historical outline of post-war Britain.

The post-war period (1945–80) saw the decline of British imperial power. The country was faced with the economic necessity of joining Europe as just another nation, while still possessing widespread residual social attitudes of dominant Anglo-centric nationalism and imperial pride.

The period of imperial power had also seen the extension of British citizenship to many groups and races throughout the Empire. While it existed, there was little movement of these citizens to the mother country, although such a right existed, under the notion of the Commonwealth of Nations. By 1964, however, many non-white groups bcgan to emigrate to Britain. Some, such as the West Indians, were drawn for economic reasons, to work in industries such as transport which British workers found uncongenial. Others, such as the Kenyan and Ugandan Asians, emigrated because of discrimination against them in their home nations.

Britain, like most liberal democracies of the post-war period, had become a Keynesian welfare state. The dominant liberalism of the period stressed the co-operative social contract between capital and labour, and the notion of a multicultural society. This was in contradistinction to the philosophy of the Anglo-centric assimilationist society of the nineteenth century and later.

The first moves to form the National Front came from a philosophic position opposed to multiculturalism, which was seen to be attacking the very basis of the single culture/single 'race state' and society. Liberalism was viewed as the first step in the death of the organic unity of the British cultural soul.

There is no doubt that a political movement such as the National Front would have been marginal in good economic times. Britain, however, like most Western liberal democracies was at the time, moving out of the long post-war economic boom. The Keynesian social contract was beginning to fail. Electorally, the effect of National Front racist ideology was strongest in working class areas. It built significantly on 'competitive' racism that was created by the fear of other introduced ethnic groups competing cheaply for jobs and houses. Such racism explains the disappearance of jobs, housing, good working conditions and economic prospects in terms of competition from racially different labour. The power of labour bargaining in the social contract between labour and capital is thought to be removed or threatened by the emergence of a culturally diverse group.

The elements of National Front ideology[21] that came to the fore in British politics were, with reference to Spoonley's basic analysis: organic; exclusive; defensive of conditions.

Race as the Basis of Nationalism

The National Front saw the major threat to national racial purity as coming from the liberal emphasis upon multiculturalism. The coloured peoples are being used, they said, by a world conspiracy to oust the white worker from his rightful place in society. In essence, he is being made powerless by the destruction of his monopoly of being the *only* working class. During imperial days, the British working class may have been at the bottom of the national heap but they were granted superiority over other colonial classes (even upper classes) by virtue of their race. Now they were losing even that under the imposed policy of multiculturalism.

The internationalist big business and Bolshevik conspiracy behind multiculturalism was to destroy the very idea of the 'nation'. Eventually all nations will die, it is alleged, as they become racially mixed. Thus big business and Bolshevism will triumph.

The non-white are not the conspirators. They are being manipulated by powers behind them.

The Biological-Intelligence-Morality Link

The moral aspects of race are also stressed by the National Front. Biologism has a long history in racial thought. From the eighteenth century, ideas of the 'Great Chain of Being' and polygenic (many origins) and monogenic (single origins) notions of man's beginning, underpinned the imperial age.

As Poulantzas has said, 'Fascism cannot be understood without reference to Imperialism.' The rank ordering of races in terms of superiority/inferiority in imperialism re-emerges in National Front ideology. Morality was inherently an aspect of physical stature. Civilisation could not be expected of a lower form of human life and to mix racially with them would be to sink to a lower cultural position.

Essentially, however, the National Front ideology was a defensive one. Its purpose was to protect British 'organic' society from elements that would destroy the British character. While possessing a Nazi-like ideology and some of its tactics, it never possessed a world view (like Aryanism) which would transcend British national borders.

The National Front in Britain was a movement of elements of the alienated and marginalised working class at the end of the long post-war economic boom. Nowhere did the National Front capture large sections of the disaffected middle class which have remained within the main stream of politics. In the 1980s–1990s, the National Front, although still strong, is in decline. It is now simply one element of the radical Right.

Fascism in Australia

The New Guard

It is difficult to talk of a Fascist movement in Australia similar in ideology, size and popular support to the European fascist movements. Most Australian quasi-fascist movements are small fringe radical Right groups, with the possible historical exception of the New Guard.

The New Guard was a Sydney-based paramilitary organisation formed from a core of returned World War I Australian soldiers and members of the middle class.[22] They emerged, like the Italian and German Fascist movements, from a middle class seriously under threat, or perceived threat, from the rise of socialist governments and the impact of the great Depression of 1929-39. Their main activity was to provide a radical conservative combat organisation to oppose NSW Labor Party supporters and the Communist Party in the period of the Lang government in NSW from 1930–32.

Eric Campbell, the ex-Australian army officer who organised the New Guard, always disclaimed the 'fascist' label for his movement.[23] Campbell argued that the New Guard's ideology was Empire Loyalist, not one based on race struggle or anti-Semitism. He denied any revolutionary ideological desire for political power for the Guard. Instead, it was a self-appointed defender of the conservative style of democracy.

Nevertheless, the tactics and methods of the New Guard movement closely resembled the first stage of 'street struggle' (*Kampf Zeit*)[24] of Italian and German Fascism prior to the revolutionary destruction of the 'decadent' liberal state by the seizure of legal power in alliance with conservative elements. Whether the label of 'fascist' is correct or not, depends on a short background analysis of the historical period and a study of New Guard ideology,[25] as several authors outline.

The appearance of the New Guard took place in the crisis of the Australian economy and social structure during the Depression of 1929–39. During this period, the basic Australian 'social contract' between capital and labour i.e. the preservation of high wages for labour in return for protection to high cost industry, became disturbed due to the failure of the world economy.

Australian prosperity rested upon three intertwined fundamentals: the maintenance of membership within the imperial club, thus benefiting from imperial preferences for primary exports; the maintenance of the Australian 'social contract' first recognised by Deakinite liberalism in 1908[26]; and a hybrid nationalism which linked local patriotism with higher, mystical Empire loyalism.

Such a society as Australia's was noted for its political stability. This was particularly due to the dominant Benthamite utilitarian[27] view of the state, where it was seen as the provider of services for material benefit rather than as an ideological Hegelian *Volkstaat*, the soul of the nation. Patriotic myth and the emotional centre of the world-scattered Anglo-Saxon race focused on the Crown and person of the Monarch. The Australian state was simply a structure for the provision of good management and the maintenance of the social contract. Both dominant parties, Labor and Conservative, recognised quite early that bold experiment based upon alternative ideologies outside the liberal utilitarian state was unnecessary and unlikely to be supported.

Nevertheless, the 'social contract' had and has a serious problem. It has no control over external change which can inflict traumas upon Australian society.

The trauma theory of Australian history stresses the prime role external disaster (depressions, wars) have on the socio/political equilibrium of the country. In those periods the liberal utilitarian state is not able to manage the capital/labour contract, as most economic decisions are out of its hands. Class conflict may therefore erupt and alternative ideologies arise, due to these external events.

The great world Depression of 1891 triggered the rise in Australia of the radical Labor Party, as well as an accelerated move to Federalism. The great strikes of 1891–94 which gave birth to the Labor Party also gave birth to a conservative opposition, but one which was unorganised compared with that of the unionists.

Nevertheless, the conservative rhetoric of 1891 emphasised the attack upon British tradition, law and order, and the right to property. This was to be echoed by the New Guard in 1931–35, and indeed is still heard today. 'Labour movements, when in power, have traditionally faced a rising media temperature compared with conservative ones.'[28]

World War I was another trauma as it caused the agonies of the conscription referenda battles at home and the first major split in the Australian Labor Party over this issue. Sections of the ALP, who preferred Empire loyalism to party platform, joined with the conservatives to form a nationalist government, under Billy Hughes.

By the time the war ended and the diggers returned home, there had arisen both the Anzac legend, which combined radical and conservatives in a peculiar externally-orientated loyalist nationalism, and the legend of disloyal socialists at home who had opposed the war.[29]

The essential factor of the Anzac legend is that it has the capacity to unite both streams of political thought upon which both Labor and conservative parties had built their support: those of the worker labourist and the Empire royalist. The Anzac legend was a point of unity for both groups, above class or faction.

It was upon this new-found 'third path' that Eric Campbell was to try to base the ideology of the New Guard.

The effect of the 1929–35 Depression was the worst shock to the Australian political structure since 1891. In NSW, the Labor Party had produced an enormously vigorous and combative Premier in Jack Lang. From 1925, Lang's party introduced numerous welfare services and battled constantly to reduce conservative power, particularly in banking and the media. He earned himself the enmity of the press and the disquiet of the conservative middle class as a result.

In 1930, Lang was returned to power. The Depression was in full flight, and pressure mounted on the Federal government from overseas banks to cut government expenditure and wages and raise interest rates. Lang opposed this plan. Instead, he proposed an alternative plan which centred on not paying foreign loans until the Depression was over. Conservative opinion was outraged. Lang was using the liberal state for non-traditional purposes. Conservative forces therefore began to organise for the defence of property and the conservative version of the role of the liberal state.

Two outcomes of Lang's actions were the emergence of the New Guard, and the eventual dismissal of Lang by Governor Game in an unprecedented constitutional move.

The New Guard was thus first organised in the defence of the conservative interpretation of the role of the liberal state and British-style democracy. As Humphrey McQueen points out,[29] the New Guard was largely drawn from the conservative middle class. The working class ex-digger did not respond to the 'third path' Anzac rhetoric.

The organisation was similar to that of previous conservative movements. Like the League of National Security and the secretive Old Guard,[30] it was formed by ex-army officers and prominent figures in business and financial circles. Such groups had begun to come together in Australia during the 1920s with the passions of Empire loyalism and defence of property and anti-Communism.

The New Guard was thus not a new movement. It was in the tradition of anti-labour conservative groups that had opposed the rise of labour since the nineteeth century. The New Guard did adopt some trappings of European fascism, such as the occasional use of the Fascist salute. But the New Guard ideology never achieved Right radicalism. The movement was in reality a body which saw its role as the defence of the conservative version of democracy.[31]

With the slow return of prosperity and the fall of Lang, the New Guard dwindled. As the trauma of the Depression disappeared in the World War II years and high post-war high employment, Australian Society returned to the Deakinite 'social contract' which had shown a remarkable resilience as long as its basic foundations of great power dependency, white racism, protectionism and award wages were not completely overturned.

Notes

1. Drucker, P. *The End of Economic Man.* London, Heinemann, 1939, pp. 123–24 as referred to in Kedward, H.R. *Fascism in Western Europe 1990–45.* London, Blackie, 1969, pp. 217–18.
2. Wilke, G. 'Village Life in Nazi Germany' *History Today* 36, October 1985, p. 24.
3. Watkins, F.M. *The Age of Ideology — Political Thought 1750 to the Present.* New Jersey, Englewood Cliffs, 1964, p. 95.

4. Kedward, H.R. *Fascism in Western Europe 1900–45*. London, Blackie, 1969, p. 48.
5. Kedward, pp. 6–34.
6. Watkins, pp. 41–45.
7. Preston, Nathaniel Stone *Politics, Economics and Power*. USA, Macmillan, 1969, p. 203.
8. Kedward, p. 111.
9. Gilbert, G.M. *The Psychology of Dictatorship*. New York, Ronald Press, 1959 as quoted in Kedward, p. 186.
10. Cross, R. (ed.) *20th Century*. London, Purnell Reference Books, Vol. 13, 1982, p. 1376.
11. Geyer, M. 'The Nazi State: Machine or Morass' *History Today* 35, October 1985.
12. Bissel, R. 'Political Violence and the Nazi Seizure of Power' *History Today* 35, October 1985, pp. 8–14.
13. Geyer, M. 'The Nazi State: Machine or Morass' *History Today* 36, January 1986, pp. 35–39.
14. Geyer, p. 37.
15. Geyer, p. 39.
16. Allen, Gary *None Dare Call it Conspiracy*. California, Concord Press, 1973.
17. Chomsky, N. *The Washington Connection and Third World Fascism*, Vol. 1. Boston, South End Press, 1979, p. 250.
18. Catholic Commission for Justice and Peace *National Security Regimes in Latin America: A Guide for Discussion*. March 1980, p. 166.
19. Atkin, R. *Revolution: Mexico 1910–20*. London, Panther, 1972, p. 49.
20. Jones, G. *Social Darwinism and English Thought*. New Jersey, Harvester, 1980.
21. Spoonley, P. 'The National Front: Ideology and Race' *Journal of Intercultural Studies*, Vol. I, (1) 1980, pp. 59–65.
22. McQueen, H. 'The Social Origins of the New Guard' *Arena* 40, 1975.
23. Campbell, E. *The Rallying Point: My Story of the New Guard*. Victoria, Melbourne University Press, 1975, pp. 129–39.
24. Mollo, A. *To the Death's Head True: The Story of the SS*. UK, Thames/Methuen, 1982, p. 25.
25. See McQueen.
26. Putting up the Tariff Wall *Australia's Heritage* Vol. 9. Third Edition. Sydney, Lansdowne, 1982. p. 1556.
27. Collins, H. 'Political Ideology in Australia: The Distinctiveness of a Benthamite Society' *Deadalus* Winter 1985.
28. See McQueen.
29. Ibid.
30. Ibid.
31. Amos, K. *The New Guard Movement 1931–35*. Victoria, Melbourne University Press, 1976, pp.]8-19.

References

General

Brady, R.A. *The Spirit and Structure of German Fascism*. New York, Citadel Press, 1971.
Bissel, R. 'Political Violence and the Nazi Seizure of Power' *History Today* 35, October 1985.
Cross, R. (ed.) *20th Century*. London, Purnell Reference Books, Vol. 13, 1982.

De Grand, A. *Italian Fascism: Its Origins and development*. USA, Lincoln University of Nebraska, 1982.

Ebenstein, W. *Today's Isms* Sixth Edition. Englewood Cliffs, Prentice-Hall, 1970.

Gamble, A. *An Introduction to Modern Social and Political Thought*. London, Macmillan, 1981.

Geyer, M. 'The Nazi State: Machine or Morass' *History Today* 36, January 1986.

Glaser, H. *The Cultural Roots of National Socialism*, London, Croom Helm, 1978.

Gossett, T.F. *Race: The History of an Idea in America*. USA Schocken Press, 1978.

Gross, B. *Friendly Fascism: The New Face of Power in America*. New York, South End Press, 1980.

Gregor, A.J. *The Ideology of Fascism*. New York, Free Press, 1969.

Kedward, H. *Fascism in Western Europe 1900–45*. London, Blackie, 1969.

Kitchen, M. *Fascism*. London, Macmillan, 1976.

Lubasz, H. (ed.) *Fascism: Three Major Regimes*. New York, Wiley, 1973.

Mollo, A. *To the Death's Head True: The Story of the SS* UK, Thames/Methuen, 1982.

O'Sullivan, N. *Fascism*. London, Dent, 1983.

Preston, N.S. *Politics, Economics and Power*. USA, Macmillan, 1969.

Purcell, H. *Fascism*. Melbourne, Nelson, 1981.

Sargent, L.T. *Contemporary Political Ideologies*. Illinois, Dorsey, 1969.

Watkins, F.M. *The Age of Ideology — Political thought 1750 to the Present*. New Jersey, Englewood Cliffs, 1964.

Wilke, G. 'Village Life in Nazi Germany' *History Today* 36, October 1985. *Western Political Theory* Part 3. New York, Harcourt Brace Jovanovich, 1968.

Contemporary Trends

Allen, Gary, *None Dare Call it Conspiracy*. USA, Concord Press, 1973.

Amos, K. *The New Guard Movement 1931–35*. Victoria, Melbourne University Press, 1976.

Atkin, P. *Revolution: Mexico 1910–20*. London, Panther, 1972.

Australia's Heritage Vol. 9. Third Edition. Sydney, Landsdowne Press, 1982.

Billig, M. *Fascists: A Social Psychological View of the National Front*. London, Academic Press, 1978.

Calvo, Roberto 'The Church and Doctrine of National Security' *Journal of Inter-American Studies and World Affairs* 2 (1), 1979, pp. 69–88.

Campbell, A.A. *The Australian League of Rights*. Victoria, Outback Press, 1978.

Campbell, E. *The Rallying Point: The Story of the New Guard*. Victoria, Melbourne University Press, 1965.

Chomsky, N. and Hermann, E.S. *The Washington Connection and Third World Fascism* Vol. 1. Boston, South End Press, 1979.

Collins, H. 'Political Ideology in Australia: The Distinctiveness of a Benthamite Society' *Daedalus* Winter 1985, Boston, USA.

Fielding, N. *The National Front*. London, Routledge and Kegan Paul, 1981.

Gossett, T.F. *Race: The History of an Idea in America*. New York, Schocken Books, 1971.

Jones, G. *Social Darwinism and English Thought*. New Jersey, Harvester, 1980.

McQueen, H. 'The Social Character of the New Guard' *Arena* 40, 1975.

National Security Regimes in Latin America: A Guide for Discussion. Catholic Commission for Justice and Peace, March 1980.

Spoonley, P. 'The National Front: Ideology and Race' *Journal of Intercultural Studies* 1 (1) 1980.

Truitt, R.D. 'Defining Latin American Security Issues' Military Affairs, 1976, 40(4), pp. 169–175.

Walker, M. *The National Front* Second Edition. London, Fontana, 1978.

Recommended Reading

Kedward, H. *Fascism in Western Europe 1900–45*. London, Blackie, 1969.

Mollo, A. *To the Death's Head True' The Story of the SS*. UK, Thames/Methuen, 1982

Sargent, L.T. *Contemporary Political Ideologies*. Illinois, Dorsey, 1969.

Chomsky, N. and Hermann, E.S. *The Washington Connection and Third World Fascism* Vol. 1. Boston, South End Press, 1979.

Amos, K. *The New Guard Movement 1931–35*. Australia, Melbourne University Press, 1976.

2

Conservatism

> I attest the retiring, I attest the advancing generations
> between which, as a link in the great chain of external order,
> we stand.
>
> Edmund Burke in Warren Hastings,
> *Works*, Vol. VIII, p. 439[1]

The ideology of conservatism has puzzled many scholars
determined to identify its salient points. In essence, 'it is largely
a psychological preference rather than a rational ideology'.[2] As
such, conservatives can appear even inside radical politics,
usually as the 'Right wing' or 'pragmatist' section of the movement, or as the proponents of the correct traditional methods.

This phenomenon is particularly noted in post-revolutionary
societies, where the old culture has been destroyed or degraded
by colonialism or the revolutionary act itself. There is thus no old
cultural/political tradition to preserve. After a short giddy period
of rapid change when radicals are in charge of the revolutionary
process (e.g. Maoist China), the conservative mentality reasserts
itself within the revolutionary movement as the guardian of
the correct ideological line. The conservative searches eternally
for the security of habit which becomes tradition and later
prescription.

Conservatism, however, for the purposes of this study, can be
generalised into three basic types:

1. *Reactionary conservatism* which opposes without discussion,
   or views with immediate suspicion, any proposed change
   in all political, economic or socio-cultural matters, reacting
   with blind opposition. Such reactionary or 'passive' conservatism offers few ideological reasons for such opposition.
   It usually resorts to mysticism such as 'the nation's way of
   life' or 'God-given morality'. Its appeal is usually to the
   need for security and simple correct answers in a complex
   world.
2. *Radical conservatism* develops a recognisable set of ideological principles, usually built around the notions of some
   moral and economic paradise from which society has
   fallen. It stresses the need for action, will and the cleansing

of the body politic of agitators, malcontents and conspirators in order to achieve once more the correct path.
3. *Organic (mainstream) conservatism* is a subtler form. It is adaptable to change, but only on its own terms which aim at the preservation of the status quo. Such a conservatism is suspicious of any ideology which commits it to fixed goals and policies. It prefers instead a vaguer set of 'principles', stressing honour, order, morality, economic values etc. which, of course, are identified with this group's set of values. Both 'organic' and 'radical' conservatism can be 'active' conservatisms. They can both seek to propagandise and capture public support, although both groups may have different ultimate objectives.

An ideology of defined conservative principles tends to exist in those countries with continuous or near-continuous development. This is particularly true of those which have escaped the corrosion of colonialism and modern social revolution. Such countries are usually historically dominant 'First World' core countries such as the UK, the USA, and, to a lesser degree Western Europe, Japan and such semi-peripheral countries as Australia, Canada and New Zealand.

In the latter cases, as well as in the USA, conservatism tends to be a form of liberalism, as the residual feudal elements of aristocracy, the landed gentry and a state church were not transferred or reproduced in any influential manner. Tradition and precedent are not, therefore, fundamental factors in conservatism in such countries. There is a greater commitment to express conservatism in the economic terms of *laisser-faire* capitalism (Whiggism), and to support the extension of the franchise slowly to all, rather than support for the other, 'Tory' stream of conservatism.

The Tory stream stressed the mystical union of all classes in the organic order; the responsibility of the élite towards the weaker members of society in return for obedience; and the limitation of democracy to those 'born to rule', as indicated by class or social status. It also stressed the preservation of a defined mode of social morality. It originally viewed the uncontrolled workings and morals of *laisser-faire* capitalism with some distaste and suspicion.

Conservative ideology in the West thus tends to have two basic emphases:

1. *Social morality* which conforms to traditional standards of responsible family life and upright personal life-style. Social discipline exists when one code of social morality is

enforced. It is reinforced when the pursuit of one 'ideal type' of citizen (e.g. the English gentleman or the church-going family man) permeates the cultural and educational training of all members of the society.

2. *Freedom is indivisible from private property.* The existence of private property is held to be the cornerstone of all other freedoms. This is a universal theme in Western conservatism.

Each country with an outlined conservative ideology has, of course, culture-specific approaches to these basics. Nevertheless, both elements provide the foundations of world-wide conservative ideology.

Conservatism can thus initially be recognised by its concern with social morality and private property. However, it also has a definite style:

1. *It represents an attitude to change.* Conservatism prefers to oppose or control change, desiring change that is incremental and adapted to the existing order. Mainstream conservatism thus differs from reactionary conservatism in that it does not simply oppose for opposition's sake, and from radical conservatism in that it does not wish to return to some pre-existing legendary society or state (See the Radical Right).

2. *It has a veneration for process and ordered tradition.* In many ways, conservatism is pre-industrial in its style. It possesses a mystical belief in the unity of the state, society and government, all growing organically through the historical experiences of the nation or race. Intuitively, therefore, the conservative searches for those institutions (such as royalty) and myths (such as nationalism) which are above class conflict or a demeaning political arena. History is thus very important in the eyes of the conservative. Differing historical interpretations of key people, institutions or events can often be received with deep disapproval or even rejection. It is important to preserve the mystical link with the past in an ideal manner. A nation must not lose its self-confidence.

3. *It possesses a deep suspicion of the rationalist ideologies.* Liberalism and socialism are the offspring of the European Enlightenment. They are ideologies born from the Enlightenment cult of rationality and later from the Industrial Revolution with its focus on 'progress' based on technocracy and development.

   The conservative has come to terms with developmentalism in modern times, since the rise of nineteenth-century socialism has driven the industrial middle class into his arms. However, the suspicion of humanist (or human-centred) rationalist ideologies still exists.

To a conservative, both liberalism and socialism have laid hands on the order of things. These ideologies have elevated reason to first place in man's existence. They have used the state to implement vast changes in pursuit of their utopias. They have introduced dissension into such things as education and culture under the guise of enquiry and realism. This is the 'treason of the intellectuals' and the modern education-based 'new middle class'. They have deprived the masses of the comfort of their national and cultural myths.

The conservative duty is thus defined as opposition to this process. This opposition, as stated, can be simply passive. It can be based upon irrational fear of change, loyalty to old ways or defence of existing property arrangements. Conservatives can find themselves stubbornly defending the 'irrational' or 'illogical', simply because it *is*.

On the other hand, conservative opposition can be active and ideologically articulate. This is particularly the case with the 'New Right'. With the exhaustion in the West of the liberal utopia[3] and its ideal type of 'rational man', conservatives (especially libertarian conservatives) have been increasingly loud in pointing the way back to their Paradise Lost.

4. *Conservatism is an anti-ideology.*[4] Conservatism arose slowly, in opposition to Enlightenment proposals of reason, natural justice and rights. It was appalled by Rousseau's picture of the individual trapped and corrupted by an unjust society, for the conservative venerated that very society, formed by the experiences of centuries.

The notion that progress would follow if the individual could break the shackles that community laid on him seemed to the conservative to be an act of sacrilege. Opponents seemed lunatics, a word that conservatives have always used to describe radicals.

It was the shock of the French Revolution that forced conservatism to outline its precepts and seek mass ideological support. This great liberal revolution put the European ruling classes on the defensive, in which situation conservatism needed to express itself as an antirevolutionary and anti-liberal ideology.

Yet at the same time, it was obvious to many that the idea of material progress, which implied a better life for the masses through the application of science, was an attractive idea.

Conservatism set out to show that such progress was best achieved with order. The old and new should be reconciled by adapting existing institutions — thus foiling the utopian thinkers. Incremental progress preserved tradition, social harmony and the ruling power structure that had evolved.

Origins

Edmund Burke and British Conservatism

It was Edmund Burke who first outlined the precepts that form the basis of conservative ideology to this day. The fact that Britain was the source of the first articulated Conservative ideology was probably inevitable. The empiricist tradition of British philosophy rejected the European Continental rationalist mode descended from Descartes, which argued that we can know the world through reason alone. To Cartesians, 'the real world is characterized by order and rationality ... Truth about reality lies in the logic of the theory.'[5]

British empiricist tradition from Locke to Hume rejected this assertion. Reality could only be known through experience. Hume in particular stressed that rights and justice stemmed not from 'natural law' but from the conventions of society which changed only when their usefulness to that society ceased. Change was therefore incremental and culture-specific, each society operating by its own 'logic of sentiment'.[6] There were no universal truths.

This was part of the philosophical background of Edmund Burke. He, however, was not simply reflecting empiricist philosophy, but also articulated the values of the dominant class, the English landed gentry.

Since the English Civil War (1642–49), the landed gentry had dominated British political power. English political thinkers of this period (such as Harrington)[7] had welcomed its rise, since it was seen as the basis of stability and order. These thinkers outlined an ideal of limited democracy. The franchise would be property-based, not universal, and each section of English society would know its place. The élite, who would rule, would do so in a decent and responsible fashion, in return for power.

This 'social contract' with the lesser orders stressed paternalism. Lesser people would be protected if they did their loyal duty to the whole and their masters. Rights existed for all at each level, part of their birthright as Englishmen. Such rights would be protected by law as it was convenient and necessary to the maintenance of the whole. They did not exist as individual 'natural' rights, as rationalists and liberals stressed, but as part of the balance of the whole social machine. Men had hit upon this balance in the past and, as long as it worked, it should be maintained.

Liberalism, with its stress upon individualism, would destroy this machine. It would atomise society. Worse, it would, under the false liberal ideology of individual reason and equality, cast the weak and ignorant masses into a world where they would not survive. The French Revolution was thus a mortal threat to the English system of values in a way that the American Revolution of 1775–83 had not been.

Burke and many of his Whig Party had defended the right of the American revolutionaries to oppose the extension of royal power. He saw the American Revolution as simply the defence by overseas Englishmen of their traditional liberties against the Crown. They had not lost these by becoming colonials.

English political life was a balance between the power of the Crown and the rights of the Commons. The Crown, in upsetting this balance in America, had brought revolution down upon its own head.

The new American republic continued the notion of counter-weighted power and slow constitutional change. To English conservatives, society was safe even if American conservatism was eventually to take on the form of business-based liberalism. The power of the American 'gentry' class did not last long past the Revolution, if such a class ever powerfully existed at all there.

The French Revolution, however, was a leap into a new rationalist era.

Burke was thus an enemy of France and a friend of America. In his book counter-attacking the French Revolution *Reflections on the French Revolution* (1790), he laid down the broad foundations of conservative ideology:

The Theory of the State

The state is the guardian of society and the repository of the wisdom of the nation. The government of the day is simply a trustee, and should not initiate change if it can be avoided, but await its social generation.

However, the government of the day should not ignore its duty. Government should be firm, indeed ruthless, in its protection of society against the lawless and anti-social. It should bolster the power of religion and tradition. It should reform when the state, government and society are in agreement.

The state and its government are one part of the nation, but not its dominant one (although conservatives could differ over the leading role of the state). Freedom emerges from the existence of private institutions — the family, community groups etc., which have emerged over time. The state and its government are the guardians of their free association and lawful conduct. The state and its government can and indeed, should prevent anti-social conduct. But the state and its government should not be guided in this by revolutionary or rationalist ideology.

Indeed, such ideological fervour is seen as the worst anti-social conduct of all. This type of fervour in government strips society of the protection of precedent and the comfort of tradition. The citizenry will become victims of those who possess the state and an ideology which justifies all actions including murder, in the name of reason.

Force, based upon immediate expediency, would eventually guide the actions of such a state. It would declare war on society in the name of reason.

The Theory of Society

In order to understand this dire prophecy, we must look to Burke's assumptions and English history. The English Revolution (1642–60) had indeed resulted in the dictatorship of Cromwell and his army, despite the initial hopes of English republicans and supporters of the Commonwealth. This precedent was not lost upon Burke.

But Burke was primarily basing his conservative defence of civilisation on a different belief in man's nature than that which underlay the French *Declaration of the Rights of Man* (1789).

The French Revolution stressed Rousseau's notion of 'man in chains'. The innocent nature of man was twisted and deformed by a social *nurture* into which he was born but which he did not make. It was a system of unjust power, wealth and class bias. Yet man was supposed not to question this structure but to conform to 'the wisdom of the ages'.

Tom Paine (1737–1809) outlined liberal objections to Burke in *The Rights of Man* (1791) and railed against Burke's idea that the present should conform to the strictures of dead generations. Much later, too, Karl Marx was to repudiate this notion of rule by precedent, habit and tradition, writing in *The German Ideology*, 'And so the muck of ages weighs like a nightmare on the mind of the living'. Both upheld Rousseau's view that by improving social nurture (or society), man's good nature would be released. This Burke simply did not believe.

To him, society was the creation of little men and little adaptations. It was too large and complex to be changed by the state. If Rousseau's 'chains' were released, viciousness, not altruism, would be the dominant drive. Man had been born evil. His nature was corrupt. He was civilised by the state, tradition, coercion and habit. Social discipline created what was good in man. Therefore the 'true' conservative saw himself as the guardian of *social morality*.

This is the fundamental concern of the conservative 'Old Right' in contemporary times. There exist strong differences between the Tory and Whig Old Right perspectives on social morality.[8] The Tory view is that social morality rests upon frail human nature, which should be understood for its hypocrisies and sins, though not condoned. The most we can do for human nature, Tories believe, is to guide it towards self-improvement.

The Whig view, however, is influenced by its Protestant Puritan and Irish Catholic ancestry in English-speaking countries. It stresses the role of the state in the prohibition of human sins of the flesh, but not necessarily economic inequality. These views often emerged in repressive social legislation and prescriptive practices. Puritanism and conservatism often thus became synonymous.

The contemporary New Right, while making political alliance with such moral conservatives, is more attached to the subideology of libertarian capitalism.[9] The New Right wishes to return to the other aspect of the lost Whig Puritan utopia. This was the society of the free economic man, untrammelled by state interference.

To a true Burkeian conservative, suspicious of any ideology or fervour, the New Right is a source of great misgivings.

The Theory of Progress in Economics and History

The conservative views himself as the 'sea anchor' of history. In Burke's time, conservative opposition to the liberal theory of progress was largely opposed to the liberal notion of progress via Individual reason.

In the nineteenth century, however, British conservatives were faced with the deeper and more enduring challenge of industrialism riding upon technical progress. New social classes such as the industrial working class and the liberal-minded manufacturing business class were rising to the fore. The numerical base of original conservative power — the landed gentry and the rural voter — went into decline.

It is at this point that mainstream conservatism shows its natural adaptability in seeking new supportive coalitions. In the advanced countries of Western Europe, in the USA, the UK and the British-influenced countries of the Commonwealth, there has been a steady shift by conservatives from rural to urban support. While still preserving old rural bases, conservative ideology has received votes from an increasingly wide spectrum of social classes. In the twentieth century, in particular, conservative support has emerged strongly from the upwardly mobile lower middle class — the small business man and the ambitious or socially conservative worker.

Conservative ideology, serves a purpose when approaching the problem of 'progress' in the industrial age, offering as it does institutional and economic certainty in an age of rapid technical change for such security-conscious social classes. Through it, 'progress' can be handled without institutional destabilisation, and in a *respectable* manner. This is the great conservative ideological attraction — its domination of the 'standards' or 'boundaries of decency' or mainstream values.

The British Conservative Party was the first to meet the challenge of technological progress and its consequent social change, under Disraeli in 1867. It moved to capture as much of the new industrial worker vote as possible, undercutting the emerging liberal/labour partnership that was to be the major radical force in industrialising countries.

Disraeli shrewdly concluded that the desire for order and respectability was not confined to the upper and middle classes. He propounded a new social contract to attract the conservative elements of the British working class.

This outlined a gradual share for all classes as the productivity cake grew, while still preserving the rights of the employer and property rights. It also offered a share in Imperial status, by virtue of race, and a reflection of glory from the Imperial idea of the British civilising mission. This kind of 'closed' nationalist myth, stressing the uniqueness of national culture, and the need for unity to attain national progress, quickly became one of the tenets of conservative ideology in all Western countries.

Conservative approaches to this national progress varied according to cultural heritages. The USA adopted the full blooded Whig developmental mentality compared with the more re-strained British Tory conservatism and the often reactionary European variety of conservatism.

European Conservatism

European conservatism was highly suspicious of liberalism after the experience of the French Revolution. The old monarchical conservatism of Europe had been removed or shaken by

Napoleon and then restored by the Council of Europe (1815), influenced by the Austrian Count Metternich.

Restored conservatism had its confidence shaken to the roots. Under Metternich, it attempted to maintain itself against liberalism by the executioner and the police spy instead of the shrewd English method of adaptation.

What conservative Europe truly feared was the triumph of the masses — the little, common people — which had been vaguely experienced in the Jacobin and earlier periods of the French Revolution. Political writers such as the Frenchman De Tocqueville (1805–59) studied such 'mass' democracies as the USA, warning of their levelling effect (*Democracy in America*, 1840) if the concept of 'progress' was uncontrolled by an élite and linked to universal suffrage and hence the common man. De Tocqueville, like modern writers such as Aldous Huxley (*Brave New World*) was a cultural conservative identifying quality values with élite rule. Mass democracy would only degrade taste.

As Winthrop and Lovell indicate,[10] nineteenth-century European political writers such as Gaetano Mosca, Vilfredo Pareto and Ortega y Gasset (*The Revolt of the Masses*) were obsessed with the role of élites in maintaining standards of civilisation against 'the great unwashed'. This depended on élite control of political power. Ortega y Gasset, especially, argued that this was always possible due to the existence of two types of citizen, a 'self-made, self-disciplined' and often rational elite. The other was a mass citizenry — fearful and lacking in independent thought. 'Such mass minds could be found across all social classes, so class theory was irrelevant'. Leaders came from all classes. They were courageous and self-confident, stepping blithely into the existential void of life despite codes of morality, conduct and conformity. Thus democracy should encourage the mobility of such leaders to the top, but no more.

Such conservative democratic élitist theory, together with the necessity for such élites to manipulate the masses (deriving from Mosca and Pareto), expressed a contempt for and fear of the common man not so evident in English Toryism. The roots of Fascism are evident in the conservative élitist approach to the rise of the European masses on the back of 'industrial progress'.

Thus the notion of 'progress' was a grave problem for social control in much of European conservative thought. Would it cause a repeat of the French Revolution? In Germany, the answer was found in the romantic nationalism of Herder and Treitscke. This adapted to the rise of the masses and 'progress' by steering them into a union with the conservative Prussian state around ethnocentric notions of 'destiny', *kultur* and the idealisation of the German warrior.

All conservative ideology, however, in all countries stressed that progress in history was linked to the soul of the nation. It might or might not be linked to economics. Conservatism was thus quite willing to use the state to tinker with the capitalist system to preserve that soul. For, ultimately, what was important was élite leadership. Leadership ensured the unity of state and society; the preservation of the institutions of state and society; and that all classes were loyal to the task. Ideology was, at all times, expendable. What was important was the preservation of political power in conservative hands.

If such a smooth-running unity of the nation was not occurring, such disruption was not necessarily due to poor conservative management, but to the existence of the agitator, the anti-social and the misled. The nation is best defended, therefore, with the elimination or marginalisation of the conspirator and the defence of the 'natural' system of private property.

The history of conservative ideology over the nineteenth and twentieth centuries is thus littered with a succession of perceived conspirators and threats. These begin with the French revolutionaries and the *Declaration of the Rights of Man*, which so aroused Burke, and go right up to present-day communist, humanist and unionist 'conspiracies'.

Conservatives are not alone in the use of political 'conspiracy theory'. However, rarely has an ideology depended so much on what it opposes. And, indeed, rarely has an ideology so deftly used an instrument such as 'conspiracy' and social ostracism to slow down the pace of social 'progress'; to adapt it to respectability, and to cleanse it of all elements hostile to the status quo.

In contemporary politics, this conservative method has become double-pronged. Under the New Right label, conservatism has seized the initiative from the tired liberal Welfare State. The social moralist conservative and the *laissez-faire* free enterpriser have tried to come back together in a Whig Puritan unity. In doing so, ideology and capitalism have intertwined.[11]

Thus conservatism has come full circle, enmeshing the conservative sense of social morality with the *laissez-faire* economic system[12] whose ideological ancestor was the very liberalism that Burke opposed.

Contemporary Trends: The New Right

One of the most interesting intellectual effects of the decline of the post-war social democratic and Keynesian consensus ... has been to reveal the divergence within the political Right between conservative and libertarian tendencies. Whereas most conservatives have remained attached to several aspects of the consensus, most obviously the welfare state and wide ranging government regulation of the economy, libertarians have advocated either abolishing the welfare state or restricting (welfare), deregulating the economy and relying instead on the forces of the free market ... [13]

Quadrant, June 1983

Background

The New Right (or neo-conservatism) is the name given to conservative ideological thought behind Right-wing resurgence of ideas in the 1970–80s.

In order to understand this phenomenon, it is first necessary to trace a short historical outline of the clash between liberalism and conservatism in the late nineteenth and early twentieth centuries.

Generally speaking, there was a growth in the role of the state in all advanced Western countries in this period. The idea of the regulatory state grew largely from nineteenth-century liberal ideology. Liberal ideology of this period broke from the original eighteenth-century liberal capitalist model first outlined by Adam Smith in *The Wealth of Nations*. The original model of liberal democracy confined the state to defence, law enforcement and the bare necessities of state economic involvement.

Under the influence of such nineteenth-century liberal philosophers as Green and Hobson, the second phase of liberal thought saw this 'pure' Adam Smith liberal state as 'heartless'. The state was in a position to forge a 'capitalism with a human face'. It could regulate safety standards, working conditions and wages and tariffs, to provide security and some predictability to an otherwise chaotic 'market' economy system.

Many conservatives, too, were attracted to this notion of the regulatory state which forges a new social contract with an otherwise restive labour force. From Burke's day, 'many conservatives [saw] the state as uniquely charged with perceiving and realising the "common good"'. This protective role of the state 'requires that there should be no limitations on its powers'.[14]

Thus, during the historical rise of the liberal welfare state in the twentieth century, one conservative element, (that known in contemporary British conservatism as the 'Wets') adapted ideologically to its emergence. While great increases in state power were often opposed by conservatives, nevertheless most mainstream conservatives, when in government, tended to continue, or even add to, this same power of the state.

Increasingly, therefore, by the post-world War 11 period, the differences between liberal/social democratic and conservative governments were to be found in social morality areas (divorce, abortion, etc.), human rights issues or foreign policies. Consensus largely ruled in the area of economic management and market control.

Reasons for Convergence

This progress of liberal/conservative convergence in practice over the Welfare State was expedited by several historical factors. The most important were: first, the rise of nineteenth and twentieth-century *mercantilism* (or protectionist policies) boosted the role of the liberal regulatory state. This process was speeded up by the formation of the great nineteenth-century European empires and the competition between industrial nations, as new rivals such as Germany and the USA joined the search for export markets. The state was called upon to protect national and infant industries from 'unfair' foreign competition. The worker movements of such countries concurred in these regulations, since jobs were protected. Even Britain, which had been the first industrial nation and proponent of nineteenth-century free trade, was by 1902 forced into a mercantilist position.

Secondly, the *extension of the franchise to the working classes* in liberal democracies meant the rise of working class parties or parties responsive to such voters. Such social democratic parties or union-led interest groups pushed for a 'social democrat/ liberal consensus' formed around the liberal Welfare State. This consensus or social contract cushioned the workers and the poor by providing such things as pensions, public education, and free hospitals. These were to be paid for by taxes drawn from the rich and the middle classes. This 'social wage' was seen as a means of social equity, as well. Taxes would ensure that there would be no-one too rich and no-one too poor.

This was not a Marxist 'Left' state, but a liberal 'Left' one. Capitalism still existed, even if it was regulated and forced to recycle its profits to other groups in society by the state's wage fixing apparatus and public spending. The free market was now a 'fair' one.

This trend to the Welfare State was speeded up by the trauma of the Great Depression (1929–39) and World War II. The Great Depression brought the 'free market' theories of economics into disrepute. It also radicalised many of that generation, who then sought solutions from the Left. World War II also brought into disrepute such ideologies as Fascism as antidotes to the excesses of market capitalism.

World War II, particularly, underlined the regulatory and directive role of the state in economic planning. Old empires were declining after the war and markets were being thrown open to export-oriented firms of international capital. The rise of big business also endorsed the regulatory role of the liberal state. It preferred long-term planning, security of labour inputs and well-managed fiscal and monetary policy.

Thus, in post-war Western democracies, the liberal state became more and more the preserve of big bureaucracies, big business and big unions. Under the influence of the economic policies of Lord Keynes, the post-war liberal democratic state took on an air of having solved capitalism's ills. By the late 1960s, there was prosperity, and employment flourished. Where economic conservatism (libertarianism) did exist, it was usually confined to a few querulous intellectuals.

The libertarian stream of conservatism, that of the 'Drys', had been quite submerged as a viable stream of conservative ideology since the Great Depression. Libertarians endorsed the Adam Smith-style limited state. The free market should prevail in all things including the public services through privatisation. They attacked their fellow conservative Wets for using the state to pursue something called 'the common good'.

To a libertarian, there is no such thing. As Levin states, 'the common good is a figment of political imagination'. Society is seen as a mass of different interests all vying to buy and sell in one common economic market. A state pursuing 'the common good' is really, on investigation, 'pushing one interest group's desires at the expense of others'.[15] Or such a state will be blackmailed by a group of big interests (business, labour and bureaucracy) colluding at the expense of smaller ones.[16]

However, in the face of the success of the liberal Welfare State between 1945–73, such libertarian talk did not find public support. The social democratic/liberal consensus or social contract held firm as long as post-war prosperity endured.[17]

The Crisis of Liberalism

By 1973. however, cracks were appearing in the fabric of the liberal state. There was a *decline in productivity*. Since the Bretton Woods Agreement of 1944, Keynesian economics had stressed the interventionist model of the state. It would use fiscal and monetary policies to dampen inflation and avoid deflation. Production would thus be fairly continuous, without the great market slumps of the past.

Out of this growing production would emerge a liberal utopia. Tax monies would increase, as all grew richer. There would be enough public money to increase public wages and also increase welfare, as well as integrating ex-consensus or alienated minorities, such as blacks, into the system. The prevailing welfare view of both conservative and liberal/social democrat was that after big business, government and unions got their share, a regulated trickle-down effect would boost these 'out groups' of the poor and alienated. There would also be enough to finance arms expenditure against the rival Soviet system.

By the early 1970s, however, productivity began to decline in many of the advanced Western economies. The high cost of labour and increasing taxation and inflation saw the flight of capital to countries with lower labour costs, longer working hours and more labour discipline. Government spending on welfare plus wages (both private and the 'social wage') was higher, by 1975, than production,[18] signalling serious and continuing inflation. Similarly, the replacement of high-cost labour by industrial technology meant the rise of a permanent pool of unemployables. This group was limited by their skill levels in attaining new employment. They were doomed to a permanent dole existence which the moral conservatives, especially, condemned for its alienating and anti-social tendencies.

Prospects for the continuation of the liberal state were also not increased by the OPEC petrol cartel of 1973. After that, the liberal welfare state could not depend on cheap fuel to underwrite continued prosperity. The petrol-producing nations of the Third World saw their petroleum as a rapidly decreasing asset used to prop up a false First World standard of living. Such countries meant to make the First World pay to underwrite their own industrial development.

There was a crisis of the ideology of liberalism. So strong had the belief become in the West, in the permanence of the social democrat/liberal consensus and the Welfare State, that many politicians and scholars pronounced political ideology dead. The liberal welfare consensus ruled both conservative and liberal parties. Those radicals of the Left and Right who did not move pragmatically towards this consensus were thought doomed to remain on the fringe of politics.

Even Marxist thinkers such as Marcuse (*One Dimensional Man*)[19] thought that the function of the liberal Welfare State was to buy off and dampen the radicalism of the Western working classes. Radicalism was thus confined as an oddity of some of the intelligentsia. It also became a 'fringe' movement, concentrating on quality of life issues such as the environment rather than questioning the economic consensus. Liberalism had triumphed.

Throughout the 1970s, however, the liberal framework of values began to be questioned. Linked to the general economic crisis of the liberal welfare state, a rising tide of social conservatism emerged. This found increasing mass support due to the impact of the liberal social legislation in the 1970s. Such liberal legislation or value proliferation centred around feminism, human rights issues such as homosexuality, divorce and abortion; multiculturalism; 'child based' education; pacifism; non-punitive criminal codes and what seemed a general decline in standards of law and order.

A *new conservative partnership*[20] was to be forged between the libertarian and social conservatives in the 1970s–80s, around the link between the free market and the family. The Old Right — conservatives of social morality of all hues — found their scapegoat in the liberal state. The libertarian conservative abhorred this state because of its 'false' *economic* policies. The social conservative now abhorred it because of its 'false' *moral* values. These values were, it was alleged, destroying the cornerstone of society — the family. If the family was destroyed by the personal freedom philosophy of liberalism/humanism then, it was believed, only the state could pick up the pieces. Thus socialism would come by stealth, through the back door.[21] The patriarchal family must be defended. Its existence opposed the final triumph of the liberal state. Liberalism, then, became the true ideological enemy of the New Right partnership.

Beginning in 1979–80, the Thatcher goverment in the UK and the Reagan one in the USA rode to power on New Right ideological principles. The victory was limited in its voting support and certainly neither politican fully implemented the ideology of the New Right. Nevertheless, New Right ideology now sets the ideological agenda of debate.[22]

The debate is a conservative one, due to the crisis of the liberal welfare state and its underlying ideology, and the present inability of liberal theorists to recover the ideological initiative. What, then, are the elements of New Right, or neoconservative ideology?

The Ideology of the New Right

The ideology of the New Right focuses on three elements: family; market; and the defence of the West. This last factor is now a problem for conservatives with the disappearance of the USSR. The threat to these three stems from the existence of two basic ideological enemies — the liberal Welfare State ethos and the 'New Middle Class'.

Throughout New Right ideology,[23] which links both culture and economics in a value reinforcing manner, these factors are considered to be the basis of the decline of the state, society and culture.

The Theory of State and Society. The New Right regards the post-World War II liberal Welfare State as a wrong turning. The Great Depression had frightened Western liberals and conservatives into the liberal Welfare State because of the fear of communism. However, the New Right argues that socialism is no longer an attractive alternative to the Western working class.

The New Right claims that the Western working class is small-capitalist-minded and property orientated. A New Right state, therefore, should not simply return to *laissez faire* attitudes but actively encourage the involvement of the working class in capitalism. It should encourage wide ownership, profit sharing and stock holding. Public housing should be sold. Workers in public enterprises such as telephone companies, should be encouraged to welcome their privatisation and to share in this process. By such means, the state will encourage the entre-preneurial spirit. The alienation of the worker from capitalism is said to emerge from the lack of sharing in the profit process. The state must act positively to build a consciousness of engagement. To do this, however, will require the curtailment of the power of big interests — business, bureaucracy and, particularly, unions.

Unions are a special target. This is not solely because of their power to block the free market, but also because they are considered to be vehicles for the alternative ideologies of class conflict and socialism. At the least, legislation should confine their operation to non-political areas. At best, unions should be destroyed or forced into signing 'no strike' agreements.

Libertarians, in particular, stress the need to reverse the liberal welfare mentality of the post-war decades that has allegedly 'affected' labour productivity. This can only be done by contract-style employment, variable wage legislation and minimum state control of conditions. This would reverse the liberal welfare ethos of dependence, and replace it with a competitive, if not Social Darwinist, spirit.

The free market state would go hand in hand with the patriarchal family and its system of values. Every man and woman's first duty would be to their family and not to a wider collective loyalty such as unions or class. Thus libertarianism, conservative social morality and a trenchant anti-Communism have been drawn together into a new political force. The basic enemy in all of this is the 'New Middle Class'.

The New Middle Class. The New Right emphasises that Western society has become dominated by a post-war phenomenon. Public spending on the expansion of the liberal Welfare State has created a new 'public' middle class of teachers, lawyers, socio-logists, public servants etc. The liberal Welfare State has not only provided this class with jobs but also with an interest in maintaining such state spending. Unlike the old pre-war business middle class, the New Right libertarian argues that this group is unproductive and preaches values contrary to the reality of competitive life and man's aggressive nature.

The New Right conservative who endorses social morality takes an ever dimmer view. This New Middle Class, they claim, is also the new ruling class.[24] It attempts to impose its own set of humanist/liberal values in economics, morality and history, which are totally at variance with what social conservatives see as 'mainstream' values. This new élite, according to the New Right, has come to dominate the media, government bureaucracies, the academies, union leadership and even some business management.[25] So there exists a battle for conceptual hegemony i.e. that 'standards' or 'the boundaries of decency' will be reformulated and taken out of their traditional conservative domain.

The New Right thus reflects the ideological heritage of Mosca and Pareto (élites leading masses) and the traditional conservative usage of 'conspiracy theory', to explain the failure or crisis of the socio-economic system. The 'New Middle Class' has been identified as the cause of this crisis.

To the New Right, this group is an important problem. For years, the New Right maintained the West and was caught up in a struggle with the Soviet system. They argued that the 'New Class' of liberal minded public ideologies weakened the West. It is the duty of conservatives to be active now that liberalism seems to be failing and to reverse the trends of the last forty years which this New Class endorses in its 'New Politics'. The collapse of communism has dampened this conservative critique which now argues that liberalism simply cannot be afforded rather than 'it is soft on communism'.

Table 2.1   Australian New Right Beliefs

Cultural concerns that divide us

The rescue of Australian history

Symbol	Leftist 'orthodoxy' that the New Right attacks	'Mainstream' tradition that New Right asserts
1788	Invasion	Settlement
Aboriginal Contact	Genocide	Fragile native culture
Pioneers	Environmental rapists	Undaunted visionaries

Symbol	Leftist 'orthodoxy' that the New Right attacks	'Mainstream' tradition that New Right asserts
Colonial Women	Oppressed and victimised	Pillars of hearth and home
Working class	Condemned to exploitation	Well-organised and socially mobile
Explorers	Incompetent or possessed	Sturdy adventurers
Eureka Stockade rebels	Working class heroes	Emergent entrepreneurs
British Investment	Economic dependency	Condition for progress
Early capitalists and politicians	Lackeys of London	Enterprising and outward looking
Anzacs	Innocent victims	Conscious patriots
Depressions	Weevils in the flour	'Susso' provided and fascism averted
Menzies	McCarthyism and cultural despair	A home of your own
USA	Source of evil	Natural allies
Immigration	Factory fodder	Land of opportunity

Reasserting traditional social values

Theme	Leftist Interpretation	Mainstream Interpretation
Economic development	Destructive	Creative
Family	Source of conflict	Fundamental social haven
Rights	Minority rights	Responsibilities
Church	Consciousness raiser	Spiritual welfare
Patriotism	Unhealthy, militaristic	Foundation of citizenship
Sexual morality	Alternative lifestyles	Heterosexuality
British heritage and Crown	Colonial anachronism	Lifeline to world's best legal and political institutions

Theme	Leftist Interpretation	Mainstream Interpretation
Australians	Racist	Assimilationist
Australian society	Multicultural	Integrated
Education	Child centred, creative	Standards and citizenship
Ideal man	Sensitive, caring, collectivist	Independent
Australia's future	Solar not nuclear	A secure job

The future of mankind

Theme	Orthodoxy as now taught in schools	Current reality as promoted by New Right
Population	Breeding out of control. Within our lifetime famine, riots, poverty, wars and catastrophe	Rate of growth of population is slowing. Growth of food production outstripping growth of population.
Wealth	Because of the greed of the West the Third World is condemned to be poor	Western economies produce the most food. Third world produces the least due to market inefficiencies.
Resources	Running out of the lot. It's almost all gone	More resources available now then ever before. Doomsday has been predicted for 10,000 years.
Pollution	World becoming filthier and dirtier every day, life more precarious	People are living longer than ever before and in good health. This is the best indicator of a viable environment.
Energy	None left for the Third World or for your kids	Energy cheaper now because there is so much of it. If oil gets more expensive it will become redundant.
Nuclear energy	Dangerous in operation, dangerous wastes and won't take off anyway	Fastest growing form of energy in the world today. Virtually unlimited supply.

Theme	Orthodoxy as now taught in schools	Current reality as promoted by New Right
Practice	That there is an arms race, that it will inevitably terminate life as we know it. It hangs over all our lives.	If the arms race hangs over all our lives this is because the prophets of doom ensure that it does and they ignore the last 40 years of relative peace for the west, unparalledled in the 20th century.
Capitalism	Consumerism and commercialisation are harmful because they encourage over-consumption and stand in the way of a sustainable society.	Commercialisation has democratised the world's best innovations by making them the property of the masses, thus liberating them from drudgery. If you don't believe it try walking.
Ideal society	A 'sustainable' society, living within its means, conserving for future generations and living simply.	A sustainable society is an ecological dreamtime — something which has never happened in human history but whose likeness can be found at times of maximum human impoverishment and misery.
Economic growth	Cannot continue growing as in the past. There has to be a plateau. We are at the pinnacle and should wind back. Life is at its fullest now and that is too unstable.	There are no physical or economic constraints to continued progress. The only constraint is the current self-imposed constraint of ideology and will.
Technology change	Destroys dignity, jobs and lives.	Eases the burdens of centuries and creates completely new sorts of jobs.

Source: Duncan and McAdam, 'The New Right: where it stands and what it means', *Bulletin*, 10 December 1985, p. 39

Conclusion

To many students of ideology, however, the 'New Right' represents simply a return to classic or pre-Keynesian capitalist economics of the *laissez-faire* variety endorsed by Adam Smith, and a resurgence of conservative moral authoritarianism. For such students of politics, this 'New Right' libertarian capitalism places its proponents on the Right wing of liberalism, not within conservatism. 'New Right' libertarian capitalists, or 'dries' (after the term first used by the British Conservative government under Mrs Thatcher in the 1980s) are different from those members of her party who wanted to continue such state regulation. These 'dries' dismiss traditional conservatism for possessing too great an eagerness to use the state as do socialists, communists and 'wet' or state liberals.

On the other hand, the alliance of such libertarian 'New Right' liberals with resurgent conservative moral authoritarians, and their focus on the traditional social values, places the 'New Right' movement within a conservative mould and constituency. For the purposes of this text, therefore, the 'New Right' has been discussed under conservatism.

However, this alliance underlines the truism that ideologies are fluid. The vacuum of ideas caused by the slow collapse of the post-war social democratic-liberal consensus in the West is being filled by the 'New Right' (who now have their own ideological crisis with the collapse of their Soviet enermy). Unlike the period during the Great Depression, liberalism and/or the radical Left have not yet developed an ideological response.

The greatest part of this ideological battle, which is held by the New Right to be raging throughout the Western world, concerns the battle for the mind, the 'consciousness' or concept interpretation of the electorate.

This is, of course, part of the reality that whatever ideology is held to be hegemonic or dominant in offering solutions to economic problems, it will also endeavour to take the initiative in areas of conceptual usage such as history, elbowing aside other perspectives. Outlined in Table 2.1 are the mutually 'antagonistic' positions on beliefs and concept usage taken by the 'New Right' and 'New Class' interpretations. Conservative values are automatically ascribed to 'New Right' and mainstream values.

Contemporary Conservatism in Australia: The New Right

It is evident from what the New Right is saying about Australian Society and national identity that its theorists are convinced they possess great potential to appeal to the conservative middle ground of voters . . .

(Duncan and McAdam, the *Bulletin*,
10 December 1985, p. 38)

The peculiarity of Australian conservatism and its ideological underpinnings lies in its historical development as a dependency of Britain and a white racial dominion. This has led to some cultural unity of the ideas of the mainstream 'Right' and 'Left'. These common elements — British loyalism and White supremacy — were present during the formation of Australian political ideologies from the nineteenth century onwards. A commitment to the developmental mentality also pervaded both sides of the political spectrum, forming another common (if unspoken) bond between parties of the Left and Right.

There had been, of course, a fierce political struggle for control of the nineteenth century state, between land and urban interests. In the early years of colonial self-government, the Australian squattocracy made some attempt to ape the Tory conservative precedent in England. Landed interests attempted to dominate the state and its economic direction by confining the franchise by age, wealth and other forms of limitation. They were initially defeated however, between 1850–1901, by the effects of the gold rushes, with their vast infusion of settlers.

These settlers demanded their share of land as the gold ran out. The rise of urban business (especially in Victoria) provided money and leaders for this dissent, around the Free Selection movements. The British government, after the Eureka Stockade Rebellion (1854), and influenced by Lord Durham's *Report on the Affairs of British North America* (1839) on Canada, with its advice on holding colonies by élite sentiment and education rather than force, was quite favourable to the extension of the franchise.

This was also, of course, the Victorian Age. A widespread philosophy of Benthamite utilitarianism[26] permeated the thinking of Australian capital and labour. The stress in this philosophy was 'the greatest good for the greatest number'. The state should be an active partner in this process and encourage 'fair' capitalism. Capital and labour should seek negotiation, not conflict, and 'accord' over the division of the economic pie. Such division could be determined by a state court if necessary.

Benthamism was a controlled, co-operative ideology of liberalism which did not reflect the apocalyptic class struggle central to the Marxist ideology.

Political conservatism in the British Tory or European reactionary sense, found Australia poor ideological ground in which to take root, although social conservatism flourished. Nevertheless, political conservative forces managed to dominate state upper houses until well into the twentieth century. Known as Houses of Review, these bodies often existed upon limited franchise and gerrymandered electorates. They offered, especially, a haven for 'passive' conservatism in the periods when liberal/ labour governments were in power.

Thus the political style and ideological core of Australia had been largely formed by 1901. All parties agreed to some degree with the common goals of White Australia, British dependency and developmentalism. Benthamite utilitarianism was becoming the most common view of political parties, to the near exclusion of *laisser faire* libertarianism and Marxist class war.

The liberal regulatory and Welfare State was a natural outcome of this common seedbed. Alfred Deakin not only reflected on common racial bonds, with all their cross-class implications,[27] but by 1907–08 had initiated a conservative/liberal ideological front against Labor. This amalgamation was not long-lasting, but Deakin outlined the style of regulatory state that was to dominate Australian political thinking for the next seventy years.

The liberal Welfare State with its protectionist role, and its image as an interest group negotiation arena, became increasingly the mode. Essentially, this mode identified the state as a utilitarian provider of services,[28] not a battlefield of ideology. The purpose of Australian parties was to capture the state, not to provide ideological alternatives. Parties were to be judged by their management of the state, not their dreams.

The structure of this state suited the emerging Australian way of life ('fair' capitalism) and the bargaining of big business; big labour, and farmers with government via their interest groups. By the 1950s, this process had reached its apogee. Conservatives were part of this liberal universe. Even the Country-National Party, formed in 1919, saw its role as part of the liberal regulatory/Welfare State, with access to control of government tariffs and subsidies.

By 1976, cracks were appearing in the Australian liberal Welfare State structure. During the 1960s, dependency on Britain, and hence the security of imperial defence and trade, began to fade. Australia had to meet the challenge of restructuring its economy to the new Pacific Basin region, dominated by Japan and America.[29] This has put enormous pressures on the post-World War II 'social contract' between labour, land and capital. A New Right ideology has arisen in Australia to match the rise of neo-conservatism overseas.

This New Right reflects much of the ideological elements found in overseas criticisms of the liberal welfare state. Eventually, however, it is shaped by Australian conditions and by streams of conservative thought historically present in this culture.

As G. Sheridan points out,[30] there are three major elements in the Australian 'New Right'. These comprise:

(a) the libertarian economic conservatives;
(b) the cultural conservatives;
(c) the Catholic Social Doctrine tradition (or Corporationists).

These streams are not necessarily harmonious and need further elaboration.

The Libertarian Economic Conservatives

As T. Caswell indicates,[31] what is new in the Australian New Right is libertarianism. Historically, Welfare Statism has been dominant. Now, serious consideration is being taken of the hard-headed market liberalism of 'supply side' economic thinkers such as Milton Friedman.

Australian conservatism has long been 'Wet' conservatism with an emphasis on state regulation and social morality. The latter is due to the historical influence of Whig Puritanism and Irish Catholic Jansenism.[32] The dominant ideology of Benthamite utilitarianism had submerged such classical economic theories as *laissez faire* capitalism until the present world-wide economic crisis.

This crisis has emerged due to the end of the long boom which has sustained the Australian economy since 1949. The Chifley-Menzies era saw the rise of Australian prosperity based upon world demand for raw resources. The rural and mining sector were dominant as earners in the export trade in the post-war period. The internal economy was sustained by import replacement industries staffed to a large degree by migrant labour, and protected by tariffs. While Britain remained the imperial mentor, protected markets could be found for primary products in the UK. The Vietnam War also sustained demand for primary products for much of the period while Britain entered the EEC.

The downslide of the Australian economy begins with the end of this long boom, around 1973–76. The libertarian New Right argues that the ideology of liberal Welfare State protection must be broken. Old standards of living derived from the dependent British-Australian link must decline. In particular the Benthamite state ideology of 'the greatest good for the greatest number', ensuring a liberal version of the corporate state which regulated the economic share of business, labour and farming, must be ousted. Australia must return to market liberalism. Therefore, Australian libertarian ideology stresses:

The Dismantling of the historical liberal Welfare state. Libertarians stress the export trade and the internationalisation of the Australian economy. In many ways, they are the resurrection of the Free Traders whom Deakin and his Liberal Protectionists defeated in 1908. Indeed, libertarians deplore the classic industrial law Harvester Case Judgement of Judge Higgins (1907) which set up the notion of the basic wage based on needs and not productivity. From this, they argue, has stemmed the rigidity of Australian wage fixing and industrial relations. In another sense, free trade libertarianism represents the triumph of international over contemporary national capital interests.

The Labour Market. The central demand of the economic New Right is a decentralised labour market. In a new age of a Pacific Basin economy and conglomerate international capital, a uniform and legalistic wage sector would be a problem to enclave and fractionalised development. The solution is a contract labour market, and, if necessary, a dual labour system. This would allow for the existence of a fixed high wage sector of unionised labour. Next to them would exist a fluid labour market of lower paid groups contracting in and out of parttime/short-term jobs.

In effect the libertarian New Right wants to change the traditional Australian-European system of unionised labour to the American individualised system. As Senator Button has written:

> [The contest is between] the United States model where trade unions have been reduced to the status of an ineffectual rump and the European model where traditions of consultation and cooperation have led to the trade union movement being a progressive and significant participant in economic affairs. There are plenty of people in Australia who aspire to the US model as the solution to our problems . . .
>
> (Senator Button, *Institute of Public Affairs Review*,
> 40 (1) Autumn 1986: 3)

Privatisation and Downgrading the Public Sector. Libertarian ideology also challenges the public sector. Historically, this has absorbed much unemployment in Australia. The government and its Public Service has been a vital partner in Australian capitalism since penal days. Libertarians regard the public sector, however, as having grown too wasteful under the liberal Welfare State. The Public Service should be trimmed back to fundamentals such as defence, administration and roads.

Too much public spending has developed a dependent mentality in Australians who have come to look to the government to cushion or deflect economic reality. This public sector (the libertarians also claim) has done more to develop a 'new' class, rather than help the true poor.

Libertarians are particularly strong on the call for privatisation of public bodies, such as Telecom. They argue that such bodies should be sold to private investors or to the bodies' own workers, as in Thatcher's Britain. This will develop worker productivity and the loyalty to capitalism that is presently lacking.

While not proposing worker's power or co-operative communism, it is interesting to see how the New Right recognises the need to overcome alienation as the first role of a successful ideology. In this they are close to anarchism and syndicalist socialist thought, with its emphasis on the meaning of working life. New Right changes to public bodies intend, however, to strengthen capitalism and its adherents, not to replace it.

The first problem for 'Dry' libertarianism is to convince conservative 'Wets' of the electoral viability of their ideology. These conservatives view with grave disquiet the dismantling of such things as rural subsidies.

The New Right libertarians have also singled out the liberal New Middle Class, with its set of economic and cultural values, as antagonists. In so doing, they have come into partnership with other traditional streams of conservatism.

The Cultural Conservatives

A long-term Australian conservative influence has been the intellectual strand centred around the preservation of conservative cultural values, such as the family, race and British links, as evidenced by such symbols as the flag and the Queen.

During the post-World War II period, the intellectual arena in Australia was dominated by liberal ideology in tandem with the dominant liberal Welfare State. Cultural conservatives felt themselves to be marginal. Nevertheless, they persisted over the postwar period with their central tenet of anti-communism and their desire to sustain conservative social morality. The decay of this morality, which they believe is due to mass unemployment, the drug culture, education problems, feminism etc., has been their greatest concern.

The blame for this decay has been located by cultural conservatives in the New Middle Class. This has been singled out as the fountainhead of alternative 'myths' in such areas as literature, history and the media, compared with 'mainstream' ones.[33]

Cultural conservatives have traditionally seen their battleground to be in society and not the state. Like traditional economic conservatives (Wets), cultural conservatives have allocated an active role to the state to uphold the moral 'common good'. Thus cultural conservatives have usually found little common ground with libertarians over the role of the state. Libertarians, for instance, dispute that the state has a duty in social arenas such as divorce, abortion and homosexuality.

The close ideological allies of the cultural conservatives rest more in the historical stream of Catholic Social Doctrine.

Catholic Social Doctrine

The oldest politically organised stream in Australian New Right conservatism stems from political Catholicism. This has its ideological origins in the reaction of the Catholic Church to the liberalism of the French Revolution.

European Catholicism in the period 1789 to the rise of nationalism in Germany and Italy (1870) was thoroughly anti-liberal. The church became enmeshed with the reactionary conservatism of Metternich, leading to the virulent and still-enduring anti-clericalism of European liberals and socialists, so thoroughly reflected in Marxism.

The stream of Irish Catholic migration to Australia in the nineteenth century brought with it both the anti-liberal Catholic political stance and the puritan social conservatism of Catholic Jansenism.

Church anti-liberalism (and anti-socialism) in Australia, however, was in a peculiar position. The Catholic Church stressed that 'without the assistance of church and God, human reason is incapable of reaching its true perfection. For men to dream of achieving a kingdom of heaven on earth, by their own unaided efforts is wicked and reckless presumption.'[34]

But most Irish Catholic migrants were working class. They were a minority in a largely liberal-minded English environment but, with their peculiarly Irish talent for politics, were heavily involved in worker politics and unionisation. As Australian industrialisation, urbanisation and unionisation proceeded rapidly in the late nineteenth century, it was feared that the siren call of socialism might lure this group into the arms of atheism and liberalism.

The Papacy reacted to this historical challenge by the evolution of Social Doctrine ideology by Pope Leo XIII (1878–1903), who sought to evolve a doctrine midway between capitalism and socialism. This Christian Socialism (outlined initially in *Rerum Novarum* (1891), a Papal Bull or statement, enjoined employers and workers to co-operate in an atmosphere of brotherhood. Class warfare was unnatural, as it alleged, were the ideologies that taught this belief.

Catholic Social Doctrine elaborated on 'class collaboration', maintained that the first aim of a Catholic worker or employer should be to fight the individualism of liberalism and the anti-private property thrust of socialism.[35] In Australia, such teachings fitted in well with the dominant Benthamite liberalism of state-managed, 'fair' capitalism, and much of the English Chartist tradition of master/man collaboration, along understood legalist principles. Catholic Social Doctrine elements were absorbed into this Australian labourist/social democratic melting pot. It was in anti-communism and social conservatism that Australian Catholic Social Doctrine made its major impact.

By the 1930s, Social Doctrine formed an important part of ALP ideology. With the onset of the Great Depression of 1929–39 and the rise of Marxist socialism, many catholics within the ALP began to organise to combat the increasing popularity of Marxist thought and the rising influence of the Communist Party.

With differing support from the various state Catholic Church hierarchies, many Social Doctrine adherents during and after World War II organised the Catholic Social Movement which came to be known as the Movement. This was a semisecret body linked ideologically to the National Civic Council. The purpose of the Movement was to oust communists or their sympathisers from the unions and the ALP in conjunction with elements of the ALP Right Wing.[35] The National Civic Council provided ideological and directional guidance.

Even in this period (1945–57), the Movement's ideology was philosophically universalist. It saw its members' struggle as part of the world-wide crusade against communism. The liberal humanist moral structure was also seen as an enemy. The Movement was ejected from the ALP in 1955–57, causing a great rupture in that party's membership and electoral support.

Ideologically, however, the moral conservatism and the anti-communist tenet of Social Doctrine continued in the National Civic Council and the rump party formed by ALP defectors in 1955–57, which took the name of the Democratic Labor Party. At no time, did Social Doctrinists abandon the original ideology of the interventionist state operating to harmonise the interests of employer and employee.

As Considine indicates, in the 1980s, however, this Australian version of Catholic Social Doctrine has begun to change. Sensing the demise of the post-World War II dominant liberal consensus and recognising the drift of many catholic conservatives into the middle classes, this stream of conservatism has begun to move closer to the 'New Right'. Industrial politics and unionism no longer possess the same emphasis.[36] The future for conservatism lies with the new conservative suburban middle class, first recognised electorally by Robert Menzies in 1949 as 'the forgotten people'.

In the age of the failure of liberal ideology, Social Doctrinists sense that the electorate is open to new conservative ideological ideas. These they see as being provided by the New Right. As

Considine further outlines, Social Doctrinists are more and more purging their old ideology of the central role of the state and adopting the values of neo-conservatism[37] with

(a) a re-emphasis on the values of traditional family;
(b) arguments for privatisation;
(c) attacks on trade union power;
(d) the embracing of unregulated business.

A coalition of three streams of conservatism is thus emerging in the Australian New Right. It would seem that for the first time in forty years, a 'new' ideology seems intent on capturing a major political party and dominating the political arena of ideas. Conservatism seems to have become 'active'.

But, alternatively,[38] 'new conservatism' could be seen as part of the dominant effect of external economic and ideological change upon the Australian socio-political culture.

Conservatism replaced the radical nationalist Australian myth of Henry Lawson with the vague 'Australian way of life' ideology of the 1950s. This fostered a sense of uniform community and urban consumerism based upon 'the car, the family, the garden and the uniformly middle-class way of life'.[39] This was eventually questioned by the rise of liberal and New Left views brought on by the divisiveness of the Vietnam war (the external trauma factor); the reality of a multi-cultural society (many of whose members did not relate to the Anglocentric 'Australian way of life'); and the widespread dissatisfaction of many women with a social ideology limiting them to mother/wife role models in a nuclear and patriarchal family.

But just as the Lawson view of Australia was undercut and replaced by the conservative 'way of life' myths in the 1950s, now the struggle is seen by the New Right as one to replace the liberal myths of the post-Vietnam period.

The rise of New Right ideology can be seen as part of the cycle of liberal versus conservative ideological struggle for hegemony in the Australian national consciousness.

Notes

1. Sabine, G. and Thorsen, T. *A History of Political Theory* Fourth Edition. Illinois, Dryden, 1973, p. 566.
2. *Encyclopedia Britannica* Vol. 5, Fifteen Edition. USA, Barton, 1984, p. 63.
3. Gray, S. 'Conservatism on Campus' *Australian Society* June 1986, pp. 30–31.
4. Watkins, F.M. *The Age of Ideology: 1750 to the Present*. New Jersey, Prentice-Hall, 1964, p. 29.

5. Wilber, C.K. 'Methodological Debate in Economics: Editor's Introduction' *World Development* 14 (2) 1986, p. 143.
6. Sabine, and Thorsen, p. 55.
7. Sabine and Thorsen, pp. 459–69.
8. Conway, R. in Manne, R. *The New Conservatism in Australia*. Melbourne, Oxford University Press, 1982, pp. 255–75.
9. Caswell, T. 'The New Right is New' *Australian Left Review* 95, Autumn 1986, p. 20.
10. Winthrop, N. (ed.) *Liberal Democratic Theory and Its Critics*. London, Croom Helm, 1983, p. 141.
11. Gray, pp. 30–31.
12. Christenson, R.M. *et al. Ideologies and Modern Politics*. London, Nelson, 1971, p. 219.
13. James, M. 'Conservatism Wet and Dry' *Quadrant* June, 1983, p. 29.
14. Ibid.
15. Lowi, T.J. *The End of Liberalism: Ideology, Policy and the Crisis of Public Authority*. NY, W.W. Norton, 1969.
16. West, K. *The Revolution in Australian Politics*. Ringwood, Victoria, Panguin, 1984.
17. Levin, M. 'The Two Conservatisms' *Quadrant*, December 1983, p. 39.
18. Lowell-Field, G. and Higley, J. 'Reagan, Thatcher and the Unemployed' *Quadrant* April 1982, p. 41.
19. Christens, R. *et al.* p. 293.
20. Duncan, T. and McAdam, A. 'The New Right: Where it Stands and What it Means' *The Bulletin* 10 December 1985, p. 44.
21. Levin, p. 40.
22. Duncan, T. and McAdam, p. 38.
23. Greville, P.J. (Brigadier) 'The Enemy Within' *Pacific Defence Reporter* XII (1) July 1986, pp. 6–9.
24. Tanner, L. 'The Radical Right' *Fabian Newsletter* 24 (5) November 1985, p. 20.
25. Tanner, p. 19.
26. Collins, H. 'Political Ideology in Australia: The Distinctiveness of a Benthamite Society' *Daedalus*, Winter 1985.
27. Courtenay, P.P. *Northern Australia*. Sydney, Longman Cheshire, 1982, p. 20.
28. Davis, S.R. *The Government of the Australian States*, Melbourne, Longman, 1960.
29. Leach, R. 'Balkanization of Australia' *Dyason House Papers*. Autumn 1978.
30. Sheridan, G. 'Time for the Right to Unite' *The Australian* 12–13 July 1986, p. 40.
31. Caswell, pp. 20–23.
32. Carroll, J. 'Paranoid & Remissive: The Treason of the Upper Middle Class' Manne (ed.), p. 14.
33. Greville, P.J. (Brigadier,) p. 9.
34. Watkins, p. 66.
35. Considine, M. 'The National Civil Council; Politics Inside Out' *Politics* 20 (1) May 1985, p. 49.
36. Considine, p. 57.
37. Ibid.
38 See Leach.
39. White, R. *Inventing Australia*. Boston, Allen and Unwin, 1981. p. 166.

References

Caswell, T. 'The New Right is New' *Australian Left Review* 95, Autumn 1986.
Christenson, R.M. *et al. Ideologies and Modern Politics*. London, Nelson, 1971.

Collins, H. 'Political Ideology in Australia: The Distinctiveness of a Benthamite Society' *Daedalus*, Winter 1985.

Considine, M. 'The National Civic Council: Politics Inside Out' *Politics* 20 (1) May 1985, pp. 48–58.

Courtenay, P.P. *Northern Australia*. Sydney, Longman Cheshire, 1982.

Cronin, J. and De Crespigny, A. *Ideologies of Politics*. London, Oxford University Press, 1975.

Davis, S.R. *The Government of the Australian States*. Longman, Melbourne, 1960.

Decter, M. 'Mugged by Reality: An Introduction to Neo-Conservatism' *Quadrant* January-February 1982, pp. 32–37.

Duncan, T. and McAdam, A. 'New Right: Where it Stands and What it Means' *The Bulletin* December 10, 1985, pp. 38–45.

Gilmour, I. *Inside Right: A Study of Conservatism*. London, Hutchinson, 1977.

Greville, P.J. (Brigadier) 'The Enemy Within' *Pacific Defence Reporter*, XIII (1) July 1986, pp. 6–9.

Hazlehurst, C. (ed.) *Australian Conservatism*. Canberra, ANU Press, 1979.

Henderson, G. 'Conservatism Wet and Dry' *Quadrant*, June 1983, pp. 29–37.

Leach, R.H. 'The Balkanization of Australia' *Dyason House Papers*, Autumn 1978.

Levin, M. 'The Two Conservatisms' Quadrant December 1983, pp. 39–42.

Loney, M. *The Politics of Greed: The New Right and The Welfare State*. London, Pluto Press, 1985.

Lowi, T.J. *The End of Liberalism: Ideology, Policy and the Crisis of Public Authority*. NY, W.W. Norton, 1969.

Manne, R. (ed.) *The New Conservatism in Australia*, Melbourne, Oxford University Press, 1982.

Sawer, M. (ed.) *Australia and The New Right*. Sydney, Allen and Unwin, 1982.

Sabine, G. and Thorsen, T. A *History of Political Theory* Fourth Edition. Illinois, Dryden, 1973.

Scruton, R. *The Meaning of Conservatism*. New Jersey, Barnes and Noble, 1980.

Sheridan, G. 'Time for the Right to Unite' *The Australian*, 12–13, July 1986.

Summers, A. 'Comments on the New Conservatism' *Quadrant*, March 1982, pp. 43–46.

Tanner, L. 'The Radical Right' *Fabian Newsletter*, 24 (5) November 1985, pp. 19–22.

Watkins, F.M. *The Age of Ideology: 1750 to the Present*. New Jersey, Prentice-Hall, 1964.

West, K. *The Revolution in Australian Politics*. Ringwood, Victoria, Penguin, 1984.

White, R. *Inventing Australia*. Sydney, Allen and Unwin, 1981.

Winthrop, N. (ed.) *Liberal Democratic Theory and its Critics*. London, Croom Helm, 1983.

Willis, S. and Norda, L. 'Women and New Right' *Intervention* 18, 1984, pp. 58–77.

Recommended Reading

O'Sullivan, N. *Conservatism*. St Martin's Press, NY, 1976.

Manne, R. (ed.) *The New Conservatism in Australia*. Melbourne, Oxford University Press, 1982.

Sawer, M. (ed.) *Australia and the New Right*. Sydney, Allen and Unwin, 1982.

3

Liberalism

By 'liberalism' I shall understand here the conception of a desirable political order which in the first instance was developed in England by the time of the old Whigs in the latter part of the seventeenth century to that of Gladstone at the end of the nineteenth century ... It was this conception of individual liberty under the law which ... became the basis of the American political tradition ... This liberalism must be clearly distinguished from another, originally Continental European tradition, also called 'liberalism' of which what now claims this name in the US [and Australia] is a direct descendant. This latter view, although beginning with an attempt to initiate the first tradition, interpreted it in the spirit of a constructionist rationalism prevalent in France ... , and in the end, instead of advocating limitations on the powers of government, ended up with the ideal of the unlimited powers of this majority. This is the tradition of ... the French Revolution which has become the ancestor of modern Socialism. English utilitarianism has taken over much of this Continental tradition ... Liberalism and democracy, although compatible, are not the same. The first is concerned with the extent of governmental power, the second with, who holds this power ... The second kind of 'liberalism' ... has in effect become democratism rather than liberalism ... and by demanding *unlimited* power of the majority, has become essentially anti-liberal.

(F.A. Hayek 'The Principles of a Liberal Social Order', in de Crespigny and Cronin, 1975)

This quote from F.A. Hayek quite clearly defines the problem with the ideology of liberalism. The concept lends itself to two different perspectives.

One perspective, which Hayek supported, stresses the need to return to early or classic liberalism. It supports the ideas of a deregulated market; a passive non-interventionist state; defined rights of property; laissez-faire economics and an emphasis on conservative social morality. This conservative liberalism looks backward, to the origins of liberalism as a market and merchant philosophy, before the rise of the activist state.

State liberalism provides the other perspective. As Hayek points out, the rise of the activist and interventionist liberal state was not envisaged in classic liberalism. The state in classic liberalism was to be confined, strictly limited and locked up by law and convention while a 'spontaneous' society went about its business.[1]

To conservative liberals such as Hayek, this past vision of a free 'nomocratic' (law governed) society was slowly replaced by a new definition of liberalism, influenced by the rise of democracy. It gave birth to a 'telocratic' (purpose-governed) society dominated by a state dedicated to a long-term social purpose ('the common good') and run by a new class of liberal technocrats.[2]

State liberals have endorsed this kind of 'telocratic' society for two reasons. First, the 'chaos' of free market capitalism is seen as socially injurious and potentially the cause of mass alienation from a liberal society. Secondly, many state liberals (especially radical democrats) identify this ideology of liberalism with its democratic aspect, i.e. the increasing and meaningful participation of all citizens at all levels of collective interaction, from the family to the nation. The purpose is to democratise the decision making power within capitalism and the parallel social system. Meanwhile, they still maintain the capitalist economic system. While there is division amongst state liberals concerning the extent of power to be wielded by the state technocracy in its social engineering, and the extent of mass democratic participation in decision making, nevertheless there is wide agreement on the necessity for an activist state.

Thus there exist two counterpoised tendencies within liberalism. Classic liberalism theorises limits to the state. It also proposes limits to the liberal pursuit of reason and progress, especially when this strays into the realm of imposing equality. Equality exists only before the law.

To the state liberal, especially the radical democrat, the application of reason to human life and the pursuit of democratic equality is the essence of liberalism. Nothing should remain unquestioned by human rationality. If privilege is claimed by virtue of custom, wealth, birth, class, religion, race or (more recently) sex, then privilege should answer in the court of reason why its assumed special position should remain unchallenged.

Liberalism thus contains two opposed streams of historical development. Nevertheless, their ontological roots are the same. Both share a common foundation in the assumption of pre-existing individual rights. They emphasise the need to create a rational society where individuals can impose their wills and create their own lives within the boundaries of sensible and constructive law. The purpose of society is agreed to be the progress of the human species along the path of constitutional law and order.

Differences may arise over the nature of this social progress in both moral and economic areas. But the major source of controversy concerns the role of the state — should it be limited or initiatory? This is the centre of ideological conflict within liberal democracies which extends into contemporary times.

Liberalism is the first modern ideology.[3] It has been the matrix of the modern political spectrum of Left/Right ideologies. Socialism and other non-liberal Left positions can arguably be seen as offshoots of the technocratic (state) or radical democratic (participatory) liberal positions. Similarly, conservative liberalism, where it defends privilege and property, can find echoes and allies on the authoritarian right.

In common sense terms, then, classic liberalism may be seen as liberalism of the Right, while state and participatory liberalism occupy positions on the Left. Public opinion may swing electorally in a liberal democracy between these poles, given the demands of the historical period. It is unlikely, however, where liberal values are socially hegemonic, that there would be a complete abandonment of the liberal democratic system of values. Thus, electorally, there may be a technical rather than a metaphysical change of government and social values. There may be two or more parties, but all are simply attempting different versions of the same liberal state.[4]

What is necessary for liberalism to survive as a system, therefore, is not the possession of some form of utopian ideological goal, but the existence of forms of government and dominant civic attitudes (or consensus of values) that will allow this peaceful transition between conservative and radical liberal poles, while ignoring other ideological alternatives.

Liberalism is thus an attitudinal ideology. It seeks to develop within its citizenry a critical pragmatism and a sense of moral brotherhood while still emphasising the need for self-help. It stresses the notions of the utilitarian nature of the state rather than its omnipotence; the basic equality of all citizens; the need for democratic involvement in decision making (at least at the political level) and a belief in the worth and natural rights of the individual.[5]

The governmental structure through which these civic attitudes are expressed tend to be similar institutionally and procedurally in most liberal democracies. They incorporate some or all of the ideas of constitutional government: division of legislative, judicial and executive powers; freedoms of speech, assembly and participation (either enunciated in a Bill of Rights or preserved by custom); and the encouragement of pluralist interests and parties.

Thus liberalism is primarily interested in creating the conditions for a *style* of democracy. It stresses 'how' a liberal democratic society should operate and declines to provide a total answer to 'where' it should go. Nevertheless, it defends the notions of 'freedom' and 'equality' before the law as woven into these procedures. These concepts provide the *dynamic* of liberalism. Each historical or individual problem that arises is meant to be handled by a theoretically mature, educated, citizenry, secure in these cherished beliefs of 'freedom' and 'equality' before the law, and using them as the touchstone for their interpretation and approach to political problems.

If such a solution does not emerge, given this theoretically mature citizenry, liberals can only assume the lack of educated reason amongst the masses, or the manipulation of events and opinion by malevolent élites.

Liberalism is thus a flexible doctrine whose basis is a rational humanist approach to life. The essentials of early or classic liberalism are associated with freedom more than pure equality. Equality was a concept linked with the rise of democracy throughout the Age of Revolutions, from the seventeenth to the twentieth centuries. Classic liberalism therefore had to adapt to the demands of democracy, leading to the rise of the welfare State and the radical democratic notions of equal civic participation in decision making.

Essentially, classic liberalism[6] can be defined as a political philosophy concerned with 'freedom', stressing:

(a)   'civil freedom of the individual
(b)   free political institutions
(c)   freedom of religion
(d)   free enterprise and free trade'.

The history of the ideology is an account of the adaptation of its values and political institutions in order to answer the differing historical demands of society for more individualism (freedom) or more collectivism (equality). The focal point for controversy thus becomes the role of the state.

At one pole, libertarians (the New Right) emerge demanding limitation of the state and the fullest liberty for individual enterprise. This is in the tradition of the British 'whig' ideology which argued for a weak state and strong individualism. The New Right argues that we have 'fallen' from this ideal by the misuse of the state. At the other pole, the exponents of the Welfare State may demand a comprehensive state machinery run by a liberal technocracy. This state is seen as the tamer and guide for capitalism and the provider of a welfare safety net for the unfortunate. The state becomes a co-ordinator for business, labour and the organ-isations of the land. An interest group democracy[7] emerges, run upon 'scientific' notions of efficiency set by the standards of the 'new class' of technocrats. However, it is beset with a peculiar stagnancy.

As Hall states:[8]
Liberal politics were linked with liberties and with economic development ... This commonly entails the initial suppression of pluralism (democracy) which clearly has no elective affinity with liberal politics. Nevertheless, social develop-ment will itself increase and strengthen pluralism ... [but] a strengthening of pluralism may result in some sort of power stand-off ... For liberties has changed its meaning in Western society in a disturbing manner, being currently used to describe privileges [of groups] ... which are held against the public interest and thereby resulting in a power stand off.

The definition of liberalism changes subtly under this new Welfare State influence and interest group democracy. Both labour and capital find their innate class conflict reduced by the bound-aries of respectable action within the liberal Welfare State.[9] The definition of liberalism changes to:

(a) civil freedom of the individual within boundaries of 'the greater good' defined by the state.
(b) The recognition of the importance of interest groups over and above individuals.
(c) Freedom of religion.
(d) 'Fair' enterprise and controlled trade.
(e) Free political institutions, dedicated to managerial not ideological politics.

The possession of the skills and common liberal attitudes in each citizen is essential, therefore, for the continuation of liberal society, since liberal ideology is so variable between these poles of libertarianism and technocratic state liberalism.

These common attitudes include antagonism towards the ideas of class warfare and division; acceptance of élite power; and the concept of the 'natural' inequality of citizens.

The terms which guide any political society, such as 'justice', 'the state' or 'freedom and equality' are redefined cautiously in liberal democracies, according to the terms of, and filtered by, acceptable legal procedure. As Ebenstein states, 'the interpretation of such terms differs widely along the political spectrum, from Fascism to anarchism'.[10] The cultural domination (or hegemony) of common liberal civic attitudes is therefore vital to the preservation of the liberal way of doing things.

This factor — the inculcation of common liberal-mindedness and skills — is still the basis of this least doctrinal of ideologies.

Origins

The origins of liberalism can be sought in the cultural genesis of Western society.[11] The Athenian democracy of Greece, as reported by Aristotle and Plato, was strongly influential in later European political thought. This was particularly so in the emphasis on an educated citizenry for the attainment of wise government.

Similarly, as Christenson outlines,[12] Greek Sophist philosophy was influential in its stress upon individual consent to any law. This was to influence the central tenet of classic liberalism, stressing the social contract between citizens and government.

Roman law injected the seeds of belief in pre-existing natural law. By virtue of birth into the human race, each individual possessed the protection of natural law.[13]

But the essential factor of individuality arose from Christianity. Throughout the Christian era, the idea of the single soul achieving or losing its salvation by its own efforts permeated Western consciousness. Similarly, the belief arose that it was incumbent on this 'good' society to educate the ignorant, so that their individual reason and conscience would be aware of choice between sin and virtue.

The Bible also taught the message of the equality of souls before God and that earthly Caesars were ultimately paper princes. The role of the state (Caesar's realm) was diminished. It was there merely to provide peace and order, so that souls could be free to get on with their real purpose — the afterlife.[14] In return the state got obedience as a 'Divine Right':

> Give unto Caesar the things that are Caesar's and unto God the things that are God's.
> *New Testament*, Gospel of St Luke, 20

This essentially conservative message, stipulating resignation to earthly power was, of course, only one Biblical interpretation. The Bible could also be used to question the social order and to equip the rebel with ideological justification:

> When Adam delved and Eve span,
> Who was then the gentleman?
> (Slogan, English Peasant Rebellion, 1381)

Thus both a conservative and radical message could be found in religion. But it was not until the seventeenth century that the first political doctrine drawing on this cultural heritage emerged. The ideology of liberalism differed from religious ideology in being humanist and centred in this world. If the definition of ideology is a 'secular religion', then liberalism was the first ideology.

Classic Liberalism

In feudal times, the individual was defined as a subject owing duty to some lord. Every man had a master. By the seventeenth century, however, a new urban and trade-based class of merchants had risen to challenge this feudal view of the commoner's role. Aided by the humanist focus of the Renaissance and the Protestant emphasis upon individual salvation, a new perspective of political authority began to emerge. The legitimacy of government was held to rest upon the consent of individuals, not the Divine Right of Kings. This ideological proposition transformed the feudal subject into a responsible citizen.

One major contributor to this 'social contract' theory was John Locke (1632–1704). Locke, with his two major works, *Two Treatises on Civil Government*, was one of the great political philosophers who arose in the aftermath of the English Revolution (1642–60). The overthrow of the English monarch, Charles I, provoked an avalanche of debate between radical democracy and property-based liberalism.[15] Locke, however, focused on the nature of the English Constitution that emerged from the Glorious Revolution of 1688, which overthrew the Catholic King James II and replaced him with the Protestant monarchs William and Mary. This event also installed the basic English 'balanced' Constitution, between the monarch, the hereditary House of Lords and the elected House of Commons.

Locke's works outlined classic liberal ideals: the existence of natural law, man's birthright, which no government could remove; the authority of government resting upon the consent of the governed, consent being withdrawn if the balance is exceeded, up to and including the right to rebellion. All these are governed by a social agreement, or contract, between governed and government.

Montesquieu (1688–1755), a French political philosopher, later drew attention to the division of power inherent in the British Constitution of 1688 as the source of freedom. Montesquieu saw the weakness of the French state as being in its lack of checks and balances, the state having no limit to its reach. He drew from the English example the necessity of the division of the state into executive, judicial and legislative sections. Tyranny was avoided by such division. Thus centralised state power was frustrated, and the citizenry could go about their daily business, building a 'spontaneous' society.

The ideas of classic liberalism reached their height in the American Revolution (1776–82), which used the theories of Locke and Montesquieu in both the Declaration of Independence (1776) and the American Constitution (1787). This structure of the liberal state, later to be widely copied, was initiated by this constitution.

The American constitutional state emerged as one embodying a balance of powers. The Senate, based upon state suffrage, was elected to counter the nationally-elected Congress. Executive power rested in the President, serving a four-year term. Lastly, the Supreme Court, with judges selected for life, could decide upon the interpretation of the Constitution if the 'social contract' was under question or in need of adjustment.

This ideological structure was seen by many American conservatives (and by such English Conservatives as Edmund Burke) as simply another stage in the English Revolution of 1688. The King, by this time George III, had once again overstepped the invisible boundary of royal power. The Americans were simply transplanted Englishmen defending their rights.

Other liberal elements, however, came to influence the American Revolution.

First, American complaints against Britain reflected the anti-mercantilist, pro-free trade sentiments of the colonial merchant class. The world of 1776 was locked into a European-based imperial mercantile system. Core nations such as the two superpowers, France and Britain, dominated peripheral colonies like the future United States. Laissez-faire economies, however, expressed in a coherent form in Adam Smith's *Wealth of Nations* (1776) stressed the non-interference of the state in economics and the ideal of the 'spontaneous' capitalist society. Laissez-faire theory proved a handy element in American revolutionary thought.

Adam Smith intended that his doctrine was to be, essentially, a merchant class ideology, not a doctrine for the masses.[16] In the American Revolutionary war, however, classic liberalism had to come to terms with radical democracy. This was a war of liberation against a colonial power. Free trade became a revolutionary slogan, therefore, not of a class, but of a nation.

Radical New England democracy entered the picture with the writings of Tom Paine (*Common Sense* 1776). As Walker notes,[17] Paine did not stress a dominating state. Nevertheless his notions of far-reaching democracy had implications for men of property and classic liberalism.

Paine's radical democratic writings indicate the dilemma for classic liberals when forced, in a national crisis, to seek mass support for their rather narrow definition of liberalism. Few will die for *laissez-faire* economics, or the notion of a society dominated by merchants, while many will sacrifice themselves for democracy and equality.

Paine's explanation for the rise of tyranny 'stressed the role of manipulative, self-interested élites who distorted society by their possession of superior wealth and status'. Privilege, or the claim of groups for special treatment, was always a sign that equal rights were being misused. Therefore it is common sense for the people to overthrow such élites and assume government.

Classic liberalism, however, based upon Adam Smith's entrepreneurial spirit, endorsed such an élite, a business one, as the motor of change. Here was the source of a future confrontation between classic liberalism and radical democracy, for as Hayek stated (see opening quote), 'liberalism and democracy, though compatible, are not the same'. As Brugger writes, classic liberalism saw democracy only as a means to an end — the attainment and protection of individual rights, especially property rights. These were deduced from 'natural rights' (Locke) or later from 'utility' (Bentham). 'Classic liberals saw democracy simply as an instrument to attain a set of static human rights.' Once achieved, these rights reflected the highest attainment to which men could aspire. Any further developments in human rights were false,[18] because classic liberalism saw human nature as unchanging. It was competitive, gain-seeking and selfish. '[Adam] Smith's democracy was indeed a shareholder's meeting write large.'[19] Democracy without limitation was dangerous. It would give power to the ignorant and envious masses who might be swayed by alternative views concerning the road to human development. It was necessary to protect oneself from democracy by a limiting constitution, one almost impossible to change; a law system based upon property; and a state whose power was dispersed in case it became a tool for mass democracy.

Radical democracy was to prove the enemy of such liberalism. It endorsed a creative role for the state, which would increase the potential of each individual via education, by increase in participation in government and the provision of welfare for the poor. Liberty could only be real for the masses if the state acted creatively to rid society of privilege, poverty and disease. Only then could the individual practise true freedoms. The state must be given increased powers, not curtailed. Otherwise, freedoms would remain a minority practice of the rich and powerful.

The initiative in liberalism after the American Revolution passed to such state liberalism via the French Revolution and its

Jacobin leaders. It reached nineteenth-century England through utilitarianism.

State Liberalism

The French Revolution of 1789 drew liberalism into the continental tradition of government dominated by statism (*étatisme*); bureaucratic directionalism (*dirigisme*) and the idea of the benevolent despot. This style of government had been embedded by centuries of the royal centralisation of power. Such a tradition of paternalism for the 'common good' was not lost upon the new republic.

While the inherited style of government was important for the rise of the state in continental liberalism, the influence of the philosophers of the Enlightenment was also enormous. The writings of Jean-Jacques Rousseau (1712–78) were of great importance, especially in his book *The Social Contract*.

Rousseau believed that people were born pure and good but were corrupted by the evil society into which they were born. This society was made unjust by élites historically taking power by force, and then solidifying their privileges in law, hierarchy and custom. The civilisation and institutions of these élites enslaved people. Rousseau emphasised the need to set people free by applying reason to the restructuring of society's institutions.

Rousseau also added to the original Lockeian notion of the social contract between government and citizen by introducing the notion of the 'general will'. This was a democratic idea. It stressed the fact that a community as a whole knew its own best interests. It could be translated by the political ideas of majority rule, referendum or plebiscite to endorse change, once the old order had been swept away.

The 'general will' concept, of course, meant that no generation was bound by the decisions of past ones. Tom Paine stressed this in his pamphlet on *The Rights of Man*. But what was necessary to burst the boundaries of the old society and make a clean break with the past before a true democratic 'general will' unfettered by previous ideas of history would evolve, was a revolution. The problem was the low level of awareness of the masses.

Implicit in Rousseau is the nagging thought that 'the masses are too unenlightened to carry out a revolution'[20] which is both a political and a social break with the past. With the French Revolution begins the history of Jacobinism as a means of solving this dilemma.

Jacobinism describes the philosophy of a group of delegates to the French National Convention (1792–95) who were determined to carry through the Revolution in all its social and political implications. Coalescing around the leadership of Robespierre (1758–94), and operating within a state given to centralisation and directionalism, the Jacobins became the driving force of the Revolution. As the external threats of invasion of the new republic increased, and as internal counter-revolution escalated, the Jacobins took power via the Committee of Public Safety. The use of force and terror, rationalised by patriotism, revolutionary ideology and the dream of an egalitarian new democracy that would emerge after their guardianship, reinforced their rule. While there is no doubt that Jacobinism saved France from counter-revolution, it also endorsed the idea of the dictatorship of the few who knew best the route that humanist, rationalist politics should take.

The American Revolution had been led by a coalition of conservatives, moderates and radicals fighting an external foe. It had been a political struggle only. The French Revolution was the first *social* revolution. For the first time, the ordinary man and the radical mob, especially the Parisian masses, entered history endorsing the use of revolutionary state power. Revolutionary state liberalism had let the genie of radical democracy out of the bottle.

Unlike in America, where it was contained by the Constitution, radical democracy on the continent had been shown the way to power via the state. For liberalism, the choice was to adapt to the equalising demands of democracy, culminating in the twentieth-century Welfare State, or to be pushed from the centre of the political stage by nationalism, radical democrat or Jacobin styles of socialism (Leninism).

The path followed by most Western liberals was towards the new idea of a liberal Welfare State.

Nineteenth-Century State Liberalism

The great year of European Revolution, 1848, was the turning point for liberalism. For the next forty years, European classic liberalism went into decline as it failed to deliver hope to the new propertyless industrial masses.

In Britain, the Conservative Party under Peel and Disraeli, especially after 1867, reached out for mass support by offering its conservative version of the paternalist state. In Germany, after 1870, Bismarck followed a similar path of state welfarism, tying Germans to the monarchical/nationalist state. In France, the Revolution of 1848 revealed the ideological inability of classic liberalism to fill the needs of the peasant and the worker who required material change to their circumstances before freedom of the individual could emerge. The masses began to turn instead to the new doctrines of socialism and anarchism.

Liberalism, particularly in Britain, began to divide. Classic liberals continued to stress free trade, a limited state and individual freedom. Others, however, stressed the need to control the social structure so that true individual freedom could begin, and mass voting support could increase.

It is the latter trend which created the ideology of the liberal Welfare State or state liberalism. Three main elements influenced this ideology:

The first was the *utilitarianism* of Jeremy Bentham (1748–1832). According to him, the state should allocate a 'fair' distribution of wealth. This distribution would not come from changes in the existing wealth structure but from shares in constantly increasing production.[21]

The state thus became chained to a developmental psychology, but this was done under the rationale of 'the greatest good for the greatest number'. The state's purpose was not to exist simply for the benefit of the owners of property to which classic liberalism alluded. Its duty was to all citizens. Social progress and harmony could best be achieved by increasing affluence and by dispersing the benefits of this to increasing numbers, thus bringing excluded and alienated groups into a sense of economic and political loyalty to the system. Also, an increasingly complex social system needed a professionalised state and accompanying experts to co-ordinate and rationalise its workings.

Essentially, 'utilitarianism was a means of preserving the social status quo.' It deflected radical democratic questioning of an unequal social system. Instead of Locke's classic liberal demand for state protection of 'existing individual interests', e.g., individual property,[22] the Benthamite state urged endless industrialism, whose benefits should be available to all. These, such as free education, health and welfare and industrial legislation, were *useful* rather than simply humanitarian. They increased the sum total of pleasure, contentment and harmony in the community as well as stimulating more production as people got healthier, more skilled, richer.

Peace from class warfare would thus be bought by increasing mass income. In such a state, therefore, as depression would be a disaster and re-open class antagonism, politicians became managers and economic technocrats rather than purveyors of morality or political philosophies which might offer alternatives such as 'local development' or 'workers' democracy rather than 'endless growth'. The question is whether such a system can get off its voracious industrial treadmill?

The second element, from the writings of J.S. Mill, stressed notions of *individual potentiality*. It was the duty of the state to provide education, culture and 'ideal types', towards which each individual should be orientated. By developing individual potential from all classes along those lines, natural creativity would be released. Liberal civilisation would also be reinforced as people adhered to universal norms of reason, tolerance and pluralism to be stressed in such liberal education and culture. Ultimately, people would lose the competitive and aggressive attitudes fostered by the world of capitalism.[23] 'Mainstream' competitive values would eventually be supplanted by humanist/ co-operative norms. History would be changed by all men and women, especially the masses, identifying with the new values. The state, by education, would have brought an end to the conflict[24] between 'haves and have-nots'. Unfortunately, Benthamite values in education stressing 'education in useful things' are constantly at war with such Millsian ideas in liberal education. Also unfortunate would be the fact that the 'new values' would be those dictated by the middle class.

The third element, the *New Liberalism* of the 1890s led by thinkers such as T.H. Green, J.A. Hobson and L.T. Hobhouse, began to theorise the thorny questions (associated with socialism) of the *planned society* and the *Welfare State*.

These New Liberals rejected the Marxist class warfare and economic determinism analysis of history. Systems could survive by the application of 'ideas' and 'will' to reform.

In particular, L.T. Hobhouse in his work *Liberalism* outlined the foundations of state liberalism and its historical path. Hobhouse reformulated liberalism into its clearest modern form. Politics for Hobhouse' was not the authoritarian state nor the Jacobin philosopher kings, 'not an issue of man against the state, but of man working through the state as an instrument of social organisation to achieve personal and social fulfilment'.[25]

The major break with classic liberalism was the redefinition of freedom. Full freedom (for the New Liberals) could only be achieved with increasing equality. Privilege must therefore be restrained by social control.[26]

Hobhouse and his contemporaries pointed the way forward to the mixed economy, the liberal Welfare State and the liberal socialism[27] of the twentieth century.

To some, this kind of liberalism represented a means of saving capitalism and classic liberalism from the political disaster to which their inegalitarian dogmas might have consigned them. It was a triumph for democracy in an area where some compromise had to be made.

To others, especially today's New Right, this liberalism was the outcome of the historic pursuit of 'reason' in the West, which had delivered the state and political power into the hands of neither capital nor labour, but into those of the liberal intelligentsia — a new public middle class of social engineering technocrats and a knowledge-based bureaucracy.[28] Political power (in this opinion) should be returned to the wealth makers, defined as the men of property, capital and enterprise.

Finally, to some Marxists, this New Liberalism, culminating in the modern liberal Welfare State, represents a phase in the needs of capitalism to freeze class war after the Russian Revolution and the Great Depression. The liberal Welfare State has not, however, removed the antagonism of capital and labour. It has now exhausted its post-war liberal/social democrat political consensus,[29] built upon the delivery to the working class of increased wages, credit and welfare.[30] This welfare state is now simply too expensive for capitalism to maintain.

To the Marxists, the New Right's determination to dismantle the liberal Welfare State will, in fact, rob capitalism of its major political and economic protection. The New Right, in its blindness, will speed up the release of the class warfare genie from its welfare bottle.

Figure 3.1 Characteristics of Classic and State Liberalism

	Classic Liberalism	State (New) Liberalism
Theory of State	1. A limited state.	1. An initiatory state.
	2. A confined constitution, which defends individual 'freedom' against the state and collectivism.	2. Open constitution endorsing positive action by the state in enforcing equality.
	3. A state and its bureaucracy will not attempt social engineering.	3. The state must be allowed to build the conditions for personal freedom.
	4. The state should operate under law, not consensus.	4. The state is the arbiter between interest groups within the consensus.

	Classic Liberalism	State (New) Liberalism
Theory of Society	1. People are born flawed (nature)	1. A flawed society causes evil (nurture)
	2. The individual is a rational being and his rights precede social rights.	2. The individual is rational but needs to operate with full knowledge of social rights within a fair system.
	3. Social contract exists between individual and government.	3. A social contract exists between individual and government and other citizens.
	4. A spontaneous society is superior.	4. The 'common good' precedes spontaneity which may reinforce privilege.
	5. Preservation of 'mainstream' cultural heritage and social structure.	5. Multiculturalism
Theory of History	1. History is made by rational individuals pursuing individual interests.	1. History is made by rational individuals pursuing 'freedom' and 'equality'.
	2. History is survival of the fittest, but this is a progressive force.	2. History is a story of increasing civilisation through the learning and application of reason and co-operative values by individuals.
Theory of Economics	1. Social welfare destroys initiative.	1. Welfare is necessary for political and moral reasons.
	2. A deregulated market is necessary in labour and resources.	2. State regulation is necessary for planning and welfare reasons.
	3. Free trade.	3. Protection where necessary.
	4. Emphasis should be on private capitalism as the economic motor.	4. The partnership of business and labour (unions) under government direction is more utilitarian.
	5. Mankind responds to economic rationality.	5. Mankind responds to other motives besides economics, such as morality.

Contemporary Liberalism: The Liberal Welfare State and Left/Right Critiques

Classic liberalism was in decline from around 1848. The rise of 'New' or State Liberalism was accelerated by the demands of history in the period 1890–1945. This was one of grave crisis for Western capitalism, although the system of Parliamentary democracy was to survive unscathed, if adapted. This was particularly true of countries such as the USA and the UK, where the liberal ethos was strong:[31] where the working and farmer classes were not marginalised; and where their organisations or classes had leaders integrated into the political consensus.

As outlined, the ideology of state liberalism had expanded in the late nineteenth century under the influence of political thinkers such as Green and Hobhouse. The ideological framework which they expounded rationalised the basic transformation of traditional liberal principles to include the notion of a welfare and interventionist state.

This transformation was fortuitous. The demands for social reform in the period between 1900–45 was accelerated by the great historical crises of the time: World War 1, the crisis of mercantilism in the Great Depression (1929–40), and World War II. The rise of the Welfare State thus had an aura of historical necessity which attracted a range of supporters from Left and Right.[32]

First there were the rising non-revolutionary labour and social democrat parties. Socialism, to them, was interpreted originally as social reform, with some fair distribution of wealth for the masses and a welfare net for the unfortunate. The actual idea of the co-ordination of capitalist production by an interventionist state was to emerge in reality with the post-World War II Keynesian economic revolution. Such an interventionist economic tool as Keynesianism of course presumed the independence of the nation state in a world of increasing international capitalism.

Next, there was the movement by both conservative and state liberals to tame the labour force and give it a sense of responsibility to the capitalist system. Labour could not control capitalism unless it was revolutionary and expropriated property. If it eschewed this, its leaders at least could be made to see that the growth of welfare and wages could only come from increasing co-operation with capital and a lessening of conflict. The welfare state would numb class antagonism and reduce labour irresponsibility. As Aubrey Jones, an English Conservative is quoted, as saying,[33] 'This irresponsibility [of labour] can be overcome if labour is made to feel it has the same purpose as capital, and that while they remain rivals, this rivalry is subordinate to a unity'.

From 1900, social reform in Western democracies by governments of all colours triggered further expectations. Riding the crest of this wave of reform, state liberalism took on the image of an idea whose time had come.

The welfare state in particular represented common ground for both Left and Right. After 1945, there was also a convergence of Left and Right over the acceptance of the basic structure of the interventionist state. The concept of the unity of welfarism and the interventionist state was thus an unwritten basis from which politics began.

The majority Left began to define socialism, not using class politics, but with the terms of state liberalism. Similarly, the Right largely abandoned classic liberalism to embrace the ideological notions of the 'civilised market'.

Thus there was to emerge over the period 1900–75 bipartisan support for the ideology of the Welfare State. As Gough outlines,[34] 'this ideology postulated a harmony or convergence of the interests of capital and labour', even though the historical reality was one of bitter struggle 'over which group would control services, who would be eligible for them, and what level of service would be offered'.

This ideology of harmony underlay some of the 'end of ideology' debates of the 1950s.[35] These argued that both traditional Left and Right parties had been inexorably drawn to the centre[36] by the managerial demands of the Welfare State. A phenomenon of liberal/labour partnerships of the centre (the state liberal/social democrat consensus) had emerged. Government was now about good management. Politics was now about issues and movements which tinkered with, and added to, the solid basis of the dominant ideology of the liberal Welfare State. Thus the purpose of politics was first to educate and then to equip groups and individuals with compensatory rights and money transfers to allow them to compete more adequately within the given system. The old days of politics being about the transformation of the system itself and developing the potentiality of every human being by this transformation, was gone.

The Keynesian Economic Revolution

The capstone of the structure of state liberalism was the emergence of Keynesian economics. The Great Depression showed the inadequacy of classic market economies in handling the world of existing political and human reality. The world between the wars was a protectionist one. Great European empires practised mercantilism within closed colonial boundaries. Many great capitalist firms were monopolies or oligopolies. They were price makers not price takers, as no free market existed in their closed national or imperial worlds.[37] When demand fell for goods after World War I, these firms could resist the downward pressure on their prices. The decline in demand inexorably meant a decline in production. Costs had to be cut. This fell inevitably on the most mobile and weakest factor of production — labour.

Classic economists seized quickly on unionism as the major reason for decline in demand. Unionism to them kept wages artificially high. Reduce wages and employers would hire more workers. As there was little desire to attack large firms and monopolies, much of the weight of the suffering of this depression therefore fell on the politically weaker labour factor. Governments cut wages and government spending, unionism was attacked and unemployment became the 'safety valve' for an overheated system.

But in effect, increasing unemployment cut demand still further as the ability to consume declined. Governments added to this downward spiral by following protectionism and thus sabotaging the export trade. Imperial or national interests came first. Capitalism was in crisis.

Classic market economies simply could not work in the existing historical stage of capital organised on a national and closed 1930s imperial basis.

To work correctly, classic capitalist market economies had to transcend nationalism and the state. They needed a perfect market. The world had to become one big emporium with the national state reduced to an executive for managing the national economy according to signals sent from the major stock markets and commercial or capital centres. Currency had to be deregulated. National capitalist groups concerned with their own small markets had to be absorbed or overcome. World capitalism had to become one, rather than several, competing imperial cores. In 1929, however, unlike the tendency in the 1990s, this political situation did not exist.

Great social upheavals thus threatened the world of 1929. The Marxist prognosis about the future of capitalism ending in its own collapse, which had been written off as farcical by late nineteenth century capitalism, seemed to loom ominously.[38]

A new form of economics which would suit the needs of capital survival at this stage of national and imperial organisation, was needed. Coinciding with previous social reformist tendencies, the Welfare State philosophy now crossed into the arena of the interventionist state.

John Maynard Keynes (1883–1964) was a British economist steeped in the demands of Empire. His book *General Theory of Employment, Interest and Money* attacked classic economic thinking because it represented the way capitalist-minded people would *like* the economy to behave,[39] and not how it was. Other groups existed in society whose economic desires might be different to those of businessmen and whose democratic political power might be stronger. Yet classic economics felt that to speak for the market was to speak for all.

Keynes came close to Marx in his political insights into the workings of capitalist economies, but he was at pains to dissociate himself from Marx's contention that capitalism was doomed. 'The essentials of capitalism could be preserved if reforms were made on time.' Other classes, especially labour and the intelligentsia, had to be let into decision making.

His suggested reforms were largely macro-economic. The nation had to use its fiscal powers of taxation and spending, plus manipulation of the interest rate on lending and the flow of money, to stimulate demand.

Building on earlier Benthamism, Keynesianism stressed ever-increasing production as good in itself, as it would provide the extra income for the worker whose spending would then stimulate production in a never-ending cycle. Government spending on welfare now became not just a matter of morality but also an economic necessity to stimulate the market.

Internationally, through the Bretton Woods Agreement (1944) there would be agreements on tariffs, protectionism and international banking, which would preserve some autonomy for the nation states but at the same time lock them into a world monetary system. Much political independence had to be foregone to avoid the trauma of another Depression. Many nationalists observed that a terrible price would be paid for the surrender of economic control leading to a new dependency:

> The very sovereignty of this nation [Australia] is in jeopardy ... The Bretton Woods Agreement will enthrone a World Dictatorship of private finance ... [it] quite blatantly sets up controls which will reduce the smaller nations to vassal status and make every government the mouthpiece and tool of international finance ... World collaboration of private financial interests can only mean mass unemployment, slavery, misery, degradation and final destruction.[40]
> (E.J. Ward, ABC broadcast, 27 March 1946)

Others saw this Keynesian development of state liberalism to include the partnerships and co-ordination of capital and labour, as a welcome factor. The growing technocratic civil service and middle class intelligentsia saw it as a victory for liberal rationalism and utilitarianism over the chaos of market capitalism. Capitalists, it was assumed, were narrow and stupid. Clever scholars and civil servants, a mandarin class,[41] would iron out the mistakes capitalists constantly made. Reason would triumph.

As Hall points out, big business welcomed Keynesian economics as a recognition of the priority of the corporate over the model of small business and family capitalism so beloved of classic market economics. Corporate capitalism preferred stability and the orderly macro-economic planning which Keynesian economics provided.

Others applauded the ideology of harmonisation which Keynesianism underwrote. This ideology destroyed the old capital/labour tribalism. It expedited social mobility[42] and strengthened the centre of politics. A solid middle classing effect occurred, with rising wages and material comfort. The boundaries of cultural respectability, and therefore acceptability, became dominantly middle class. The role model became increasingly the middle class family man/woman, with his/her implicit moral superiority over other forms of civil life.

The view of James Mill in his *Essay on Government*, that 'the middle class would show the working class what was in its best interest',[43] finally seemed to be attainable. All could now attain middle class levels of affluence. Middle class culture would flow from that basis to all.

For three decades, from 1945, and with Left and Right support, the liberal welfare and interventionist state has dominated Western democracies. To many it has been an attempt to reconcile capitalism with democracy: 'A bargain was implicitly struck whereby capital accepted certain welfare provisions while labour accepted the market economy.'[44] The ideology of *harmonisation* emerged from this assumed cohesion.

Labour unrest and internal challenges to the system were held off by a Benthamite emphasis on growth in both private and social wages, and government services, as Hall and Beilharz outline. State liberalism emphasised the negotiatory and arbitrational role of national governments to adjudicate and disperse shares of this growth.

Accordingly, an pluralistic interest group policy, rather than a class system of politics, began to emerge. Highly organised groupings of labour and differing factions of capital, based upon different commodity production (e.g. mining) rather than class, fought a series of endless battles over their share of growth, under the paternal eye of the state. 'Conflict was endemic but relatively harmless,' due to its regulation and containment.[45]

The liberal welfare state was not to be shaken by internal factors from its ideology of harmonisation. The real shock came from the international economic structure.

The oil crisis of 1973 staggered the whole system of post-1945 Keynesian world trade, with its national arrangements for 'growth sharing' between capital and labour. Cheap energy was no longer available due to price rises from the formation of an oil cartel. Without cheap energy, continuous growth was problematic. Inflation surged as governments also attempted to maintain welfare payments.

As oil prices fell through over-supply in the 1980s, the huge debts of Third World commodity countries such as Mexico caused great problems for world trade. Imports were cut by such debtor nations. Such cut-backs multiplied their effects internationally. In the 1980s, therefore, protectionism and subsidised commodity sales have made their international reemergence in some core countries, with depressing effects on weaker trading nations.

Deregulation and privatisation of the liberal interventionist state and its instruments have been one of the means for Western democratic capitalist states to fight back and to regain a leaner and more competitive trading economy. Inevitably such states have also cast eyes on the welfare aspects of their system and the share of growth which has traditionally gone to labour in wages and the Keynesian social welfare wage.

The last item of 'share of growth' is crucial. Labour in the social contract of state liberalism can probably live with the deregulation of the interventionist state, often introduced (such as the fixed exchange rate) for the benefit of capital. Even welfare cuts can probably be borne, especially by the skilled and professional elements of the workforce. Welfare and the poor are a long way from the reality of such elements, which may indeed share attitudes of superiority and work ethic based disapproval of welfare receivers along with the 'mainstream' traditional entrepreneurial middle class. But the crucial test for state liberalism and its ideology of social harmonisation will be in the 'share of growth'.

In summary, the liberal welfare/interventionist state is based upon Benthamite expansionism. Society is held steady by incorporating the poor and ex-consensus groups into the existing structure.[46] Growth is essential for class peace.

But growth itself is faltering after forty years of continuous postwar expansion, along with an increasing environmental crisis which can contain little more growth. Thus, critiques from both Left and Right have emerged to analyse the causes of the present crisis of state liberalism and its growth-based ideology of social harmony.

Critiques of Liberalism

Critique of the Left

The Left critique of state liberalism stems originally from a Marxist analysis which mostly focused on the decline of class consciousness and working class militancy. The radical democrat New Left of the 1960s also emphasised elements of structural determinism in the state liberal 'growth' model which immobilised human development and quality of life issues. Like Rousseau, the New Left saw the democratic system as an aid to the development of the human spirit. To them, the new liberal welfare state aided materialism, not democracy. It added the faceless bureaucracy to the authoritarian capitalist structure as an enemy of broad democracy. Many of the New Left critics took the anarchist path of analysis, stressing the state as a companion or prime actor in oppression.

Other critics, such as Bahro[47] were later to stress the problem of industrialism itself, and its disastrous environmental link to the 'growth' mentality. He meant that both the capitalist and Soviet systems (liberal Welfare States and socialist ones) were products of industrialism, and equally bad. They were both doomed to the treadmill of 'growth' to maintain themselves as political successes. In the end, the earth itself would rebel against their misuse.

The major elements of the Left critique of state liberalism are: first, *incorporatism*.[48] The liberal welfare state has stressed the ideology of harmonisation. Many leaders of political parties and unions have actively striven for incorporation (such as the Australian Accord), dampening worker militancy. This has led to the corporate state ideology under the direction of the technocracy. The worker is neglected or receives rewards in an uneven manner according to skill level. A dual labour economy may emerge. Worker leaders who object to this process or use different methods of resistance may suffer marginalisation or penalties.

The second element is *social imperialism*.[49] The liberal welfare state has acted to impose the norms of capitalist middle class behaviour and social roles, particularly on the working class. It has legislated for, and upheld, the notions of the patriarchal nuclear family, the suburban home, and the respectable reproduction gender roles of men and women as the dominant ideology.[50] The liberal welfare state has sought a cultural unity on 'ideal types' as a means for self-censorship and social stability. 'One dimensional man' (as Marcuse called this creation) was a shallow being dedicated to a treadmill of 'growth', production and consumption. The existential boundaries of humanity, with their infinite possibilities, became confined (as J.P. Sartre stated) to inauthenticity. A '9 to 5' existence, dedicated to work and family, meant to live as if there were nothing beyond production and reproduction. Human beings had given up their potential. They had been imperialised by the dominant capitalist work ethic originally belonging to the small business class.

The third element concerns *environment*. The liberal Welfare State was chained to a model of growth and development, an endless Benthamite cycle of reaching for more technology, more affluence, and more government services to absorb more people into the consumption/production structure. This whole growth model is premissed on the continuation of environmental stability and the availability of resources. This is proving to be a myth.

Unfortunately, both the capitalist, the worker and the socialist are caught up in the ideas of industrialism. No support can be expected from the traditional Soviet systems (or their replacements) in redesigning industrialism in harmony with nature. Therefore to replace the liberal welfare system with a socialist system of industrialism may be meaningless.

Critique of the Right

The Right critique of the liberal Welfare State has largely echoed the classic market or libertarian economic line (see section on the New Right in the Conservatism chapter). This was an attempt to return to pre-Keynesian market structures which possessed no internal national structural rigidities of labour legislation and monopoly price fixing. In an age of increasing transnational capitalism and core country domination, the pressure for international division of labour is enormous. Nations should go along with this inevitable procedure and rid themselves of historically obsolete national economic structures. If this means a temporary or permanent drop in standards for some social elements e.g. unskilled labour, women, or Aboriginals, this is inevitable in this new stage of untrammelled and non-imperial free trade.

Much of the Right critique was also aimed at the cultural threats unleashed by the New Left, especially feminism. Right-wing notions of freedom and 'defensive' liberty (or protection from an interventionist state) are linked with ideas of protection from moral and cultural change. The traditional family, with traditional gender roles and social morality are seen to be under attack from a liberal Welfare State and its controlling 'new class'.

The major Right critiques of the liberal welfare state are: first, *market interference and efficiency*.[51] Right-wing libertarians claim that the interventionist state has institutionalised rigidities in the market. These include: labour awards, nationalised industry, and publicly-owned utilities. These last should be privatised, or sold off to capital. The market problems of the 1930s such as world mercantile empires or national capital no longer apply with their former intensity. Therefore the Keynesian state which was the 1930s' cure is the cause of the problem of the 1980s.

The second critique is of *the New Class*. The liberal Welfare State has created a new public middle class of state technocrats and bureaucrats and professionals, between capital and labour. These 'new mandarins' are a direct creation of the Keynesian state and Hobhouse's state liberalism. They have taken over economic and political decision making. But capital and labour will be freer and more prosperous if this class is confined to the classic liberal state interests.

This class has also attempted a cultural revolution in mainstream values in the name of reason. This holds dangers for the patriot, those who are content with suburban life, and those who fear social engineering.

The third critique includes *socialism*. The major struggle in the world today is against the Soviet bloc, which is the source of anti-capitalist ideology. This is particularly dangerous because of the attraction of this model to the modernising Third World. However, this argument has become muted with the collapse of the USSR.

The liberal Welfare State, even though it is not true socialism, has softened the Western citizen and created a welfare mentality, a forerunner of the state socialist mentality.

As for the appeal of socialism to the Western worker, this is now dead.[52] This is not the 1930s. A return to classic market economies will not mean a rise in socialist ideology amongst Western workers. Today's worker, especially the skilled labourer, is a small capitalist. This section of the workforce will do well under market economies. The state should therefore sell off its utilities and privatise them, creating thousands of stock holding small capitalists. It should allow the worker to negotiate his wage in a contract labour market. A dual labour market will then emerge, with a large middle class and skilled labour group on high wages, a semi-skilled and un-skilled part-time labour market, and some welfare poor.

This type of competitive society is impervious to socialism or welfarism. However, there will be battles in the Third World against socialism. Therefore nationalism, competitiveness and natural aggression (all cultural elements which the 'New Class' and the liberal welfare state tends to oppose) should be encouraged in culture and education.

Liberalism in Australia

The dominant political ideology in any country derives from its cultural history and its cherished social myths. This forms the basis of Burkes' 'logic of sentiment'.

The 'Logic of Sentiment'

In Australia, the English imperial link[53] was vital in the creation of social myth and the historical movement by both conservative and radical Australian forces towards a consensus of support for state liberalism.

As White points out,[54] English social myths concerning Australia begin in the 1840s. The old convict 'Hell on Earth' stereotype fell away, giving place to twin beliefs that Australia was 'salvation for all' and 'a working man's paradise'. In Australia, English social divisions could be escaped. Egalitarianism reigned and opportunities flourished for the industrious.

Nostalgia also shaped the political expectancies of migrants to Australia. White outlines[55] how the country was to provide an opportunity to recapture the yeoman farmer society of pre-industrial England. This yeoman myth was to underlie much of the post-Gold Rush free selection movements initiated by colonial governments. These governments were seen as service providers and instrumentalities to achieve popular social myths, despite market limitations. In an age when large-scale agriculture was becoming more economic, Australian governments persisted in the pursuit of the ideological aims of settling small farmers on the land. The moral superiority of rural life over urban living was never questioned.

This physiocrat belief in the moral pre-eminence of rural life dogs contemporary Australian politics and underlies much country/town antagonism. Indeed, the belief in the moral superiority of the yeoman ideal type also lies behind much of the suburban peasant mentality. West, in *The Revolution in Australian Politics* stresses the suburban peasants with their yeoman dream as the basis of support for the long reign of Robert Menzies. This dream stresses the near self-sufficient nuclear family (half urban/half yeoman) on increasingly large acreages, with room for the horse, children and the vegetable patch.

The underlying belief linking the middle class, worker and prospective yeoman emigrant to Australia was that 'all of their differing class dreams — new riches, a paradise for working men, and a farm — could be achieved'. Australia offered 'opportunity for all'.

Unlike England, the existing distribution of wealth in Australia was not a major question. Indeed, such wealth in the colonies was an object of admiration rather than envy. With hard work, new wealth could be created from the endless supply of both land and opportunities. In the nineteenth century, therefore, Australian colonials were agreed that the provision of 'opportunity for the industrious' was the foremost duty of government. Citizens of all political persuasions would identify with Alfred Deakin's 1903 election rhetoric: 'We have illimitable resources. They are only waiting for stimulation.'[56] From the beginning, a Benthamite doctrine of growth was a common political basis.

Mainstream radicals, too, endorsed the Benthamite doctrine of growth. But they were more suspicious of the role of privileged élites in ruining the 'working man's paradise' and the 'yeoman' arcadia. Echoing Tom Paine rather than Karl Marx, Australian mainstream radicals pursued democracy rather than anti-capitalism. They pursued 'fair' enterprise rather than 'free' enterprise. 'Opportunity for all' would be had by the control, not removal of the malignant élites of the rich and powerful. Increased democracy was the best safeguard to ensure control by the 'masses' over other 'interests'.

Freedom on the Wallaby

Our fathers toiled for bitter bread
    While idlers thrived beside them;
But food to eat and clothes to wear
    Their native land denied them.
They left their native land in spite
    Of royalties' regalia,
And so they came, or if they stole
    Were sent out to Australia.

They struggled hard to make a home,
    Hard grubbing 'twas in clearing.
They weren't troubled much with toffs
    When they were pioneering;
And now that we have made the land
    A garden full of promise,
Old greed must crook his dirty hand
    And come to take it from us.

But Freedom's on the Wallaby,
    She'll knock the tyrants silly,
She's going to light another fire
    And boil another billy.
We'll make the tyrants feel the sting
    Of those that they would throttle;
They needn't say the fault is ours
    If blood should stain the wattle.

Henry Lawson

Australian mainstream myths, despite the reality of continuous class struggle, stressed the fundamental unity of all classes grouped together in endless development and growth provided that a sensible cross-class government acted in a manner to benefit all by encouraging growth. Thus Benthamite utilitarianism provided the hegemonic political foundations of the Australian 'logic of sentiment'.[57] This unity of sentiment helped preserve the social order.[58]

The Role of the State

Inevitably, the state's 'main' role was 'to expedite opportunity and to provide support for personal industry.[59] It was seen as a partner in development, and an aid towards the attainment of the Australian dream.

Since penal times, the state had co-operated with, and partnered capital in the distribution and allocation of land and labour. In the nineteenth century, Australian colonial governments were instrumental in infrastructure development and import replacement schemes, via public funding of services and mercantilist policies.[60] Governments were judged in terms of their efficient provision of such services.[61]

The nineteenth century thus quite early indicated the road of socially desired development and the need for state liberalism. Social myths stressed the perfection of Australian society *as it was*. Only industry was required[62] to attain the quintessential Australian dream, incorporating ideas of the 'good woman', the respectable nuclear family, the independent yeoman, and the honest working man, all jumbled together on a suburban block. This decent life was to be serviced, not dominated, by the state.

The rigidity of the Australian mainstream social myths was to push conservative, liberal and radical ideologies into a historical compromise around state liberalism, with the liberal welfare/interventionist state as its instrument. The state was to service the existing Australian dream and to protect it from harmful outside forces, such as the Yellow Peril and foreign capitalists. It was not, however, to create its own ideology. The state served society, not, as in some Hegelian systems, the other way round.

Australia in the late nineteenth and early twentieth centuries was thus a laboratory of state liberalism in a growing partnership with social democracy. Such Benthamite utilitarianism via the state exercised the wonder of European socialists as *Socialisme sans doctrine* (socialism without theory). This was not the first time state liberalism was to be confused with socialism.

Australian conservatism was slowly forced to abandon much of its English aristocratic basis[63] and to seek accommodation with state liberalism around the welfare and interventionist state. It continued, however, to dominate the moral and cultural 'boundaries of respectability', as well as preserving the imperial idea. To the conservative, this idea offered a transcendent patriotism, glory and mystic race unity.

Radicalism, too, was locked into the liberal myth of the 'working man's paradise'. As White explains,[64] this myth idealised the successful skilled worker or independent yeoman as typical of the Australian worker. 'Such an ideal was far from the reality of unskilled or semi-skilled labour, migrants or Aboriginals, or, especially, women.' Radicalism in a general sense in Australia has been a series of historical 'bitter struggles' by these groups to gain entry into the 'working man's paradise' and to be given a share of the growth, power and 'opportunities for all'. At the same time, the mainstream struggle for a greater share for the working man (defined as white, male, Anglo-Celtic, family-centred and suburban) has continued.

Radicalism therefore was largely a process of breaking *into* the system or attaining more once in. Only a few, dismissed as of the extreme Left or Right (such as genuine Marxists or the contemporary New Right) have proposed breaking *up* the system.

Both mainstream Left and Right on the Australian political spectrum have thus been drawn by the dominant myths of the 'logic of sentiment' and the nature of external dependency, into a common pragmatic system of state liberalism. The divisions between such parties concerned the management of this system, group favouritism and what elements and issues should be emphasised:

> However, a basic distinction over the role of the state [does emerge]. Conservatives oppose any extension of the state activity into areas being competently managed by private enterprise. Radicals argue that activities of national concern should be under public control.[65]

Deakin, Menzies and Beyond

State liberalism and its instruments of welfarism and interventionism has both a conservative and radical history in Australia. Amongst the panoply of conservative leaders, two — Alfred Deakin and Robert Menzies — are outstanding for their enunciation of an ideological vision of Right-wing state liberalism.

It is difficult to categorise Deakin as a conservative in the classic European sense dedicated to a cultural élite, landed gentry or aristocratic class. He was forced to the Right of the Australian political spectrum, and into coalition with his political enemies by the demands of economic and imperial history,[66] and by the rise of the Australian Labor Party. From this position, he nevertheless outlines a clear state liberalism redolent of Green, Bentham, and Hobhouse, and based on a sense of humanity rather than economic hardheadness.

First Deakin 'spoke of a policy of progress with equal laws and opportunity for all. [There would be] healthy lives, honest toil, fair wages and hours, fair prices and conditions of employment and the abolition of antagonism and prejudice.'[67] Whatever economic development occurred, its main aim was the achievement of human happiness.

This initial spurt of humane liberalism was to lay the economic foundations and guidelines for the slow emergence of the Australian Welfare State. Classic Benthamite turning points in the process were found, for instance, in the creation of the basic wage, first made part of the nationwide award in the Harvester Case of 1907. Such a wage stipulates a dignified level of income which every employer must pay. There would be no negotiation to lower this common level. Similarly, means-tested pensions and welfare payments were initiated as an aspect of a humane society.

Secondly, Deakin was fully aware of the need for manufacturing development to underwrite the truly liberal society. 'Opportunity for all' and a 'working man's paradise' could only be built upon a balanced economy. A rural commodity-based economy would be disastrous in a world of fluctuating prices. This had been vividly experienced in the Great Depression of 1890 and was to be experienced again in the 1921 prices slump after World War I.

Deakin stressed protection. A protected manufacturing sector would provide jobs for the native and migrant worker. Increasing prosperity would lead to national greatness. Tariffs would avoid the dumping of foreign goods on the Australian market at non-competitive prices and preserve Australian assets in national hands. Both prestige and security would be achieved.

Deakin was quick to link protection with the social myths of 'opportunity for all' and the 'working man's paradise'. Australia as a blessed land was in danger from two things — foreign capitalism and cheap foreign labour. Protection and the White Australia Policy would guard against these corrosive elements. At the establishment of the Commonwealth Parliament in 1901, Deakin, reaching back to ideas concurrent with Lord Ripon's mid-nineteenth-century desire for a new Britannia in the South Seas,[68] stressed the 'whiteness' of this new nation. The state would ensure racial purity, and Australia would be 'one people, and remain one people without the admixture of other races'.[69]

The imperial idea was being subtly redesigned in this period. Britain was losing its free trade, nineteenth-century preeminence. It was forced into Chamberlain's 'New Protection' posture (1902) to defend itself against the rising production of Wilhelmine or Imperial Germany and the USA. The British Empire was subtly shifting to a new arrangement of the junior partners (confined to the White Dominions) negotiating different deals with the core country (Britain) within an overall Empire autarchy.[70] Protectionism in Australia became negotiable with Britain, and the tool for the creation of the ideal society, while free trade was often depicted as the policies of economic traitors or at least the ideas of those who did not uphold the social myth of the 'working man's paradise'.[71]

The importance of Deakin was his articulation of the policies of state liberalism, both external and internal. These were to last largely unchallenged for eighty years, and were to be the seed bed from which Australian institutions such as the arbitration system were to grow.[72]

This seed bed of racism, imperial trade and defence links, protectionism and state welfarism, was the ambit of Australian state liberalism. Both right and left, state liberals and social democrats, were to operate within these parameters, becoming increasingly indistinguishable from each other for the next eight decades.

Right-wing state liberalism and its approach to Deakinism had to wait for its proper outline with the liberalism of Menzies. Robert Menzies not only established the approving 'Wet' conservative[73] position towards the liberal welfare/interventionist state, but also the coalition of social forces that supported the 'Wet' conservative or Right-wing state liberal Ideology.

Between the wars from 1919 to 1939 the slow growth of the liberal welfare/interventionist state in Australia was impaired by the usual external dependency factor in the Australian economy. Despite the efforts of protectionism, immigration and government provided infrastructure, Australia was (and is) a country with a primary commodity-based export trade. Movements in such world commodity trade have a multiplier effect on the Australian economy and a 'trauma' effect on the achievability of the Australian dream.

In 1921, Australian prices collapsed after the inflated demand of World War 1. Real wages recovered, and, for a time, Australian governments pursued old Australian social myths, such as the yeoman dream via the soldier settler schemes.

Rural prices went into depression however. By 1928, as wartorn countries recovered from their devastation, and overproduction took effect, marginal farmers could not compete due to rising costs. Rural collapse preceded world Depression.

With the Great Depression of 1929 the Australian state had to cut back on its expenditure. As award wages fell by 20 per cent, and as farm depression worsened, the dominant Australian ideology of Benthamite liberalism began to be shaken.

A 'trauma' effect took place, as disillusionment with the Australian dream, 'opportunity for all' and 'the working man's paradise', reached down into the Depression generation. For the first time since the 1890s, alternative explanatory ideologies such as Marxism penetrated some way into the world outlined by Deakin. Even some quasi-Fascism made its appearance, but this was (on the surface) a defensive conservative, rather than radical Fascist movement. (See 'New Guard'.)

The post-World War II coming of Keynesian economics was a timely rescue for state liberalism. For Right-wing state liberals, however, the problem was how to create a coalition of supporters who would support such a Keynesian world. Right-wing politics had declined in Australia from 1940–47. The main conservative party, the UAP had split, largely over personalities but also over pure capitalist versus state liberal economic and political tactics.

Menzies realized that he faced two problems. Firstly, he had to re-define the Right-wing state liberal ideological position in an attractive way which would tap deep Australian social myths such as 'opportunity for all' and recapture the ideological high ground from the social democrats. This would give him increased electoral support.

Secondly, he had to construct a party of committed numbers from disparate conservative groups such as moral conservatives, cultural conservatives and economic conservatives, and have them come to terms with the arrival of the Keynesian state. This would give him a coalition of interest groups throughout the community to match the Labor Party's deep social contacts and its ascendency with the young. All this had to occur within the Deakinite ambit.

The Menzies solution was to be successful for the next twenty-five years. It was aided by the luck of world-wide capitalist applications of Keynesianism, steadying commodity prices and the occurrence of small wars (such as the Korean War of 1951–53) stimulating a boom in such commodities.

The Menzies solution was encapsulated in the ideology of the Liberal Party from 1947. The party ideology dismissed a class analysis of Australian society in favour of a broad ideology stressing 'free enterprise' with state assistance, broad support for protectionist policies, and an emphasis upon traditional political institutions and loyalties, such as the British royalist sentiment. Allied to this was a deep commitment to the patriarchal nuclear family. The notion of a welfare net for the poor was incorporated into this vision, but only in terms of need rather than right. A Right-wing state liberal government was expected 'to create the circumstances for personal initiative and success rather than provide a wide welfare structure. Poverty was narrowly defined.'

By emphasis upon traditional mainstream moral and cultural values, the liberalism of Menzies captured the majority of Australia's expanding suburban middle class. The Menzies program struck the right note in the era of the idolisation of the 'family'[74] and the 'suburban peasant'.[75] In addition, economic conservatives were satisfied with the expanding internal market, the rise of consumerism, and the dedication of the state to the wellbeing, rather than the replacement, of private enterprise. Menzies-style 'liberal socialism' became successfully identified in Australia with the long post-war boom of Western capitalism. It operated successfully within the Deakinite policies of state liberalism, but adapted these policies to the politics of growth, towards consumerism, and a static image of lower middle class suburban Australia as the real Australia.

Such an image was to come under increasing attack in the 1960s and 1970s by ex-consensus groups such as homosexuals, feminists and blacks. Ethnic minorities, also excluded from the Deakinite list of priorities of state liberalism, were to become increasingly active. They were increasingly to turn to the alternative state liberal party — the Labor Party — and provide it with an extra constituency. This new coalition, together with the impact of the Vietnam War on middle Australia, was part of the reason for the Whitlam breakthrough in 1972.

Conclusions

Robert Menzies was long gone from the political stage, however, when the post-World War II boom ended and the Labor Party gained power. His creation, the Liberal Party, has undergone an ideological reformulation in the 1980s. It has moved on the surface outside the Deakinite structure of policies into the doctrinal world of the New Right and classic liberalism. The abandonment of the state liberalism of Hobhouse, Green and Deakin now seems, at least to Liberal Party ideologues, a welcome prospect.

This may be a historical necessity due to the disappearance of the British Empire, the decline of Keynesianism in capitalist practice, and the re-structuring and re-integration of Australia into the Pacific Basin economy. Deakinism and the ideology of Menzies represented a liberalism suitable for an Australia at a certain import replacement historical period in relation to the British Empire and the world core countries. The increasing re-emergence of classic liberalism may represent the adjustment of political ideas to the harsher capitalist demands of post-imperial realities.

Whether the democratic mass of Australians, with their traditional commitment to 'opportunities for all' and a 'working man's paradise' will accept a move to classic liberalism is a political gamble. It flies in the face of some of their deepest social myths.

The move to classic liberalism will therefore be incremental.[76] It will be accompanied by a massive program and campaign to change these deep popular social myths which are founded on original Deakinite policies that have guided Australian policies for eighty years in both Left and Right state liberalism. Such a campaign must also mean political realignments and opportunities.

Notes

1. Hayek, F.A. in De Crespigny, A. and Cronin, J. (eds) *Ideologies of Politics.* Capetown, Oxford University Press, 1975, p. 59.
2. Beilharz, P. 'Theorizing the Middle Class' *Arena* 72, 1985, pp. 92–105 and De Crespigny and Cronin, p. 59.
3. Walker, F.M. *The Age of Ideology: Political Thought 1750-Present.* New Jersey, Prentice-Hall, 1964, p. 11.
4. Catley, R. and McFarlane, B. *Australian Capitalism in Boom and Depression.* Sydney, Alternative Book Publishing, 1981, p. 9.
5. Ebenstein, W. *Todays Isms* seventh Edition. New Jersey, Prentice-Hall, 1973, p. 142.
6. Bullock, A. and Stallybrass, 0. *The Fontana Dictionary of Modern Thought.* London, Fontanal Collins, 1977, P. 347.
7. Lowi, T.J. *The End of Liberalism.* USA, Norton, 1969.
8. Hall, J.A. *Powers and Liberties.* UK Pelican, 1986, p. 22.
9. Gough, I. *The Political Economy of The Welfare State.* London, Macmillan, 1981. p. 11.
10. Ebenstein, p. 154.
11. Hall, pp. 158–63.
12. Christenson, R.M. *et al. Ideologies and Modern Politics.* London, Nelson, 1971, p. 191.
13. Ibid.
14. Ibid.
15. Hampton, C. (ed.) *A Radical Reader: The Struggle for Change in England 1381–1914.* UK, Penguin, 1984, pp. 188–200.
16. Walker, p. 13.
17. Walker, pp. 15–17.
18. Winthrop, N. (ed.) *Liberal Democratic Theory and its Critics.* Sydney, Croom Helm, 1983, pp. 36–37.
19. Winthrop, pp. 25–26.
20. Bullock and Stallybrass, p. 325.
21. Clark, M. 'Flawed Heroes' *History of Australia* Vol. VI as referred to in *Australian Society* September 1986, p. 24.
22. Winthrop, p. 29.
23. Winthrop, pp. 32–33.
24. Ibid.
25. Hobhouse, L.T. *Liberalism.* NY, Oxford University Press, 1969, p. 8.
26. Hobhouse, pp. 6–7.
27. Hobhouse, p. 87.
28. See Beilharz.
29. Catley and McFarlane, p. 225.
30. Marcuse, H. in Christenson *et al.,* p. 293.
31. Carr, R. 'Is Socialism Finished?' *Institute of Public Affairs Review* 1, 40 (2) 1986, p. 38.
32. Gough, pp. 65–68.
33. Gough, p. 67.
34. Gough, p. 66.

35. Bell, D. *The End of Ideology*. UK, Collier, 1970.
36. See Carr.
37. Barber, W. *A History of Economic Thought*. UK, Penguin, 1984, p. 224.
38. Barber, p. 223.
39. Barber, p. 230.
40. Beresford, M. and Kerr, P. 'A Turning Point for Australian Capitalism' in Wheelwright, E. and Buckley, K. *The Political Economy of Australian Capitalism* Vol. VI. Sydney, ANZ Books, 1980, p. 148.
41. Hall, p. 174.
42. Hall, p. 171.
43. Brugger, B. in Winthrop, p. 29.
44. Hall, p. 173.
45. Ibid. See also Beilharz, *Australian Society*, September 1986, p. 24.
46. —
47. Bahro, R. *The Alternative in Eastern Europe*. UK, New Left Books, 1979.
48. Gough, p. 67.
49. Gough, p. 48.
50. White, R. *Inventing Australia: Images and Identity 1688–1980*. Sydney, Allen and Unwin, 1981, pp. 160–62.
51. Hall, p. 174.
52. See Carr.
53. Jupp, J. *Party Politics: Australia 1966–81*. Sydney, Allen and Unwin, 1982, pp. 22–25.
54. White, pp. 29–47.
55. White, p. 34.
56. Horne, D. *Money Made Us*. Australia, Penguin, 1976, p. 29.
57. Collins, H. 'Political Ideology in Australia: The Distinctiveness of a Benthamite Society' *Daedalus* Winter 1985. Boston, USA.
58. White, p. 44.
59. Ibid.
60. Clark, Manning. *A Short History of Australia*. London, Heinemann, 1969.
61. Davis, S.R. *The Government of the Australian States*. Melbourne, Longman, 1960.
62. White, p. 46.
63. Jupp, pp. 23, 70.
64. White, p. 46.
65. Jupp, pp. 23, 71.
66. Horne, p. 16.
67. Horne, p. 18–19.
68. Phillipp, J. *A Great View of Things*. Melbourne, Nelson, 1971.
69. Courtenay, P.P. *Northern Australia*. Ringwood, Victoria, Longman Cheshire, 1982, p. 20.
70. Leach, R. 'The Balkanization of Australia' in *Dyason House Papers* Autumn 1978.
71. Horne, p. 151.
72. Horne, p. 17.
73. Jupp, p. 88.
74. White, pp. 158–65.
75. West, K. *The Revolution in Australian Politics*. Ringwood, Victoria, Penguin, 1984.
76. Catley and McFarlane, p. 231.

References

Australian Society, September, 1986.
Barber, W. *A Hostory of Economic Thought*. UK, Penguin, 1984.
Bahro, P. *The Alternative in Eastern Europe*. UK, New Left Books, 1979.

Barratt Brown, M. *Models in Political Economy*. UK, Penguin, 1984.

Bell, D. *The End of Ideology*. UK, Collier, 1970.

Beiharz, P. 'Theorizing the Middle Class' *Arena* 72, 1985.

Boyce, P. and Angel, J. (eds) *Independence and Alliance: Australia in World Affairs 1976–80* Sydney, Allen and Unwin, 1983.

Bullock, A. and Stallybrass, O. *The Fontana Dictionary of Modern Thought*. London, Fontana/Collins, 1977.

Catley, R. and McFarlane, B. *Australian Capitalism in Boom and Depression*. Sydney, Alternative Book Publishing, 1981.

Carr, R. 'Is Socialism Finished?' *Institute of Public Affairs Review* 1, 46 (2) Winter 1986.

Clark, Manning. *A Short History of Australia*. London, Heinemann, 1969.

Courtenay, P.P. *Northern Australia*. Ringwood, Victoria, Longman Cheshire, 1982.

Collins, H. 'Political Ideology in Australia': The Distinctiveness of a Benthamite Society' *Daedulus* Winter, Boston, USA 1985.

Davis, S.R. *The Government of the Australian States*. Melbourne, Longman, 1960.

De Crespigny, A. and Cronin, J. (eds) *Ideologies of Politics*. Capetown, Oxford University Press, 1975.

Ebenstein, W. *Today's Isms* Seventh Edition. New Jersey, Prentice-Hall, 1973.

Gibb, D.M. and Hannan, A.W. *Debate and Decision. Political Issues in Twentieth Century Australia*. Australia, Heinemann, 1975.

Gough, I. *The Political Economy of the Welfare State*. London, Macmillan, 1981.

Hampton, C. (ed.) A *Radical Reader: The Struggle for Change in England 1381–1914*. UK, Penguin, 1984.

Hayek: see de Crespigny and Cronin.

Heater, D. *Contemporary Political Ideas*. UK, Longman, 1983.

Hall, J. *Powers and Liberties*. UK, Pelican, 1986.

Hobhouse, L.T. *Liberalism*. NY, Oxford University Press, 1969.

Horne, D. *Money Made Us*. Australia, Penguin, 1976.

Horsfall, J. *The Liberal Era*. Melbourne, Sun Books, 1974.

Jessop, B. *The Capitalist State*. Oxford, Martin Robinson, 1983.

Jupp, J. *Party Politics: Australia 1966–81*. Sydney, Allen and Unwin, 1982.

Levine, A. *Liberal Democracy: A Critique of its Theory*, NY, Columbia University Press, 1981.

Lowi, T.J. *The End of Liberalism*. USA, Norton, 1969.

Macpherson, C.B. *The Political Theory of Possessive Individualism: Hobbes to Locke*. Oxford, Oxford University Press, 1964.

Manning, D.J. *Liberalism*. London, Dent, 1976.

Leach, R. 'The Balkanization of Australia' in *Dyason House Papers* Autumn 1978.

Phillipp, J. A *Great View of Things*. Melbourne, Nelson, 1971.

Rowse, T. *Australian Liberalism and National Character*. Melbourne, Kibble Books, 1978.

Sabine, G. and Thorsen, T. A *History of Political Thought* Fourth Edition. Illinois, Dorsey, 1969.

Sargent, L.T. *Contemporary Political Ideologies* Fifth Edition. Illinois, Dorsey, 1969.

Walker, F.M. *The Age of Ideology*: Political Thought 1750–Present. New Jersey, Prentice-Hall, 1964.

West, K. *The Revolution in Australian Politics*. Ringwood, Victoria Penguin, 1984.

Wheelwright, G. and Buckley, K. (eds) *Essays in The Political Economy of Australian Capitalism* Vol. VI. Sydney, ANZ Books, 1980.

White, D.M. *The Philosophy of the Australian Liberal Party*. Victoria, Hutchinson, 1978.

White, R. *Inventing Australia: Images and Identity 1688–1980*. Sydney, Allen and Unwin, 1981.

Winthrop, N. (ed.) *Liberal Democratic Theory and its Critics*. Sydney, Croom Helm, 1983.

Recommended Reading

Winthrop, N. (ed.) *Liberal Democratic Theory and its Critics*, Sydney, Croom Helm, 1983.
Hobhouse, L.T. *Liberalism*. NY, Oxford University Press, 1969.
Lowi, T.J. *The End of Liberalism*. USA, Norton, 1969.
Ebenstein, W. *Today's Isms* Seventh Edition. New Jersey, Prentice-Hall, 1973.

4

Democratic Socialism

> Socialism is a concept with many meanings but (it is) generally understood as a social system based on common ownership of the means of production and distribution. In communist theory, (socialism) is the first stage (to Communism). In socialist writings, it differs from communism by an attachment to ethical and democratic values as well as by an emphasis on the distinction between common and State ownership . . .
> (A. Bullock and D. Stallybrass,
> *The Fontana Dictionary of Modern Thought*)

Socialism has a variety of historical definitions. Like liberalism, socialism stemmed from the Enlightenment drive to apply reason to human existence. Socialism has followed two paths in this application of reason: the democratic socialist path, henceforth called 'social democracy', to concentrate attention on its most electorally successful school of thought and the Marxist/Leninist communist path with its Jacobin heritage and its development of the totalitarian state model.

This division within socialism was a late nineteenth century/ early twentieth century phenomenon. '[In fact] at times, they [have merged] as occurred with pre-World War I social democracy and more recently with Euro-communism.'[1] This division represents an analytic clash over the 'class' or 'workerist' approach to politics versus the broad socially harmonic 'citizen' approach, as a conceptual starting point, something forming a major part of the historical split between social democracy and communism, especially within the European socialist movement.

Continental European socialist democracy was, in the nineteenth century, predominantly based upon the theories of Marxism. The essence of this view is the inevitability of class conflict, between the *bourgeoisie* (capitalist class) and the *proletariat* (working class), one class or another becoming, inevitably, the ruling one, and the state being used to further the interests of this class. Later social democracy developed a stress upon social harmony between classes with the state acting as a neutral ringmaster between capital and labour.

The dismantling of its Marxist foundations was long and painful for continental West European social democracy. British socialism, however, grew from non-Marxist sources — Owenism, chartism, the liberal/labour partnership theories of T.H. Green and L.T. Hobhouse, and Benthamite utilitarianism. Its journey from working class/union foundations to modern social democrat 'technocratic managerial' politics has been easier.

This chapter will attempt to outline the major aspects of social democracy. This is important for, on the political spectrum, social democracy is the dominant Left position, opposing conservatism and liberalism in most of Western Europe, Britain, Australia and New Zealand and other countries penetrated by the ideas of state liberalism and social democracy, including the USA. Social Democracy may be re-emerging, even in the former states of the soviet bloc, as one of the dominant forms of political thought.

Essentially, social democracy can be defined as 'that part of the socialist and labour movement which accepts a democratic structure of the state and postulates social changes by means of reform rather than revolution . . .'[2]

The historical course of social democracy in pursuing reform has seen its transition from a basically working class ideology to the adoption of broad 'everyman a citizen' theories, welfare statism, and many of the trappings of liberalism itself.

This drift to the centre of politics and the historic compromise with liberalism was due largely to the pressure for consensus policies within the boundaries of the liberal welfare state.[3] 'Welfarism has largely replaced socialism as ideology within the social democratic movement.'

The real problem for contemporary social democracy is the increasing failure of welfarism. The notion of the Welfare State depends on Benthamite ideas of endless new growth. Should growth falter, what has social democracy to offer now it has shed much of its original socialist philosophy?[4]

Origins

Most nations possess a cultural history which stresses some form of social justice, fraternity and collective action. In Western Europe, writings stretching from Ancient Greece (Plato's *Republic*) to Sir Thomas More's sixteenth-century *Utopia* stressed the concept of a socially just state based upon common property and the primacy of social duty.

More's text was extremely important. Utopianism was to pass into the languages of the world as a word for an unattainable dream society. It rapidly also became a term of abuse used by its critics to describe socialism, and is often used in quarrels between socialist factions.

The problem of 'utopianism' is extremely vital to socialism. Socialism has to stay close to the needs of the people (practical ideology) while still offering an inspiring and motivating vision of the future (pure ideology).[5] To abandon pure ideology means politicians become just another set of managers of the status quo. But offer only pure solutions to the eternal political questions of social justice, democracy and equality is to be dismissed by the majority as fanatical and/or irrelevant.

Social democracy has consistently shown a majority trend towards practical ideology. Such a tendency has consistently factionalised it, between its managerial 'pragmatists' and its socialist 'pure' visionaries.

The nineteenth century was the high point of socialist thought. Many varieties of thought flourished, sifted through the pure/practical social filter and all overshadowed by the century's trend towards technocracy.

Socialist theory in the nineteenth century was fuelled by the in-human effects of the European industrial revolution and classic capitalism. It was motivated by two factors — a moral outrage at the values of classic capitalism, and a desire for industrial efficiency against market chaos. Socialism, with its criticisms, quickly captured the moral high ground. It drew upon the same Enlightenment wells as liberalism with its stress upon human betterment by extended democracy and social engineering. It went further than liberalism, however, in that it wished to tame the industrial system and, if necessary, dispense with industrialism's creator, the capitalist class, while still preserving the benefits of industrial growth.

Like the liberals, socialists approved of industrialism. The problem with the industrial system for them was the distribution of most of its benefits to the few over the many. The social system, not the machine, was in need of change. The possibilities of ecological disaster due to industrialism, except in the visions of poets, was a century away.

Socialist solutions to capitalism and industrialism took several major forms. Some stressed capitalism's complete overthrow by revolution and its replacement by a command economy and a technocratic state. Others stressed social harmony between capital and labour through an arbitrating state.[6] Some stressed an 'enabling' state which would encourage grassroots extended democracy and action by ordinary people, not by a technocratic hierarchy which made decisions from a distance. This state would devolve, not increase its powers.

Others aimed solely at labourism. This was satisfied with the achievement of an adequate income for workers and a recognition of unions. Otherwise, the capitalist could get on with running his system.

Eventually, the differences in socialist thought resolved into two major approaches to the questions of achieving democracy, efficiency and social justice. Should socialism be achieved by action from the top by experts or from the bottom by the free action of the masses? (In Maoist China in the twentieth century, this became known as the 'Red/expert' struggle.) What was needed, many thought, was a central, unifying theory.

Such a theory was to emerge, initially, with Marxism. Throughout the nineteenth century, however, the class warfare basis of Marxism was increasingly rejected by the rising 'social harmony' stream of European social democracy. In the twentieth century, this reformist theory, built upon elements of Fabianism, state capitalism and, particularly, post-World War II Keynesian welfare/interventionist theories, has replaced Marxism in social democracy. This has led to confusion and an overlapping with state liberalism.[7]

Like contemporary state liberalism, social democracy stands in some philosophical confusion, due to the crisis of their main common support — the post-war Welfare State.[8]

A generalised model of Western social democracy would follow these stages:

(a) The Utopian stage of socialism: 1800–48
(b) Marxist ideological domination: 1848–90
(c) The triumph of revisionism: the rejection of Marx: 1890–1945
(d) The Welfare State ideology: liberal/social democratic consensus: 1945

Anglo-Saxon Social Democracy drew upon middle class Fabianism with its legalist/élitist basis. It also stressed traditions of social harmony influenced by liberalism, religion and utilitarianism.[9] Marxism was a peripheral creed to Anglo-Saxon socialism.

The Utopian Stage of Socialism: 1800–48

The formative stage of Western socialism was uneven, due to different traditions; different relations to the state; and the appeal of different brands of socialist thought. For example, as G.D.H. Cole points out, Italy with its limited franchise until 1913 and its economic backwardness, was more attracted to anarchism compared with industrialised countries like Britain and Germany.[10]

Nationalism and the desire to attain respectability had a continuous effect upon socialist thought in Britain and Germany. As Gamble indicates,[11] there was a constant groping for a social consensus in such countries which would bring the new industrial masses into the existing system on the basis of legitimacy. Both the conservative moderates and most socialists wished to keep order, maintain prosperity and avoid class war. The theory of socialism was thus under constant pressure to conform to these desires and avoid the revolutionary scenario set by Marx.

The driving force behind this search by nineteenth century Western socialism to form an 'acceptable' system of ideas was both the goad of unregulated capitalism and a desire to be an effective and respected power within society.[12] Thus socialism attracted both the technocrat and the moraliser, a powerful mixture.

The Utopian stage of early socialism became a period of search for viable 'pure' and 'practical' alternatives to capitalism. It was a period of search for a Sorelian myth accepted by the masses upon which the socialist perspective would be based. Such a myth was created upon the Rousseauian view that people could be benevolent and rational beings given the 'just' society; that co-operation was more natural to people than the selfishness extolled by capitalism; and that the exploitation of capitalism was (at the least) a mere historical aberration. The world was not a Social Darwinist dog fight, but a harmonic organic society that had been temporarily misled by the chaos of market ethics and the dominance of one class, the merchants.

Continental Thought

The notion that the capitalist period was a temporary fall from the 'organic' society was particularly stressed by Henri De Saint-Simon (1760–1825) and Francois Fourier (1772–1837). Both men despised merchant values and idealised the 'organic' society of the Middle Ages. Saint-Simon recognised that the age of kings had gone, and with it the control necessary to contain the powerful competitive merchant spirit. He stressed the need to develop a new control via an impartial priesthood of scientific experts, who would co-ordinate the new industrial age for all classes. The temporary madness of capitalism was historically necessary to set this industrial process in train.[13]

Saint-Simon stressed the need for a ruling vanguard of altruistic technocrats similar to Plato's philosopher kings or the more recent, rougher example of the French Jacobins. Fourier, on the other hand, stressed the need for the release of human spontaneity and co-operation, preferably within small communities. These two views of the paths to socialism — Jacobinism or the counter-belief in mass spontaneity— still form the main divisions in socialist thought, influencing social democracy, anarchism and communism.

Britain

In Britain, pragmatism influenced early socialist thought in the tradition of empiricist British philosophy. Robert Owen (1771–1858) a Scottish capitalist, emphasised practical experiments in social organisation around industrialism. He hoped to show other capitalists that by co-operation and social harmony, rather than by exploitation, productivity would soar. All classes would benefit.

Owen was an example of the type of British socialist who was driven by religious-based moral uneasiness over the evils of industrialism. He sought a compromise, rather than accepting the Continental logic of the incompatibility of worker and capitalist. Owen was an example of the influence of Protestant Christianity upon socialist thought, with its notions that harmony could develop free souls co-operating without dogma to achieve the secular paradise.

Owen stressed an evolutionary, co-operative socialism. If necessary a parallel co-operative movement of industrial organisations should be set up alongside capitalism. This would eventually out-produce and peacefully replace the capitalist system and values, in a co-operative Commonwealth.[14] As man is a product of his environment, so improved work conditions, welfare and education and co-operative values would bring out his basic goodness. Owen believed in role sharing, in the virtues of community, and in 'the fundamental unity of capital and labour'.[15] Like the earlier British socialist, Godwin, his emphasis was upon small industry and local democracy.

Unlike Marx, Owen (like most Utopian socialists) produced no over-arching 'pure' ideology that 'provided general directives and orientations ... towards virtually every human concern'.[16] Nevertheless, his practical social and welfare experiments, together with the British Chartist stress upon organised 'labourism', or benefits for the organised workforce in return for social harmony, pointed the way for the marriage of labourism and welfarism that underlies much of contemporary social democratic thought.

Marxist Ideological Domination: (1848–90)

Marxism quickly became the dominant code of continental socialism, due to its coherence. This dominance was partly due to the violent confrontationist history of working class movements on the Continent. The French Revolution of 1789; the rise of conservative nationalism and counter-revolution; the 1830 Revolution in France; the 1848 Revolutions; the authoritarianism of Napoleon III; the rise of German Junkerism; the Paris Commune of 1871 — were all events which served to reinforce the notion of class warfare and the claims of Marxism to be the ideology of the working masses.

Much of earlier socialist thought was integrated into the great Marxist world view, even though much of it had also been dismissed by Marx himself as Utopian. This was not because of its Jacobinism (Saint-Simon), its spontaneity (Fourier) or its welfare notions (Owen). It was dismissed because it was believed to be naïve.[17]

Marx shared the earlier socialists' moral outrage at capitalism and their sense of its economic mindlessness and waste. But he despised, too, their lack of realism, and their constant appeal to capitalist reason. Groth interprets him as saying:

> They did not understand what they were up against in terms of capitalism and the state. Moreover, they did not have an understanding of what was possible and what was not in terms of leading workers against their masters . . .[18]

At the least, they offered false hopes and won easily reversed gains. At the most they got their followers killed through poor understanding of the role of the capitalist state. Morality and a romantic righteous belief in one's course proved no protection against the forces of the capitalist state.

Karl Marx (1818–83) dominated Continental socialist thought in his lifetime. Marxism was a structured philosophy using economics and class struggle as tools to analyse human history and motivation. To it, economics and class formed the hub of the wheel of life. The spokes (art, law, family relations, religion and gender relations) could all be explained by their ultimate relationship to the hub. Class struggle drove the wheel forward into history. Sometimes, exhaustion or the confusion of class forces let it roll back. But always, there was incremental progress.

Marx stressed that the socialist movement based upon the working class (proletariat) was a universal, if unevenly developed, process. History was on the side of socialism. What Marx offered was an easily understood social myth, explaining life. It was not an eternal battle between rich and poor, the powerful and powerless. The fatalistic message of the Bible 'The poor ye shall always have with ye' (Matthew 26 v. 6–13) was dismissed by the Marxists as superstition that reconciled people to their lot and the status quo. Through Marxism, history was at last comprehensible: An earthly paradise was achievable, and the lot of humankind *could* be changed.

For many, a new secular religion had been born. For others, it was a marvellous tool of understanding. As Groth points out,[19] even those such as Bertrand Russell who disputed Marxism's merits, nevertheless classified Marx as the single most influential philosopher in history.

Marxism grew constantly as a tool of analysis. It penetrated into the colonial empires, particularly via its adaptation into an explanation of imperialism. Originally, a liberal economist, J.A. Hobson[20] linked capitalism to imperialism, suggesting that capitalism, with its lopsided wealth distribution, was inherently imperialist. The rich could not consume their wealth, so their savings were excessive, and had to be put to use or the capitalist system would collapse due to a decline in purchasing power. It was useless to invest at home, as the local poor had little purchasing power. So they would invest overseas, in captive colonial or neo-colonial markets. This process involved constant risks of war with competing capitalist empires. But the system of imperialism was driven by the need for capital to make more capital — or collapse. Thus profit had little direct relationship to social needs. It could, indeed, condone the worst possible conditions in the colonies, as long as it made money.

Marxism, translated into theory explaining both capitalism and imperialism via the works of Hobson, Lenin and, later, Stalin, travelled well in the Third World. It soon became, and still remains, the major ideology of the socialist movement outside the Anglo-Saxon and West European countries.

The Triumph of Revisionism: the Rejection of Marx: 1890–1945

Revisionism represents the erosion of revolutionary Marxism due to the clash between pure and practical ideology in Europe. Marx's writings themselves exhibited this erosion. Originally the Communist Manifesto had outlined the downfall of bourgeois society and its replacement by a proletarian dictatorship. By 1870, Marx was willing to admit that wherever a worker franchise existed (as in the USA and Britain), peaceful evolution towards socialism might be possible. By the 1890s, most European social democrat parties were following non-Marxist policies in practice if not in theory. In Germany, in particular, Edward Bernstein (1850–1932) suggested a plain reformist path, dispensing with Marxism.

The reasons for reformism were many. The first was the rise in Western worker's living standards between 1840 and 1910. This contradicted the Marxist prophecy of increasing immiseration of the Western worker. Both Hobson and Lenin, of course, would argue that immiseration had been transferred to the Third World worker. Imperialism transferred wealth to the advanced Western capitalist countries and some of this wealth trickled down to the Western workers. The Western working class was thus becoming a labour aristocracy, quite happy with its dominant labour position in a world imperialist/racist system. To Marxists like Lenin, the revisionist Western social democrats were silent partners in imperialism, reaping its benefits. Thus they wished to be rid of an embarrassing Marxist ideology which stressed the universality of the working class.

Secondly, Marxist-based social democrat parties had to struggle with problems of mass acceptability in leading countries. Their Marxist ideology espoused anti-hegemonic symbols. Social scientists such as Thorstein Veblen (1875–1929) in *The Theory of the Leisure Class* drew attention to dominant ideal types of behaviour which were thrown up constantly by literature and the media, and which were emulated by lesser groups and classes in society.

These ideal types of behaviour usually belonged to the 'least useful' but most aggressive groups in society. This ruthless behaviour appealed to people immured in boring security. Such behaviour also appealed to old attitudes of admiration for someone's personal strength. Accordingly, the common folk sought to emulate their betters.[21] In the competition for electoral support, the closer social democrats came to these ideal types and the less the threat offered to this dominant ideology, the better the chance for the party.

The act of entering the electoral process forced change upon Western social democracy. The outcome was to elevate Marxism into a ceremonial rhetoric which was rarely used as a guide to practice. By 1914, only the Left wing of its parties stood for orthodox Marxism. World War I splintered the Western social democrat parties, especially in Europe, and the ideals of 'the unity of the world proletariat' were abandoned. Party after party endorsed the war. Nationalism had proved stronger than socialism.

A number of socialists clung to orthodox Marxism, In Russia, the Bolshevik section seized power in the 1917 Revolution, using a new form of 'total' party. The European Continental social democrat movement split between revolutionary communists and parliamentary social democrats. In Britain, the social democratic Labour Party did not undergo such a split, as Marxism did not form its theoretical base. Communism did not manage to penetrate into the mainstream of British politics, remaining a fringe movement.

Britain

The British social democratic movement encompassed an eclectic group of radicals, unionists, reformists and Christians. It attempted to base its strength on a coalition of interests rather than a single class, although the organised working class, via unions, would provide its central nucleus.

Labourism, with its emphasis upon the worker's share of production, was allied to a more sophisticated view of the role of the state and its management via Fabianism. This was a gradual form of élitist socialism involving the persuasion of powerful state and private figures to the cause of reform. Essentially,

'. . . the Fabians developed a form of socialism acceptable in a relatively rich country, making it easy for members of the middle class to become socialists while retaining their privileged life style.'[22]

The Fabians recognised the need to build on the sense of outrage that the nineteenth century English capitalist system had produced in the moralistic section of the English middle class. The Fabians underlined the need to exploit and tap this middle class sympathy by stressing technocratic utilitarianism — the greatest efficiency for the greatest number, not a world turned upside down.[23] They therefore stressed that no major change should take place in a society on its way to socialism unless 'it is democratic (a majority supports it); gradual (it involves minimum dislocation); ethical (it is not regarded by the majority as immoral) and constitutional'.[24]

The Fabians saw the state as an instrument of such change. It could be neutral, and not a class instrument. The key to a neutral state was to welcome the rise of dispassionate experts or technocrats. The Fabians, like Veblen,[25] saw the rise of technocracy as inevitable as long as it was needed to increase production. Veblen saw the phenomenon of technocracy hidden beneath the loud doings of 'the predatory business class'. The Fabians saw their socialism as a process of coaxing these experts out into positions of power, where, protected and controlled by a democratic socialist government, they would tame capitalism and bring planning to its chaotic production processes.

Like state liberals, the Fabians saw the necessity of mitigating the injustice of capitalism by increasing welfare services and state employment.[26] The state not only had basic functions to fulfil (e.g. defence) but it also had new social and economic functions which affected growth and production.[27]

The future Fabian state would both arbitrate and initiate socio-economic action. It would possess vast public enterprises under the rule of neutral experts. It would nationalise the heights of industry (e.g. steel and railways) in order to thwart private monopolies. A state socialism which would plan and minister to the people's holistic wants would slowly emerge. They would be consulted in periodic democratic elections, but otherwise, Fabianism endorsed Saint-Simon's 'rule by élites'.

The basic difference between Fabian social democracy and state liberalism rested upon the concepts of the 'state' and 'class': The Fabians believed, first, in reducing the role of capitalism and advancing the role of the state into the economy via national-isation, public enterprise and regulation. State liberalism stressed a market which was free of the state, except where capital could not provide the service. Secondly, Fabianism perceived capitalism's main problem to be the low buying power of the working class.[28] Cyclic booms and depressions in capitalism were due to unequal wages. The state should build up wage power, so wage expenditure would stimulate more growth at home. The state would also relieve the need for imperialist expansion. However, over-consumption could lead to a crisis of profit via inflation. This would be solved by the creation of state enterprises which planned their production and thus steadied the market. Or an interventionist state would be created which would control and balance both labour and capital, the tripartite state. (This latter suggestion was closer to the state liberalism of Green and Hobhouse than to original Fabianism.)

By 1951, most European social democrats had rejected Marxist theory. Instead, a form of fused state liberalism and social democratic thought, embracing aspects of Fabianism and the Keynesian Welfare State became the norm. Socialism for the workers via state ownership was abandoned. Instead of class analysis, a mixed economy based upon a liberal pluralist analysis of society emerged. Welfarism, administered by experts, would replace the socialist dream of a democracy run by the masses themselves.

The Welfare State Ideology: Liberal/Social Democratic Consensus, 1945–80

The post-war Welfare State of Western liberal democracies was an amalgam of state liberalism and social democratic thought. The flowing together of these two streams of ideology was perhaps inevitable for social democracy, given the dependence of Fabianism upon the technocratic caste of experts. The first aim for such a group was always the rationalisation of the capitalist market and positivist 'efficiency' rather than the 'democratic humanism' side of socialism.

Rationalisation of the market was certainly the major aim of the Keynesian economic vision,[29] which stressed the role of the state, via its experts, in the control of the trade cycles of capitalism in boom and depression. Governments would fine-tune the economy using fiscal powers (taxation, government expenditure, etc.) and monetary powers (money flow, interest rates, loan policies, etc.).

The Welfare State would be a vital aspect of this Keynesian world. Welfarism would give buying power to the unemployed, the sick and the injured. It would thus increase consumption. It could also be used to carry out non-economic policies such as population growth via child endowment schemes.

World monetary and trade agreements could be entered into, to control markets. A regulated world was possible. Both state liberals and social democrats could agree over this kind of state. Ideological conflict was thus ended.

Where differences did endure in this liberal/labour consensus, it was usually over the distribution of welfare, tax structures and foreign policy. In most cases, however, some form of negotiating institution emerged which reflected the tripartite state system.[30] This state saw itself as an arbiter between capital and labour.

Classic liberalism, whose passing some deplored,[31] had become a thing of the past. A hybrid and fairly stable consensus on fundamental values ruled the Welfare State. But this compromise has its price. It was dependent upon welfarism, which was itself dependent upon changes in international capital.[32] The whole-hearted endorsement of expertise by social democrats has caused a unity of bureaucratic values with liberal paternalism over the role of power in society. Power is held by the experts of state and the corporate bodies of capital and labour. This power is used in a rhetorically liberal humanist manner, but it is not Rousseauian in the ideal of extension of power to all.

Western social democracy has thus been

left with the legacy of Fabianism, a commitment to technocratic utilitarianism [the greatest efficiency for the greatest number]; an acceptance of managerial society and a refusal to consider capitalism as a whole.[33]

In essence, social democracy has abandoned its Utopianism for managerial politics, based on the premise that the Keynesian world system was permanent or, at least, the ultimate possibility in social harmony politics. But the Keynesian world system rested on an international world order that was fatally flawed.

Revolutionary action in the post-war period largely removed to the former Soviet bloc many of the Third World countries which had provided the system's cheap resources. The American state was not able to maintain its post-war hegemony which had co-ordinated the Keynesian system. Multipolar states and competing systems within capitalism began to emerge in the 1970s. Most importantly, the new mode of international capitalism began to rise above national state bodies. A new world system is in the making, transforming national economies into adjuncts or regional developments of this single process.

The impact of this international development upon the post-war liberal/labour, or state liberal/social democratic consensus, is twofold. First, national states are experiencing a decline in influence in the post-war planned international markets. Either they combat this with a return to protectionism, or they adopt the 'free trade' aspects of the New International Economic Order. This would theoretically mean a world-wide free market. In this situation, local small national economies may suffer from uneven development; disarticulation of various regions from the whole national economy; the emergence of de-industrialisation under the guise of restructuring and, often, dual labour economies. Thus, the welfare state 'aspect of the nation is often sacrificed in this crisis of the international market in order to preserve the capitalist system'.[34] Wages and the social wage are constantly attacked and lowered, even by social democrat governments on the grounds that sacrifice must be equally shared. Increasingly, however, sacrifice has meant simply a decline in welfare and regulation.

Enormous imbalances have thus emerged within the Welfare State. The product of Fabianism — the technocracy — cannot fulfil 'its minimum program of full employment and planned development'. Increasingly, the economics of Fabianism and state liberalism are being dominated by resurgent classic liberal monetarist economies. The egalitarian and humanist bases of the post-war consensus are also being eroded by a return to moral conservatism and by the increasing Social Darwinist views of the New Right.

If this summary is correct, is social democracy therefore finished as a vehicle for change? Contemporary social democracy in the technocratic/Welfare State mode may indeed be exhausted. It is also true that managerial politics have so dominated social democratic thought in the post-war period, to the detriment of ideological analysis, that social democracy may be unable to adapt conceptually and imaginatively to the crisis. It may split or collapse totally. On the other hand, this may be too extreme a prediction. There are many signs of a social democratic re-formulation. What then are some of these features of a possible change of direction?

Contemporary Social Democracy

There are no new and 'pure' contemporary social democratic ideas or great experiments. In the absence of a unifying theory, a mixture of ideological inheritances and eclectic proposals colour present social democratic thought. These inheritances and proposals generally reflect the historical Saint-Simon (experts) versus Fourier (spontaneity of the masses) approaches: 'This fundamental oscillation between democracy and technocracy has been part of socialist thought since its inception.'[35] It not only affects Western social democratic thought, but has by no means been eradicated from communist and post-communist theory and practice (Hungary 1956[36] and Poland 1981).

Contemporary social democratic thought therefore follows an observable pattern of emphasising technocratic or mass solutions, or a compromise formula between them. But it should be understood that the majority of these applied inheritances and proposals still take the nation state as their basis. In an age of transnational capitalism, this may be indadequate.

Social Democratic Inheritances

Clerical Socialism

Initially, this was developed in nineteenth-century Europe to oppose atheistic Marxism. A 'social harmony' doctrine was emphasised based upon Christian ethics, the family and the 'natural' order of capital and labour. This doctrine emphasised workers' participation in the decision making of production management and consumer/producer co-operatives. It has faded and re-emerged several times in recent history, as Catholic social doctrine; some elements of Spanish Carlist ideology, and post-Spanish Civil War Basque co-operative thought (Mondragon).[37] At all times, it has been promulgated as a third way between Marxism and capitalism.

A more radical variation has emerged in the contemporary Catholic theology of liberation, endorsing Christian involvement in revolution in certain cases of hopeless oppression.[38]

Workers' Participation and Workers' Control

Workers' participation in management decisions has been emphasised in social democratic thought since Robert Owen. The idea emphasises that equal (or near equal) numbers of company directors should be drawn from capital and labour in a firm. A search for harmony of interests should ensue.

The idea has fallen into disfavour under social democracy due to rise of technocratic/paternalist socialist thought; the suspicion by union leaders that such a system would integrate the workforce into half-understood decision making (they would be tricked by management), and/or bypass and make unnecessary official union leadership. The 'corporate state' model of social harmony incorporating the leadership élites of government, business and labour has been much more acceptable to such groups.

The idea has been enthusiastically endorsed, however, by New Right ideologues. In this approach there has been a different emphasis on system integration of the individual rather than social harmony of the classes. The worker would be sold or given stock in the firm, thus becoming a small capitalist. Their participation in management decisions would remain minimal. However, they would now have a personal interest in profit expansion and productivity. Workers' participation would be similar to the indirect stockholders' control over management.

Workers' Control of the means of production was a fundamental aspect of G.D.H. Cole's *guild socialism, European anarcho/syndicalism* and *anarchism*. Control of production passes into the hands of workers themselves, and they would democratically elect or hire management. This anti-technocratic power was seen as fundamental to combat worker alienation. Worker's control was essential to 'decentralised' socialism, technocratic control signifying 'centralised' socialism.

Anarcho/syndicalism and anarchism went further, rejecting the need for a parliament. Society would be run by a forum of trade unions (in anarcho/syndicalism) or by voluntary associations (anarchism).

Guild socialism, however, allowed for a role for a traditional parliament. This would control non-production matters such as defence. A parallel 'production' parliament, such as a workers'/producers' council, would control the economy.

An interesting development in the implementation of a 'workers' participation/workers' control' model in social democracy has been the rise of the Swedish Meidner plan.

As Matthews outlines,[39] this plan emerged in 1975–76 in Sweden from the Swedish union congress, in response to the excess profits (or surplus value) that many firms had gained because of centralised wage fixing. The plan envisages a percentage of these profits being allocated to labour collectively, firm by firm, as in effect these belong to labour, being wages foregone and held down by the state.

Such profit will be held in employee investment funds which will consist of money or equity (shares) in the company, the money itself being reinvested in the firm. Eventually, given the level of this 'profit tax', the workers' fund would take over the firm. First there would be workers' participation and eventually workers' control.

It is interesting that the Australian Council of Trade Unions has recommended a similar scheme, based on superannuation. A percentage of productivity gains (3%) is proposed to be paid in by employers as part of 'deferred wage' claims, into a union/employer-administered fund. The ACTU hopes to use this fund as an investment source to increase economic democracy. As Matthews points out, however, this will undoubtedly be opposed by conservative/capitalist schemes for 'privatisation' and the distribution of shares individually to workers rather than into a collective fund administered by 'union bosses'. A deep ideological split between ideals of individual and collective democracy will undoubtedly ensue in this new struggle over who controls the worker's 'surplus valus' — labour or capital. This battle will be fundamental to the future of capitalism and social democracy.

Democratic Egalitarianism

Egalitarian modes of thought infused early social democracy. These have faded in the dominant shadow of Fabian technocratic socialism. There has been a crisis of the imagination. However, many of the early democratic egalitarian ideas still emerge, even if they are cross fertilised from liberalism. Some are:

The Recall: The party or the electorate legislates for the right to recall parliamentary representatives on the written petition of a certain percentage of members or electoral votes.

The Limited Term: Politicians, union leaders, public servants etc. have only a limited term in their positions, and careerism is thus avoided.

The Initiative: A petition at local, state or Federal level, which has a certain number of electors endorsing a given proposition (e.g. 150,000) must be put to a referendum within a stated period. Citizens thus have an initiative for legislating over politicians and technocrats.

The Theory of Delegate v. Representative: This is one of the essential differences of social democracy and liberalism. A social democrat is a delegate of his or her party, bound to follow the majority vote and program. Unlike a liberal, he or she is not seen as a representative who can follow his or her own whim or conscience on votes, but is a delegate of the collective.

Other: Modern writers such as Johan Galtung, in *Self Reliance: A Strategy for Development* have revived notions of parallel parliaments or organisations. Galtung has stressed the need for a compromise between 'Alpha' organisations (such as expert technocracies) and 'Beta' organisations (such as 'worker control' or participatory grassroots citizen democracy). The aim for a modern social democracy should be to fuse both into a new gradualist ideology which understands that technology itself, such as in factories, is not value-neutral. It constantly demands hierarchy, experts and stratification.

Most of all, socialism must never again be linked with a lack of freedom.

Ideas such as workers' control have declined in Western socialism since the advent of the Keynesian state. However, some communist and post-communist countries such as e.g. what was Yugoslavia have already pioneered worker managed production, with mixed results. Some observers such as Burkitt believe (1985) workers' control is inevitable:

> It can be seen, even under capitalism, a trend towards increased labour participation in response to union demands, the needs of government and the policy demands of enlightened employers . . .

Major Contemporary Political Designs Emerging Within Social Democracy

The Technocratic Welfare State

This is the reigning social democratic/state liberal consensus model. It stresses the combination of Keynesian state intervention (less the social direction of investment), plus welfarism. The social democratic party moves away from its traditional worker base towards a broad 'managerial' party, appealing to the centre voter.[41] The party may still retain a special relationship with the working class, especially due to traditional links and the union leadership within its ranks. This relationship sometimes is close to a bipartite state.[42] This is an essential link, to contain worker dissatisfaction, and ensures that this class does not become alienated and move to a more radical party.

The Left wing of the social democratic party plays an important, if often unconscious, part in this process of containment. It articulates Left-wing traditional socialist rhetoric in order to placate its activists and Utopians and to lock them into the social democratic option. The Left wing, however, is rarely allowed to influence fundamental policy.

At the same time, the traditional 'class' analysis and language of socialism is abandoned, to be replaced by a liberal 'pluralist' model. The new social democrat progressive coalition is seen to cover broad groups of workers: women, ethnic/racial groups, conservationists etc. Legislation becomes 'issue'-oriented rather than 'class'-orientated. Progress is measured by liberal 'quality of life' legislation (e.g. conservation), which is not a direct threat to the economic status quo. Economic policies such as national-isation are abandoned for either indirect fiscal/monetary controls or total market deregulation.

The consensus is around Benthamite growth, rather than an accepted socialist economic alternative.[43] The new pluralist para-digm of society draws these groups who benefit by government expenditure into an indirect endorsement of such Benthamism. The pursuit of growth as the basis of 'greatest good' enforces a pragmatic, flexible anti-ideological approach on the party. This flexibility also applies to many ethical questions such as the distribution of wealth and power. To remain in power, the party depends more and more on a charismatic leadership who can appeal to the masses along broad populist lines over the head of the party. This way the concern of the party itself for implemen-tation of real policy can often be avoided by the leadership.

Some problems presented by this are: *the Party becomes an electoral machine* at the expense of its social movement/mass mobilisation functions. Its cadres, who are mobilised by ideology, may drift away, split into factions, or join new movements.

Oligarchy increases[44] as well as the emphasis upon managerial expertise dominated by the drive for growth. Parliament and the party lose the ability to control the cabinet/bureaucracy com-bination and, often, to impose party policy against the advice of the bureaucracy.

As Keynesianism declines, the party lacks the ideological basis to respond. 'New Right' ideology captures the ideological heights. The party adopts many of the 'New Right' proposals to stay in government, further alienating its traditional base.

Corporatism

Modern social democracy has been very attracted to corporatism as an answer to the decline of the Keynesian Welfare State. The corporate, or tripartite state stresses the integration of organised labour and business groups into advising or negotiating with government on policy. It is a popular alternative or outgrowth of the Keynesian period, since it preserves the technocratic heritage of the Keynesian and Fabian traditions. Secondly, the consensual unity and/or co-option of labour and business élites allows the government to undertake massive restructuring of the economy without effective opposition from business or labor. In many cases, this is important, as restructuring may require far-reaching protectionist or free trade propositions. Thirdly, the co-option of such bodies as unions into the consensual corporate structure diminishes radicalism. It allows for the emergence of a dual labour economy and a downturn in welfarism without effective union opposition.[45]

As Rolf Gerritson points out:

> corporatism [is] different to pluralism in that its constituent groups [are] not competitive but directive. The corporatist state [is] unique in that peak councils of business and labour obtain a representational monopoly and a concomitant disciplinary role [on those below them].[46]

Unlike the pluralist, the corporate state does not have to buy the support or votes, of each different issue group (such as migrants), or negotiate separately with them. The 'big two' are business and labour with whom the corporate state sets the parameters of the social and economic program.[47]

The leader of the corporate state becomes fundamental to its success. He or she can reach across this tripartite system and the supporting social democrat party to stir the masses through populist appeal. Such mass popularity may then be used to pressure business and labour to accept the plans of the state rather than have the state negotiate genuinely.

Essentially corporatism is seen by its exponents as the only social democratic alternative to the New Right. Two main arguments are used to gain support for the system. The first is that Nation states are facing integration into a world economy. Integration using internally negotiated social harmony between capital and labour is the best way to face the inevitable.[48] The new looming free trade world demands managerial rather than political skills. In the long run, free trade will benefit the traditional supporters of Social Democracy.

Secondly, capitalism could just as easily live with the New Right deregulated market system. Corporatism at least protects some social democratic gains and traditional labourist aims, i.e. while the economic notions of socialism are discarded, nevertheless, the *political* presence of a labour-based party is preserved in state decision making. Political power is thus not confined to business in a bipartite relationship with government.

Participatory Democracy

The oscillation[49] between the technocracy of Saint-Simon and the spontaneity of Fourier is constant in socialist thought. Participatory democracy is an aspect of grassroots democracy which was stressed strongly in the New Left period of the 1960s. However, its basic elements are traceable to the origins of socialism.

The proponents of such a mode stress the fact that 'socialism is a process ... It is self government and the scientific ways of solving problems ...'[50] People can solve their social problems by will power and possession of humanist values. The essential factor is rank and file control of all organisations.

Self-management devotees (with their anarchist and guild socialist overtones) emphasise the fact that democracy preceds socialism:

> Technocracy has destroyed the culture of democracy. Social democrats have been led astray by the smooth edifice of the welfare state and Fabian paternalism into ... a blind defense of welfarism. The public are, however, as alienated from the welfare bureaucracy as from capitalist behaviour.[51]

They are also alienated from the unions who rarely pursue social justice, just a narrow defence of their worker's perceived interests. This is particularly the curse of craft-based unionism.

The solution, according to participatory democrats, is workers' control. But it would be an expanded form that abandons the 'workerism' of traditional socialism, focusing solely on industrial and commercial workers. It stresses 'citizens' control'.

'Workerism' is condemned as it leads to corporatist social democracy that identifies socialism with saving only the workers' jobs, the workers' living standards and the workers' rights — and only unionised workers at that.

Welfare is regarded as a right in participatory democracy which is controlled, preferably, by citizens themselves. Quality of life decisions, in fields such as education and ecology remain at the initiative of the local community. They are not subject to the decisions of centralised authority which are in danger of domination by overseas or national economic cliques. Technocracy is directed by local power, not the reverse.

Participatory democrats proclaim that their form of social democracy is revolutionary, but bloody conflict does not occur between the classes. It simply transfers the decision making power in industry, civic life and so on into the hands of the many while leaving property in the hands of the few. And the possession of property without the power of disposal is meaningless.

Rainbow Coalition

The basis of a Rainbow Coalition is a vision of the unity of Greens, the environment/ecology movement, with traditional socialists (Reds) around the elements of environment, local economics, participatory democracy and social justice.

Such a coalition would hope to incorporate many social movements. These issue-based movements would work around a solid core of two basic political parties that incorporate middle and working class radicalism. The premise on which the Rainbow Coalition is formulated is that industrial society now faces new problems, and needs an up-graded socialist analysis that abandons 'workerism', or the focus upon traditional organised labour, for the wider liberal notion of 'citizen'.

Much contemporary social democracy has a lot in common with anarchist-influenced Green philosophers who emphasise self-management, citizen's power and local action. The problems between Greens and social democrats are quite deep however and mostly ideological. The differences emerge initially from the problem of defining the world. Are we to approach the world determined to dominate it (industrialism) or to find a harmony with it (ecologism)? As Beilharz and Watts outline,[52] the contradiction between Red and Green can also be placed on a male/female polarity:

> On the one hand, we have a traditional discourse (labourism), a set of political institutions (trade unions [and social democrat parties]) and a whole vast domain of human experience (wage labour) which is oriented to a normative and practical universe of male productivism and domination. On the other hand, we have a wide array of social movements, sexual movements of men and women, ecological movements etc. which to a greater or lesser extent challenge much of this male/capital/labour nexus which has traditionally dominated the Left horizon. These new movements counterpose a new vocabulary, new sets of norms ... which are typically incompatible with the older system of meaning.

The Greens' philosophy largely rejects industrialism and class analysis, the working class itself being seen as caught up in the growth model, and seen as part of the industrial problem.

Similarly, the Greens consider the Left/Right spectrum to be false: an outgrowth of the industrial age. Such a spectrum reduces humanity to adversarial positions, and means that state power must be used to overcome opposition. The state therefore has grown as a part of the industrial system as a result of its need for force. Political thought must now be reshaped totally, using a new language.

Socialists, however, find the vague Green alternatives to industrialism dubious. Industrialism is here to stay. To the socialist, industrialism can and should be controlled in its ill effects. These are usually the outcome of profit seeking or technocratic arrogance and non-responsibility. Only a socialist system, based upon wide democracy, can control the inner urge of both capitalists and technocrats to dominate and control nature and people.

Similarly, the Green attitude to the state is too ill defined for most socialists.[53] The state (as in guild socialism) does have a constructive role to play in areas such as the equalisation of educational opportunity and international relations. The elected state can be useful for democratic socialism if it is balanced by parallel parliaments (guild socialism), a bill of rights (including economic rights such as the right to tenured employment) or local autonomy via the 'Enabling State'.

The Enabling State

This mode of contemporary social democratic thought emphasises 'decentralised' over the dominant 'centralised' technocratic state.[54]

Its exponents argue that socialism has become a term of abuse in the minds of Western citizens, due to such examples as the history of technocratic vanguard states such as Stalin's Russia or the paternalism of Western bureaucratic technocracy.[55]

Socialism will only be accepted and understood in its original Utopian meaning as a society of equals in freedom by its entering into people's own lives as a result of their own willing actions.

The Enabling State operates on the belief that individual consciousness of the world is largely immediate. The nation state or the world of international relations is far away. A world view, or transcendent consciousness, is usually the monopoly of certain experts with long academic training.

To this ordinary citizen, this world is a closed universe of élite imposed levels of entry via examinations, roles, correct attitudes, birth, etc.. The citizen is alienated from his or her own existence. Existence is ordered, ruled and disciplined by manipulative and directive, yet nebulous hierarchies of technocrats and corporate bodies well outside each individual's power.

Several possibilities exist for the citizen in this situation:

(a) To leave this mode of industrial life and drop out in to an alternative lifestyle, e.g. the hippie movement of 1960–75. But powerlessness still continues.

(b) To indulge in hedonism and become Herbert Marcuse's 'one dimensional' man. Satiation is inevitable in this option. Meaninglessness must follow.

(c) To take hold of what one can in one's immediate social life both to oppose the power of élites and impose different qualities of life. This approach believes that all freedom stems from collective action. Decision making must be taken back into the area of immediate consciousness — the local community. Government and community must become one to attain socialism.

The Enabling State concept[56] perceives itself as a fusion between the ideas of Saint-Simon's 'experts' and Fourier's mass 'spontaneity'. This state would maintain its usual expert-based services, such as health. But local use of services and economic development must be citizen-initiated. This allows for local adaptation, as a centralised bureaucrat always tends to standardise solutions.

The nation state acts as a co-ordinator, equaliser and financier to a broad national plan based upon both economic and social needs, such as the provision of nurseries by all factories seeking government contracts. The implementation of this plan is passed to local councils and co-operatives. Local councils do not set up a traditional technocratic model of welfare or action. Their major aim is to stimulate and finance local action groups who are willing to follow the democratic and egalitarian guidelines built into the provision of such finances. The state has 'enabled' this devolution from experts to people power. Macro-socialism has become micro-socialism.

As Jacobs points out, discussing the case of the Greater London Council,[57] five major factors should guide the Enabling State at the local level:

(a) *Employment* is still the foremost aim of a socialist government, since it gives personal dignity and freedom. Therefore, a local enterprise bank using local government funds should be created, which would stimulate labour-intensive industries. These would be funded if they provided jobs at union rates.

(b) *Social criteria* would be demanded from firms applying for loans, e.g. workers' control or participation, equal opportunity and socially useful production.

(c) *Popular planning* (or local planning) should take the place of centralised planning. The state gives money and expertise to local groups adhering to non-sexist/non-racist guidelines to develop their own plans for services, quality of life issues and the local economy.

(d) *Welfare* must be seen as part of the broad social wage for all, and a right which is planned by the community, not as bureaucratic largesse nor a net for the unfortunate, which is part of the liberal welfarist tradition. This tradition emphasised the nuclear family as the cheap provider of most welfare services, e.g. baby-sitting. In an age of single parent families and women workers and the rapid evolution of the nuclear family, collective welfare should be seen as an integral part of the citizen's social needs.

(e) *Research* into the local economy undertaken by state experts should be on the basis of such popular planning. This should be undertaken to expedite local ideas and to advise upon them, but not to dominate them. The 'experts' are consultants, not directors.

Conclusion

As Beilharz points out in *Labour's Utopias*, the true ideal of social democracy ('The Great Republic of Equals') has persisted best where democracy was emphasised before socialism (where socialism meant planning and efficiency). The emphasis of the latter over the former has led to 'barracks socialism' where the technocrat, who was every bit as authoritarian and anti-democratic as the capitalist, dominated, even if for the best of Jacobin reasons as in the case of historical Bolshevism. An 'Enabling State' is one of the best modes of overcoming the tension between technocrat and democrat in order to achieve 'a utopia with a future'.

The achievement of socialism, as predicted by Marx, is an endless struggle between democracy and authority, rights and duties; red versus expert, all moving towards a 'civil' society where law protects the weak and not the privileged. Such a radical social democratic attitude is spurred by, but not confined to, the struggle between capital and labour. The proletariat, as emphasised in the Marxist/Leninist world analysis for revolutionary change, is still important as a class lever in world change. But as Ost points out a state socialist system built solely on this class and command system simply cannot work as events in the USSR and Eastern Europe have recently illustrated. Where crises in world capitalism have historically produced wars as solution, the first historical crisis of world socialism has produced only collapse and disillusionment. The Bolshevik phase in social democratic history is largely over. But social democracy, as a democratic mode of thinking, may actually benefit by the Bolshevik demise and disillusionment with its methods (see opening quote, Chapter 5).

Social Democracy in Australia

One of the most decisive factors in Australian politics and the role of the state, especially the Federal state, has been the external dependency factor.[58]

For over 150 years, Australia was part of the British Empire, both as an economic and a cultural dependency. Now Australia has to readjust and restructure her economy to fit the demands of the new Pacific Basin economy, based upon comparative advantage, not imperial links.

The original Australian state under British dependency was a junior partner with a managerial style state. It attempted to achieve deeply-held social myths such as 'the working man's paradise' that motivated Australian society within the boundary of empire.[59] These myths reflected an individualist rather than a collectivist society, and shaped the style and activity of Australian social democracy.

The Australian state in the period 1890–1975 represented a society built upon Deakinite foundations. Deakin articulated these foundations in the pre-Federation days as protectionism, White Australia,[60] and social harmony, via a court-controlled standard of living for workers based upon 'needs' rather than productivity. Protectionism and legislated social harmony were interlinked. As Deakin himself stated:

> The old protection contented itself with making good wages possible. The 'New' protection aims to make them actual. It aims to accord to the manufacturer that degree of exemption from unfair outside competition which will enable him to pay fair and reasonable wages ... Having put the manufacturer in a position to pay good wages, it goes on to assure the public that he does pay them.
> (*Australian Heritage* Vol. 9, Lansdowne, Sydney, p. 1,559)

The Deakinite state was the shaping force of Australian social democracy, as well as Australian state liberalism. Both Left and Right political theory had to come to terms with the Australian way of life based upon this state. As Brian Fitzpatrick outlined:

> What with industrial arbitration, the suppression of monopolies, protective tariffs, and legislation which made it unprofitable to sweat the workers, Australia was to be made a garden ... in which enlightened middle class liberalism and moderate Labor walked hand in hand with the President of the Court of Conciliation and Arbitration, smoothed by airs played by military band instruments duty free under the tariff.
> (*Australian Heritage*) p. 1,556

The cornerstone to the Deakinite state was a foreign policy of embracing 'great and powerful' friends for trade, investment and defence purposes. Within the British Empire, this cornerstone was firmly in place. But with the disappearance of this link in the post-war contemporary period and the demands for Australian integration into the Pacific Basin economy, the foundations of the Deakinite state have begun to erode or have disappeared.

But the Deakinite state endured for nearly eighty years. The Harvester Judgment of 1907, which introduced the idea of a court-controlled indexed basic wage, added this liberal notion of legislated social harmony to Deakin's protectionism and White Australia. Not until the Pacific Basin restructuring governments of Malcolm Fraser[60] and Robert Hawke were these foundations (with the exception of White Australia) to be tampered with.

The White Australia policy has, officially, gone. It has been replaced by a multicultural policy more in keeping with the Pacific Age. Protectionism is constantly being renegotiated to attain economic restructuring according to dominant monetarist economic policies. Lastly, even the indexed wage system, the cornerstone of the Australian social democrat/state liberal consensus, is to be changed for a two-tier wage system partly related to productivity.

Australian Social Democracy is thus a story of European Political ideology adapting to the four bulwarks of the Deakinite state. It has also had to come to terms with the hegemonic small capitalist/liberal myths underlying Australian social beliefs. What contemporary Australian social democracy will be like after the major changes due to historical shifts in dependency from Britain to the Pacific, will be a fascinating future story.

A generalised historical model using the external dependency factor ('Great and Powerful Friends') and the internal bipartisan foundations (protection, White Australia, wage indexation) will prove useful. It must be realised that all models are open to criticism, as they are rough and broad indicators.

External Dependency and the Role of the State in Internal Change

Colonial Dependency: 1788–1860

Australia was developed in this early period of settlement as several different enclaves. The unity of the national economy was minimal and most colonies, the present-day states, developed their major capital cities as entrepôt ports. Each colony was highly jealous of each other, something which has been preserved to some degree in the states' rights tradition.

The major struggle of labour in this period was against convict and non-white cheap labour in the developing plantation-like economy based on sheep runs.

The gold rushes of 1851–70 broke the pattern of Australian development and, temporarily, the pattern of migration. Originally, bounty migrants were brought to Australia and paid for by land sales. Land was thus dear in Australia compared with the USA. The gold rushes brought to Australia in large numbers for approximately twenty years, the artisan class and small capitalist whose normal migration dream was the USA. While it is true substantial numbers of this class existed before in Australia, the gold rush force fed the growth of this important group.

With such mainly British migrants came the doctrines of Chartism, some republicanism and socialism, and radical democracy. This group was one of the major sources determined to achieve the liberal dream of a small capitalist paradise.[62] Allied to the rising urban national capitalists, especially in Victoria after alluvial gold ran out, they pursued dreams of free selection for the farmer, fair wages for the worker and a government dedicated to servicing the achievement of such demands.[63] Protectionism, particularly in Victoria, became increasingly accepted as a cornerstone of the 'working man's paradise' and the social harmony of capital and labour. 'White Australia' policies had been imposed, but unevenly in most colonies as part of this 'social harmony' dream, with Victoria initiating such legislation in 1860.

Free trade ideology based upon classic liberal notions of the market was especially strong in NSW. These ancestors of the contemporary New Right such as George Reid[64] argued for an Australia open to world trade. Australia would be dependent in the world market on its rural trade rather than urban production. The rural price for labour was the realistic market price for all. Indeed, the modern rural/urban division in the economy was already emerging.

Farmers, dependent upon export prices for such commodities as wool or wheat were free traders. Others, who depended on government price maintenance of products, e.g. butter, state-negotiated imperial quotas (e.g. cheese) or subsidised railways and freights, were ambivalent. Throughout the late nineteenth century, such farmers were wooed by government patronage in the construction of new railways, price subsidy plans and new government infrastructure.

National Capitalist Period: 1860–1914

The free trade v. protectionist argument developed different intensities in different colonies in this period. NSW and Victoria dominated the two poles. Other states were represented in this argument over the future style of development of the Australian economy. But, by and large, the vital questions of the Australian political and economic future were going to be settled at the heart of national capitalist development: the Sydney, Melbourne and Adelaide triangle.

Australian national capitalism was itself locked into a dependent development situation with British investment.[65] The liberal style state governments dominant in this period were largely bipartite states, partnerships of business and government rather than the present labour trend to tripartite states of government, business and labour.[66]

The watershed for social democracy was the 1890 Depression and the great shearing and maritime strikes of 1891–93. The ideology of social democracy, as T. Irving points out, was necessary as an important vision and counter-mobilisation factor for the working class.[67] State socialism, in particular, was to become the vehicle to break the monopoly that liberalism had on the public political imagination. But essentially, behind the rhetoric of socialist ideology, the 1890–93 Depression and strikes were more important in launching organised labour into politics.

The 1890s Depression was the first of a long series of external traumas in Australian history which were (and are) vitally important in reshaping political forces and introducing new possibilities into the Australian political arena. All adaptations, however, until the dismantling period of Fraser/Hawke/Keating (1974–),[68] were intent on reinforcing or developing the possibilities of the Deakinite state.

The 1890s marked the appearance of social democracy onto the stage of Australian politics. Its first period in office, as part of both state and Federal governments, was notable for wide reforms, as labour carried out its basic program. This period of reform (approximately 1897–1914) has assumed,' in the mythology of the Australian labour movement, an image of heroic change and ideological soundness'. In reality, labour in this period was filling a vacuum for the working class that liberalism could not fill. The Deakinite state was adaptable, but many of the boundaries of possibility for labour, within the accepted Australian role for governments, were to be reached by World War I.

As Brugger outlines, within the limitless pragmatism that marked Labor even in this early period, were a number of enduring common perspectives that provided unity for social democratic party factions. These have often been invoked to provide the mystique that ultimately differentiates the social democratic movement from liberalism/conservatism, e.g. that Labor is the party of progress.[69]

This period also created the populist strand in Australian labourist culture which identified 'a symbolic enemy'[70] (such as 'money power' in commercial culture) which possessed both an external and internal force. Both liberals/conservatives (with their

'Australian way of life' myth) and the social democrats (with their 'working man's paradise' myth) invoked ideological demons regularly in the Deakinite state. Both sides assumed that the existing society to be the 'best of all possible worlds', beset at times of stress by factors that the state can, of course, subdue. Total change to this society and state is hardly considered.

These demons provide the basis for an Australian social democratic defensive solidarity, but not a unifying Utopian ideology. Some commonalities that emerged in this period were: *Anti-conscription*: Australian Social Democracy has a deep strain of anti-militarism or at least pro-democratic militarism. The suspicion with which imperialism and regular armies were viewed (for example, the politician King O'Malley called armies in 1901, 'these gilt spurred roosters!') was a prevalent factor of early labourism. Union experience of police and soldiers and the populist democratic notions of a people's army bore witness to suspicious attitudes towards a technocratic regular force. Conscription for war would lead to conscription for work. Conscription was thus a demon that would unite all social democratic factions, often to the distress of their own leaders. Billy Hughes, for example, came to grief on this issue and split the ALP in 1916–17. Whitlam was able to unify ALP factions and carry the country to a large degree on this issue in 1972.

Leadership and the Rank and File: The social democratic movement from the beginning applied union solidarity rules. Members faced explusion if they did not pledge, and keep, loyalty to the program. This loyalty was also expected of the party leader. He could reorder the priorities of the program but eventually he must carry it out.

The Money Power: Traditional Australian social democratic thought identified 'the commercial rather than the manufacturing side of capitalism as the enemy of social harmony'.[71] Both Lang (1931) and Chifley (1949) railed against their lack of control over foreign investment and internal banking respectively. Lang drew upon deep wells of nationalism and fear of threats to the 'working man's paradise' when he attacked the Bank of England for its demands for continuing war loan repayments in the depths of the Great Depression.

Chifley came to grief in 1949 with his referendum on bank nationalisation. Conservative forces were able to depict this move as an attack on 'the Australian way of life'. Contemporary ALP leaders sometimes depict 'trans-national companies in this "money power" tradition'. It is evident how far the present ALP has left behind the Deakinite model in that the 'money power' demon has not once been invoked. Rather, foreign money has been encouraged to enter Australia, to the consternation of the traditional rank and file.

The 'Red Threat': Australian social democracy has always been at pains to depict communism as a 'foreign creed', for both electoral and internal party reasons. Communism has been used regularly by conservatives and populists to justify foreign alliances and anti-union legislation. Australian social democracy, with its tripartite state aims and technocratic labourist perspectives, has little in common with a class analysis. It sees Marxists as marginals rather than as rivals, and even Marxist analyses are seen as irrelevant.

A large section of Catholic social doctrine-based membership of the ALP, was however, ideologically, rather than tactically, opposed to the 'foreign creed'. The 1954 ALP split was largely over this group's ideological war on communism.

Junior Partner Period: 1936–65:

This period of dependency can be exemplified by the Ottawa Agreement of 1936. The British Empire had been weakened by the expenditure of World War I. Empire autarchy (self-sufficiency) was a major aim of the post-1918 period. Grand visions such as the Empire Settlement Scheme[72] (1922) proposed the migration of the British excess population to the White Dominions, thus stimulating 'money and markets'.

Australian social democracy largely endorsed these imperial moves, as they bolstered the foundations of the Deakinite state. The Ottawa Agreement aimed at dependent development[73] within the Empire and continuing British hegemony within the whole. Within such a closed system of external stability provided by British force, protectionism, White Australia, and internal court-controlled standards of living, the 'working man's paradise' would continue to grow.

When in 1929, the Great Depression began, the British imperial system was not impervious to this world-wide upheaval. As Britain's economic system crashed, so did Australia's. The Scullin Labor government found that, ultimately, foreign dependency dictated terms over labourist ideology. The one government which proposed an alternative economic scheme which emphasised local aid before foreign repayments, the Lang Labor government of NSW was dismissed by the Governor.

The arrival of Keynesianism during World War II provided a vital factor in the post-Depression and post-war rebuilding of the social democrat/state liberal model of democratic capitalism.[74] The world-wide shift to the Keynesian state found easy bipartisan acceptance in Australia, because of the similarity of Keynesianism to historical aspects of the Deakinite state.

Rarely before has a system of government been so in tune with the boundaries of popular culture and world ideologies. The day of the 'Lucky Country' was about to dawn.

Associate Dependency: 1965–75

The election of the Menzies government in 1949 was largely due to Chifley's stubborn refusal to lift wartime controls (due to his loyalty to Britain) and the impact of the coal strikes of 1949.[75] Menzies' liberal/conservative government proved one of the luckiest and longest-lived of Australian history.

In the years between 1949 and the Reserve Bank Act of 1959, the Menzies government reaped the benefits of the four basic cornerstones of the Deakinite state. Added to these was the increasing efficiency of the technocracy behind the Keynesian Welfare State. An extra bonus for this government was the disintegration of Labor under the external impact of the Cold War.

Many members of the highly ideological Catholic Social Doctrine section of the ALP were expelled in 1954–57 for their secret moves to dominate the party. This section formed a breakaway Labor Party, the Democratic Labor Party, whose preferences aided the conservatives to hold office until 1972.

As R. White outlines,[76] the 'Australian way of life' family-centred conservative myth dominated this period. Prosperity was constant enough for this myth to take precedence over the 'working man's paradise' myth, despite hiccups in 1953 and 1961.

The major problem in this period with its 'Lucky Country' cornerstones was the fourth, external stability factor. With the shrinkage of the British Empire between 1945–65, and Britain's reversion to 'Little England' with a stated intention from 1962 onward to enter the EEC, Australia was in danger of being stranded in the Pacific with obsolete or non-existent trading and political links with its neighbours. The USA and (from 1965) Japan, were increasingly wooed as substitute partners.

Australia's subsequent associate dependency with the new Pacific powers never had the surety of the old British links. Nevertheless, the USA was avidly pursued from the period of Korea to that of Vietnam as a substitute 'Great and Powerful Friend' and a source of external trading stability.

The second Vietnam War (1965–75) was the last attempt by the USA to impose her hegemonic will upon the Pacific. It was also, to a large extent, the cause of the downfall of the last of the old-time 'Deakinite state' Labor governments.

The Whitlam Labor government (1972–75) came to power upon anti-conscription sentiments; a new 'liberal' coalition of workers, middle class radicals, women and Aboriginals; and the Labor co-option of a variation of the 'Australian way of life' myth, where only it was seen as caring for the masses of young urban dormitory suburb families and their needs. Labor was following the working class into suburbia.

It also came to power on a wave of general boredom with exhausted liberal conservatism.

The Whitlam government represented the last Labor government elected under the auspices of the Deakinite state, which it then proceeded to undermine. Protectionism was loosened in the first few weeks of the Whitlam government. The White Australia policy, which had earlier been reduced by conservative legislation, was abandoned as a government practice. Even the American external stability link received blow after blow in the Whitlam period of radical nationalism and repudiation of Cold War foreign policies. Wage control and welfare were reinforced and expanded, however, as elements of the Welfare State.

The New Pacific Basin: 1975-Present:

The defeat of the Whitlam government in 1975 was due to a massive conservative campaign coming to power over a confused electorate whose eighty-year-old Deakinite sureties had been successively attacked and whittled back by Whitlam. The new conservative government, under Malcolm Fraser, immediately set about dismantling the Keynesian/Deakinite state that (in 1975) they had indicated they would save:

> The Fraser government marked a watershed in Australian Political History, because ... a non-Labor government was in office with the express intention of undoing much social and economic policy which had hitherto seemed to have had an almost bi-partisan status.[77]

The immediate reality in the Pacific Basin was that a new regional economy was emerging.[78] Top economists and scholars such as the Japanese Jiro Tokuyama,[79] indicated that the USA and Japan would move into a senior/junior partnership in the Pacific. The remainder of Pacific Basin countries would adjust to this economic reality by virtue of existing comparative advantage, not by traditional sentiment and historical ties. Import replacement industry such as that built up in Australia during the cosy days of the British Empire would be restructured or go to the wall.

From 1983, the Hawke Labor government replaced the Fraser conservative one. Under the free trade premises of Pacific Basin restructuring, the Labor government with its succession of leaders has remained social democratic in the sense only of preserving labourist involvement in the tripartite state. Welfarism has been restructured as the bases of the Deakinite state have been steadily further eroded.

The Hawke Labor government was the first Australian social democratic government that has faced the reality of the end of Deakinism. It has had to redefine the essence of social democracy in Australia, to the confusion of many of its traditional supporters, who have too often confused Deakinism with social democracy. It has had to redefine social democracy under pressure from Pacific Basin powers to restructure, while facing the end of the post-war, long-wave boom in commodities. This Kondratieff cycle conclusion may herald the beginning of a new world depression.[80]

Such a recession–depression seems to have emerged in the latter part of the 20th century, both in Australia and worldwide. Unless the GATT (General Agreements on Tariffs and Trade) Uruguay round is partially or wholly successful, it would appear the world has a possibility of falling into three large regional trading blocs. These will include the EC (European Community) proposed to be a political as well as economic bloc in 1992; the NAFTA (North American Free Trade Association 1991) comprising the USA, Canada and Mexico with the possibility of extension into the rest of Latin America as these nations adopt free trade policies turning away from the protectionist policies of the 1970s, and, lastly, the possibility of the Japanese bloc.

While the latter is a reluctant bloc, given the dependence of Japan and ASEAN (Association of South East Asian Nations) upon low US tariffs, especially for TFC (Textiles/Footwear/ Clothing) goods, nevertheless the basic framework for such a bloc is in existence. Within Australia, such new regional groupings in Asia around the core of Japan also means a fundamental Australian re-alignment of core/periphery status. Victoria, in particular, built into the Australian industrial heartland during the Deakinite/British Empire period, is undergoing a decline. Much finance and industry is shifting north to NSW and the former periphery state of Queensland. Not only does this mean a shift from manufacturing to service industries like tourism, but it also means crisis for the Australian working class in the manufacturing states upon which Labor was founded. An increasing underclass of unemployed is emerging as in the USA and other post industrial/developed countries. For the New Right, this is a good sign as it means the cost of labour will find its true market value if only the Deakinite distortions of award wages can be dispensed with. For the ALP, it represents political disaster as their voting heartland (demanding traditional full employment) turn increasingly to Deakinite 'independent' or third force parties promising historical social democratic interventionism and pro-worker policies.

In the face of these problems, the Labor Party has defined the core of Australian social democracy as labourism, i.e. to keep and hold the dominant position for the ALP in the labour movement, and to keep and hold a position for that movement in a tripartite state. If that means the emergence of a New Right and a New Left of disillusioned supporters which will widen the political spectrum in Australian politics, this does not matter. What is important is that the ALP hierarchy dominates middle Australia. For essentially, social democracy in Australia has become a mode of managerial government rather than a Utopian movement or ideology. Increasingly the social democratic/conservative managerial system of the post-war corporate state is under pressure from the mounting contradictions between the demands of international capitalism and the political demands of a restless constituency. The circle cannot be squared, so are we seeing the emergence of a triangular political system so long predicted by the Greens (see Chapter 7) and the end of Deakinism?

A Summary of Social Democracy

The Theory of the State

(a) The state protects the 'masses' from 'interests' (organised capital, monopolies, landlords), by 'regulating' economic and social legislation.

(b) The state regulates the economy by public ownership, nationalisation or fiscal/monetary policies.

(c) The state initiates 'positive' legislation to provide services to ameliorate the public good, e.g. education; welfare, sports, etc.

(d) A neutral state technocracy will emerge under the control of an elected parliament to run the state services and the interventionist state.

(e) The state will expand its role on arbitration between pluralist bodies.

The Theory of Society

(a) Society should have democracy, equality and social justice as its dominant values rather than greed and selfishness masquerading as individualism.

(b) Private property has distorted the natural equality of humanity. A properly engineered environment can change this distortion. This includes the redistribution of wealth, education for all and a minimum standard of living.

(c)   Social harmony can exist between classes given the rule of law, consensus on egalitarian values, and respect for human rights.

The Theory of Progress

(a)   Progress will occur if growth increases both wages for labour and profits for capital.

(b)   Men and women are social creatures. Individualism in history has been predatory. All progress has occurred by social agreement or social action.

(c)   Competitive values underwrite the acceptance of privilege and the ideals of capitalism. Co-operation should be encouraged.

(d)   History is the progress of reason via increasing technology and expertise. Man must be optimistic about his future both in terms of the proper application of science to combat want and inequality, but also towards more civilised behaviour between people. Quality of life issues such as racism and sexism warrant legislation and state interference as much as traditional areas such as defence.

Notes

1. Winthrop, N. *Liberal Democratic Theory and Its Critics.* Sydney, Croom Helm, 1985, p. 7.
2. Bullock, A. and Stallybrass, O. *The Fontana Dictionary of Modern Thought.* UK, Fontanal Collins, 1977, p. 579.
3. McFarlane, B. and Catley, R. *From Tweedledum to Tweedledee.* Sydney, 1974; Gough, I. *The Political Economy of the Welfare State.* London, Macmillan, 1979.
4. Scarribelotti, G. 'Wanted: A Philosophy for the ALP Right' *Catholic Weekly* 6 June 1982, pp. 10–27.
5. Chiou, C.L. *Maoism in Action: The Cultural Revolution.* Queensland, University of Queensland Press, 1974. pp. 105–21.
6. Johnson, C. 'Social Harmony and Australian Labor: The Role of Private Industry in the Curtin and Chifley Government's Plans for Australian Economic Development' *Australian Journal of Politics and History* 32 (1) 1986, pp. 40–50.
7. Leach, R. 'Right Wing Labor' *Arena* 76, 1986, pp. 151–63.
8. Gough, pp. 149–52.
9. Cole, G.D.H. in De Crespigny, A. and Cronin, J. (eds) *Ideologies of Politics.* London, Oxford University Press, 1975, pp. 92–93.
10. Cole, p. 92.
11. Gamble, A. *An Introduction to Modern Social and Political Thought.* London, Macmillan, 1981, p. 174.
12. Ibid.
13. Heilbronner, R. *The Worldly Philosophers.* UK, Penguin, 1980, pp. 105–31.
14. 'Co–operation comes to Australia' *Australian Society* November 1986, p. 18.

15. Winthrop, pp. 230–31.
16. Groth, A.J. *Major Ideologies*. Toronto, John Wiley, 1971, p. 68.
17. Groth, p. 67.
18. Groth, p. 68.
19. Groth, pp. 67–69.
20. Heilbronner, pp. 150–52.
21. Heilbronner, p. 176.
22. Burkitt, B. *Radical Political Economy: An Introduction to the Alternative Economies*. UK, Harvester, 1985, p. 111.
23. Winthrop, p. 235.
24. Burkitt, p. 107.
25. Heilbronner, p. 176.
26. Burkitt, p. 106.
27. Winthrop, p. 234.
28. Burkitt, p. 105.
29. Barber, W. *A History of Economic Thought*. UK, Penguin, 1984, p. 250.
30. Catley, R. and McFarlane, B. *Australian Capitalism in Boom and Depression: options for the 1980s*. Australia, Alternative Publishing co-operative, 1983; passim also Leach.
31. Lowi, T.J. *The End of Liberalism: Ideology, Policy and the Crisis of Public Authority*. NY, Norton, 1969.
32. Gough, pp. 149–52.
33. Winthrop, p. 235.
34. Jessop, B. *The Capitalist State*. Oxford, Martin Robertson, 1982, pp. 79–81.
35. Winthrop, pp. 233–34.
36. Heller, A 'The Great Republic' *Praxis International* 5 (1) April 1985.
37. Watkins, F.M. *The Age of Ideology: Political Thought 1750-Present*. USA, Prentice-Hall, 1964, pp. 64–73; Clark, D. 'Employee Ownership Schemes not Rainbows for all Ideological Seasons' *Financial Times* 18 November 1986.
38. 'The Madonna as Revolutionary' *National Times* 13–19 May 1983.
39. Matthews, J. and Burkitt, p. 128 'The Push for Collective Investment' *Australian Society* January 1987, pp. 20–21.
40. See Matthews or Burkitt.
41. 'N.Z. Labor — The Move to the Right' *The Courier Mail* 18 October 1986; and Winthrop, p. 235.
42. Beilharz, P. 'Beyond the Accord' *Arena* 74, 1986, pp. 16–24.
43. Brugger, B. 'A New Style for Labor? The Hawke Government' *Current Affairs Bulletin* 63 (6) p. 5.
44. Gamble, p. 183.
45. 'The Decline of the Welfare State' *The Australian* 26 July 1986; The Move to the Right' *Courier Mail* 18 October 1986.
46. Gerittson, R. 'The Necessity of Corporatism: the Case of the Hawke Labor Government' *Politics* 21 (1) May 1986, p. 46.
47. Ibid.
48. Burrell, S. 'Labor doesn't know which way to look'. *Sydney Morning Herald* 26 July 1986, p. 25.
49. Christenson, R.M. *et al. Ideologies and Modern Politics*. London, Nelson, 1972, p. 293.
50. Summy, G. 'The Revolutionary Democracy of Dr J. Cairns' *Politics* VII, 1 May 1972, pp. 55–66.
51. Duncan, T. 'Heart to Heart attack on the Left' *The Bulletin* 19 November 1985, p. 32.
52. Beilharz, P. and Watts, R. 'The Discourse of Laborism' *Arena* 77, 1986, p. 109.
53. Camilleri, J. 'After Social Democracy' *Arena* 77, 1986.
54. Gyford, J. *The Politics of Local Socialism*. London, Allen and Unwin, 1985, pp. 108–15.

55. Self, Peter *Political Theories of Modern Government*. London, Allen and Unwin, 1985, pp. 163, 139–54.
56. Jacobs, M. 'Farewell to the Greater London Council' *Australian Society* June 1986, p. 15.
57. Ibid.
58. Leach, R. 'The Balkanization of Australia' in *Dyason House* Papers Autumn 1978.
59. White, R. *Inventing Australia-Images and Identity 1688–1980*. Sydney, Allen and Unwin, 1981, Chapter 3, pp. 29–46.
60. Courtenay, P.P. *Northern Australia*. Australia, Longman Cheshire, 1982, p. 20 and Brugger p. 10.
61. McKinlay, B. *The ALP a Short History of the ALP*. Australia, Heinemann, 1981, p. 155.
62. Clark, Manning. *A Short History of Australia*. NY, Mentor Books, 1969.
63. Davis, S.R. *The Government of the Australian States*. Melbourne, Longman, 1960.
64. Horne, D. *Money Made Us*. Australia Penguin, 1976, pp. 150–51.
65. Clark, Manning, 'The Age of the Bourgeoisie', Cochrane, P. *Industrialisation and Dependence: Australia's Road to Economic Development 1870–1939*. Australia, University of Queensland Press, 1980.
66. See Beilharz.
67. Irving, T. 'Socialism, Working Class Mobilization and the Origins of the Labor Party' in O'Meagher, B. (ed.) *The Socialist Objective: Labor and Socialism*. Sydney, Hale and Ironmonger, 1983, pp. 32–42, as referred to by Burgmann, V. *In Our Time: Socialism and the Rise of Labor 1885–1905*. Sydney, Allen and Unwin, 1985, pp. 16–17.
68. McKinley, p. 155.
69. Brugger, p. 10.
70. Ibid.
71 See Johnson.
72. Clark, Manning, p. 220.
73. Evans, P. *Dependent Development: The Alliance of Multinational*, State and Local Capital in Brazil. UK, Princeton University Press, 1979, pp. 3–55.
74. See Johnson.
75. McKinlay, p. 104.
76. White, p. 164.
77. Mckinlay, p. 155.
78. See Leach.
79. Tokuyama, J. 'The Pacific Century', *Newsweek*, 21 March 1977.
80. 'Big Depression Coming' *Courier Mail* 12 December 1986.

References

Bahro, R. *The Alternative in Eastern Europe*. UK, New Left Books, 1980.
Bahro, R. *Socialism and Survival*. London, Heretic Books, 1983.
Barber, W.J. *A History of Economic Thought*. UK, Penguin, 1984.
Barratt Brown, M. *Models in Political Economy*. UK, Penguin, 1984.
Beilharz, P. 'Beyond the Accord', *Arena*, 74. 1986.
Beilharz, P. and Watts, R. 'The Discourse of Laborism' *Arena* 77, 1986.
Brugger, B. 'A New Style for Labor? The Hawke Government' *Current Affairs Bulletin* 63 (6) 1986.
Bullock, A. and Stallybrass, O. *The Fontana Dictionary of Modern Thought*. UK, Fontana/Collins, 1977.
Burgmann, V. *In Our Time: Socialism and the Rise of Labor, 1885–1905*. Sydney, Allen and Unwin, 1985.

Burrell, S. 'Labor doesn't know which way to look' *Sydney Morning Herald*, 26 July 1986.

Burkitt, B. *Radical Political Economy: An Introduction to the Alternative Economies.* UK, Harvester, 1985.

Catley, R. and McFarlane, B. *Australian Capitalism in Boom a Depression: Options for the 1980s*, Australia, Alternative Publishing Co–operative, 1983.

Camilleri, J. 'After Social Democracy' *Arena* 77, 1986, pp. 48–88.

Chiou, C.L. *Maoism in Action: The Cultural Revolution*, Queensland, University of Queensland Press, 1974.

Christenson, R.M. *et al. Ideologies and Modern Politics*. London, Nelson, 1972.

Clark, D. 'Employee Ownership Schemes not Rainbows for all Ideological Seasons' *Financial Times* 18 November 1986.

Clark, Manning, *A Short History of Australia*. NY Mentor Books, 1969.

'Co–operation comes to Australia' *Australian Society* November 1986.

Cochrane, P. *Industrialization and Dependence: Australian Road to Economic Development 1870–1939*. Australia, University of Queensland Press, 1980.

Courtenay, P.P. *Northern Australia*, Australia, Longman Cheshire, 1982.

Crough, G., Wheelwright, E. and Wilshire, C. (eds) *Australia and World Capitalism*. Australia, Penguin, 1980.

Davis, S.R. *The Government of the Australian States*, Melbourne, Longman, 1960.

De Crespigny, A. and Cronin, J. (eds) *Ideologies of Politics*. London, Oxford University Press, 1975.

Duncan, T. 'Heart to Heart Attack on the Left' *The Bulletin* 19 November 1985.

Ebenstein, W. *Today's Isms*. USA, Prentice-Hall, 1973.

Emy, H.V. 'The Roots of Australian Politics: A Critique of Culture' *Politics* VII (1) May 1972, pp. 12–30.

Evans, P. *Dependent development: The Alliance of Multi-national, State and Local Capital in Brazil*. UK, Princeton University Press, 1979.

Evans, R. *Socialism*. London, Hamilton, 1977.

Galtung, Johan 'On the Technology of Self Reliance' in *Self Reliance: A Strategy for Development* Geneva Bogle-Liouverture, 1980.

Gamble, A. *An Introduction to Modern Social and Political Thought*. London, Macmillan, 1981.

Gerittson, R. 'The Necessity of Corporatism: The Case of the Hawke Labor Government'. *Politics* 21 (1) May 1986.

Gordon, R. (ed.) *The Australian New Left*. Australia, Heinemann, 1970.

Gough, I. *The Political Economy of the Welfare State*, London, Macmillan, 1979.

Groth, A.J. *Major Ideologies*. Toronto, John Wiley, 1971.

Gyford, J. *The Politics of Local Socialism*. London, Allen and Unwin, 1985.

Heater, D. *Contemporary Political Ideas* Second Edition. London, Longman, 1983.

Heilbronner, R. *The Worldly Philosophers*. UK Penguin, 1980.

Heller, A. 'The Great Republic' *Praxis International*, 5 (1) April 1985, pp. 23–35.

Horne, D. *Money Made Us*. Australia, Penguin, 1976.

Irving, T. 'Socialism, Working Class Mobilization and the Origins of the Labor Party' in O'Meagher, B. (ed.) *The Socialist Objective: Labor and Socialism*. Sydney, Hale and Ironmonger, 1983.

Jacobs, M. 'Farewell to the Greater London Council' *Australian Society* June 1986.

Jessop, B. *The Capitalist State*. Oxford, Martin Robertson, 1982.

Johnson, C. 'Social Harmony and Australian Labor: The Role of Private Industry in the Curtin and Chifley Government's Plans for Australian Economic Development' *Australian Journal of Politics and History* 32 (1) 1986, pp. 40–50.

Jupp, J. *Party Politics: Australia 1966–81*. Sydney, Allen and Unwin, 1982.

Kitching, G. *Rethinking Socialism*. London, Methuen, 1983.

Leach, R. 'Right Wing Labor' *Arena* 76, 1986.

Leach, R. 'The Balkanization of Australia' in Dyason House Papers, Autumn 1978.

Lowi, T.J. *The End of Liberalism: Ideology, Policy and the Crisis of Public Authority.* NY, Norton, 1969.

Matthews, J. 'The Push for Collective Investment' *Australian Society* January 1987, pp. 19–21.

McFarlane, B. and Catley, R. *From Tweedledum to Tweedledee* Sydney, 1974.

McKinlay, B. *The ALP: A Short History of the ALP,* Australia, Heinemann, 1981.

McKnight, D. (ed.) *Moving Left.* Sydney Pluto Press, 1986.

Milibrand, R. *Parliamentary Socialism* Second Edition. London, Allen and Unwin, 1961.

'N.Z. Labor moves to the Right' *The Courier Mail* 18 October 1986.

O'Meagher, B. (ed.) *The Socialist Objective: Labor and Socialism.* Sydney, Hale and Ironmonger, 1983.

Sabine, G. and Thorsen, T.L. *A History of Political Theory.* USA Dryden, 1973.

Scarrebelotti, G. 'Wanted: A Philosophy for the ALP Right' *Catholic Weekly* 6 June 1982.

Schumpeter, J. *Capitalism, Socialism and Democracy* Fifth Edition. London, Allen and Unwin, 1976.

Self, P. *Political Theories of Modern Government.* London, Allen and Unwin, 1985.

Summy, G. 'The Revolutionary Democracy of Dr J. Cairns', *Politics* VII (1) May 1972, pp. 55–66.

Tokuyama, J. 'The Pacific Century' *Newsweek* 21 March 1977.

Vaisey, J. *Social Democracy.* London, Weidenfeld and Nicholson 1971.

Watkins, F.M. *The Age of Ideology: Political Thought 1750-Present.* USA, Prentice-Hall, 1964.

White, R. *Inventing Australia — Images and Identity 1688–1980.* Sydney, Allen and Unwin, 1981.

Winthrop, N. (ed.) *Liberal Democratic Theory and its Critics.* Sydney, Croom Helm, 1985.

'The Madonna as Revolutionary' *National Times* 13 may 1983.

Recommended Reading

Beilharz, P. *Labour's Utopias: Bolshevism, Fabianism; Social Democracy.* Australia, Routledge, 1992.

Burkitt, B. *Radical Political Economy: An Introduction to the Alternative Economies.* UK, Harvester, 1985.

Friedman, E. (ed.), *Ascent and Decline in the World System.* Vol. 5, Political Economy of the World System, USA, Sage, 1982.

Watkins, F.M. *The Age of Ideology*: Political Thought 1750-Present. USA, Prentice-Hall, 1964.

Winthrop, N. (ed.) *Liberal Democratic Theory and Its Critics.* Sydney, Croom Helm, 1985.

Vaisey, J. *Social Democracy.* London, Weidenfeld and Nicholson, 1971.

White, R. *Inventing Australia — Images and Identity 1688–1980.* Sydney, Allen and Unwin, 1981.

5
Communism

Although there is a chain of intellectual dissent from Marx to Lenin, their concepts of communism are not identical. What for Marx was a system that could develop only in an advanced economy and with the enfranchisement of the entire working class in a substantive as well as a formal sense — which is what Marx apparently meant by the dictatorship of the proletariat — became for Lenin a system that could be developed out of a backward economy and on the basis of a conspiratorial party that became the vanguard of the people and that operated on the basis of a democratic centralism. Lenin's system, not Marx's, was what communism became . . .

(Morton A. Kaplan, (ed.)
The Many Faces of Communism, p. 23)

The ideology of communism will be investigated in three parts. The first part will outline some basic Marxist theory set against the figures of Karl Marx (1818–83) and Friedrich Engels (1820–95). The second part will deal briefly with the rise of Marxism/Leninism and the reasons for Lenin's (and later Stalin's) adaptation of Marxism. The role of the Communist Party (as indicated in the quote) is vital to the second phase of Marxism. The third part will deal with some of the diverse contemporary communisms and give a brief overview of Australian communism as represented by the career of the former Communist Party of Australia. In contrast to the widely held myth of monolithic communism, contemporary communism contains 'many different roads to communism that are responsive to different concrete national conditions (if they are to be successful) while they maintain the fiction of a common goal'.[1] With the collapse of Soviet communism, the issue is even more clouded. At the moment, former Soviet and East European communist nations have broken with bureaucratic one-party socialism. Nevertheless, the structure of state ownership remains dominant and it remains to be seen whether capitalism can become the dominant ideology within the new democracies or a new brand of democratic socialism will emerge.

Such diversity amongst communism is due to the changing nature of capitalism and socialism themselves, with new inputs from such sources as multinational capitalism, feminism, environmentalism, and so on. The strength of liberalism and democratic socialism as ideological opponents within the system is important. The cultural and economic background of the home society, the role of Right-wing authoritarianism, national poverty or plain chance are also important for the communist access to power. Once in power, the role of internal criticism and faction struggles between 'liberals' and 'conservative' groups with 'left and right deviationisms' adds to the complexity. This has been most obvious with the Gorbachev 'liberal' communist period in the former USSR where *perestroika* and *glasnost* led ultimately to the 'conservative' communist hard line coup attempt in Moscow in 1991.

Communism is thus a variegated movement. Some universal similarities exist, however. Orthodox communist movements are built around a commonly accepted (if differently applied) ideology, drawn from Marx, and are possessed of similar party and organisational structures, based on Lenin. These fundamental similarities of ideology and party structure are more apparent when compared with the vague ideology of democratic socialism, which often verges on liberalism, and the loose democratic socialist party structure.[2] Thus studies of Marxist theory and Leninist party structure are both imperative to describe communism.

What is Communism?

Modern communism has been seen as 'specifically linked with the ideas of Karl Marx and the concept of a classless society based upon common ownership of the means of production. This society is seen as emerging after the transitional period of the dictatorship of the proletariat and the preparatory stage of socialism.'[3]

The Communist Myth or Teleology

The basic ideas of Marx which form the foundation of a vision of society alternative to capitalism, are historical materialism and Marx's critique of capitalism.[4] Like all ideologies, the strength of communism rests on the power of its Sorelian myth and its *telos* or long-term aims. In communism, this long-term aim[5] is held to be one of liberation for all people. Divisions between classes, oppression due to riches, gender, etc. will all, it is expected, disappear through progress. Even philosophical differences between idealism and materialism, caused by ruling class illusions and values being imposed from above, alienating all for the benefit of a few, will disappear. So will all the ideologies of the political spectrum. Reality will begin after this long historical *praxis* or interaction plays itself out. According to Brugger,[5] '*praxis* for Marx entailed a practical engagement in changing reality and the building up of coherent knowledge deriving from such engagement'. Communism has achieved via Marx and Engels a powerful overview of history, giving the working class 'inevitable' centrality in the age of industrialism. This analysis of the past and vision of the future (as touched upon in the beginning quote) is powerful in its simplicity, and its identification with the mass rather than, for instance, a merchant class; a race such as the 'Aryans', or an élite of intellectuals. It is also very flexible.

The communist message can be simply outlined thus: Capitalism, like its predecessor, feudalism, is simply another dialectical stage of man's history. The process of historical movement is based upon humankind's powers of production, and will ultimately end in a classless society. Men and women can already imagine such a society but not yet attain it in material reality.

Capitalism, like previous stages of development, is doomed by its internal contradictions. The major contradiction stems from the existence of an owning class (the bourgeoisie) which controls the means of production and the social relations of production. This class thus dominates all economic and hence social decisions. It is, however, confronted by a non-owning class, the proletariat, created by it through the mode of production. There may be various other classes, such as a salaried middle class or a declining landed gentry, between these two. The epoch, however, is dominated by these two giants. The other classes will form alliances with the bourgeoisie or the proletariat in the class struggle between these two giants.

This class struggle is the motor of history, not just in the modern age, but in all previous epochs. This struggle operates by the inexorable laws of dialectical materialism. These laws assert that the basis of all human society rests upon material factors. Men and women produce. They combat nature to exist. This mute historical process underlies all change, but is hidden by history written by the ruling classes and through ruling class perspectives and values.

Ruling classes stand on the shifting sand of these changing modes of production. As these modes change, so does their position. Contradictions slowly emerge changing the *quality* of the ruling class, and these lead to its disunity. The ruling class also produces its opposite, with which it is linked by the prevailing mode of production. There is a *unity in opposites*. Finally, contradiction between these opposites can turn antagonistic. A break is made, and a new ruling class is born. The previous epoch's negation is now negated, and a revolution, a complete reversal in power relations begins and continues down the epoch.

In the case of the capitalist era, revolution led by the proletariat will occur. This event will be violent or peaceful and occur unevenly throughout capitalist countries due to the uneven stages of production throughout the regions of the world. A period of socialism will follow.

Socialism is a preparatory stage where the state will be the tutor of a new generation. It will differ from the previous bourgeois state, being dominated by the proletariat which will ensure that no residue of the old society will remain to influence the new one. Property relations, stocks and shares, finance capitalism, monopolies, inheritances, etc., together with their related oppressions such as the inferior position of women — will all be swept away by the 'dictatorship of the proletariat utilising the power of the state'. When a new generation, not raised on bourgeois corruption, takes power, the state will wither away, as force will no longer be necessary. Then, the second stage of communism will begin.

This will be marked by the demise of hierarchy, in the state, family and gender. Production will be undertaken by free association, with science linked to the co-operative good of the many, not the profit of a few. This near-anarchist stage will witness the withering of the root causes of war and greed, due to the lack of private property and the fetish of money, by which men are alienated from each other, desiring these things above community.

This stage will be marked by a parallel revolution in individual consciousness. Hitherto, the historical role of private property is seen as being to alienate people from one another. Accumulation by the few rather than the co-operation of the many has provided a sick dynamism to history. Similarly, ruling class ideology has permeated mass values, and identification with this dominant ideology has alienated the mass of people from their true interests. Further confusion, division and alienation from each other has come about through the practice of nationalist and racial, religious and gender oppression, which form vital parts of these ruling ideologies. Thus the masses have often been a class *in themselves* but not *for themselves*. The masses existed as a real class which never acted for itself, always for others. As the second stage of communism unfolded, mass consciousness would grow and these divisions would drop away.

Marx believed that such a change would occur scientifically once the social relations linked to property were changed. A change in the material world would lead to non-competitiveness. Co-operation would create the 'new communist man'. Other communisms such as Maoism have disputed this. Consciousness will not be changed simply by economic change at the base of social production. People will have to struggle with backsliders towards capitalism and bureaucracy at each advance towards the goal. Cultural revolution may, in fact, be never-ending.

Nevertheless, all communisms point to a utopian communist future where, due to commonly owned property, democracy and plenty will prevail at all levels of human endeavour — family, work and community. The state will have become irrelevant. 'True history', not that of ruling classes but of the common people, would begin.

Now the ex-Soviet states, in particular, have to come to terms with their re-integration into the capitalist world system; the rise of nationalism; pluralist democratic parties and ideas and the banning of the communist party. Is this a new aspect completely explainable by contradictions and dialectic materialism representing the triumph of democracy over a one party state leading to a new form of democratic socialism or is it a total return of the former USSR to the capitalist world system after an industrialising period where 'socialism' was simply an ideological blind for primitive accumulation of capital without capitalists?

The above outlines the Sorelian myths of communism and demonstrates the forceful religiosity of its humanism and its present crisis. The centrepieces of the communist myth are the Marxist materialist approach to history and the critique of capitalism. From these two centrepieces, via a short outline of the thought of Marx and Engels, the basic precepts of Marxism can be approached.

Marx and Engels

The major figures in the creation of Communist ideology are Karl Marx and Friedrich Engels. Marx was the dominant figure of this partnership, but, from the publication of the 'Communist Manifesto' (1848), much of the work they did was in collaboration, or at least was the product of dialogue and interaction.

Marxism was one of the last great historicist world outlines. It set out to explain world history and to analyse the capitalism of the contemporary epoch. As Heilbronner points out,[6] it is 'an inexorable critique' which, more than any other socialism, is the dire enemy of capitalism.

As leaders from Lenin to Mao have stated, there can ultimately be little long-term capitalist co-existence with a pure Marxist state. One or the other will triumph, or Marxism will have been revised, and been turned from a 'pure' into a 'practical' ideology.[7]

As Martin indicates,[8] Marx went through three life stages while developing his philosophy. The first phase was that of the young

Marx, concerned with man's *alienation*, whereby man did not achieve the ethical potential of his imagination. The second phase dealt with Marx the *revolutionary*. Here, Marx was obsessed with the possibility of action based upon a materialist view of history and with the working class as the tool of change, overcoming alienation. With the right sort of material basis, one not dominated by the distorting influence of some ruling class, all mankind will, he believed, be freed by working class action to achieve their potential. In order to achieve this aim, however, the working class had to understand its enemy, capitalism.

The third phase of thought is given over to an immense analysis and critique of capitalism.

Marx begins, therefore, with a sense of outrage and puzzlement. Why is humanity alienated from its potential for freedom and equality? Like Rousseau, Marx is perplexed that 'man is born free, but is everywhere in chains'. Through our philosophers, we can imagine a perfect world. But this is useless idealist fantasy. 'Philosophers have hitherto explained the world. The point is, however, to change it.'[9]

Marx needed a material tool to change the unsatisfactory state of affairs he perceived, not a fantasy. This tool was the working class, the 'real' class, existing in opposition to the capitalist class, with deep grievances. It could not avoid its historical fate to struggle with capitalism.[10]

However, without a deep understanding of its enemy, capitalism, and without a sense of mission, the working class would become satisfied with mere trade unionism and a share in the capitalist society rather than its overthrow. The required sense of mission was provided by historical materialism and dialetical materialism.

Historical Materialism and Dialectical Materialism

Dialectical Materialism: Marx was deeply influenced by the German philosopher Hegel who argued for an approach to philosophy based upon the world as process. Hegel stressed that the dynamism behind this process was the original 'Idea' or 'Spirit' working itself out in the material world, towards some ultimate perfection, when the 'ideal' and 'material' would be one. The material world, especially humankind, was merely the vehicle for this spirit to work through and find its own reflection, just as sculptor needs stone to express or reflect an idea within his or her head. The process lurched dialectically in an evolutionary fashion throughout the epochs of world history, for 'spirit' was blind, even if it moved inexorably, like a river.

Both Marx and Engels rejected the idealism of the Hegelian system. To them, the whole system was 'a colossal miscarriage'.[11]

Humanity was not the creature of some spirit using it as an historical instrument. In fact, men and women themselves had created such spirits from their own imagination in primitive times to explain natural phenomena and give purpose to individual life. Now in later times, they bowed down to their ancestors' creations. Men and women were further alienated from their own potential by their own historical creations. They became the servants of those who pretended to have special access to these mysticisms, such as the priesthood.

Marx and Engels rejected Hegelian idealism for materialism while enthusiastically retaining Hegel's dialectic. Dialectics combined with materialism seemed to offer the solution to Marx's long search for the source of alienation in mankind's existence.

In the first place, materialism was translated into meaning through praxis[12] — a situation where men and women make their own history as 'thinking material'.[13] However, they make it within circumstances prescribed by that stage of history. These 'circumstances' can be described as the 'political economy' so that, crudely speaking, the basis of historical materialism is the 'influence of economics upon man'.[14]

The influence of economics constitutes 'the real foundations on which rise the legal and political superstructure and to which correspond definite forms of social consciousness ... (therefore) it is not the consciousness of men that determines their existence, but their existence that determines their consciousness.'[15]

The attainment of this consciousness is a constant struggle, stemming from the human need to force a living from nature. The more surplus man can create from nature, the less precarious is his existence, and the more leisure he will have to realise his own potential for thought and the attainment of self-perfection. Thus man actualises himself by his production. But this differs from culture to culture due to different economic/geographic/climactic circumstances. 'Some societies will be pastoral or industrial or cottage industry, but whatever the form in which men solve the basic economic problem, society will require a whole super structure of non-economic activity and thought.'[16] The whole process changed constantly, due to incremental or sudden leaps in the mode of production and became known as dialectical materialism.

Marx's dialectical materialism was based upon Hegel's notion that conflict in history was 'the essential form of progress'.[17] Like Hegel, Marx saw history unfolding in a generally progressive, but zig-zag, sometimes retracting, sometimes static, manner. This procedure was called 'dialectical' and depended on several factors:

(a) Social arrangements between men and women rested upon a prevailing historical mode of production. Over time, the change in the material base caused an incremental change or change in *quality* of these arrangements, or 'thing'.

(b) Contradictions grew within the 'thing' creating its *own opposite* which formed a unity with its parent.

(c) Eventually, the original 'thing' which had been a negation of an earlier 'thing' was itself negated by a revolutionary change, and a new 'thing' was born.

To Marx, however, these 'things' belonged to the real world. They were what we 'experience in everyday life',[18] material 'things', not ideas having a life outside men and women.

Nothing abstract existed beyond these material 'things'. To Marx, these 'things' or 'powers of production' are the ways men and women set up their productive system to tear at nature. Such systems vary with time and new technology. As they change materially, so man changes the nature of his own existence within nature. A new relation between 'matter and mind' comes into being,[19] and with it new ruling classes and ruling values.

This process can be modelled thus:

(a) An existing 'power of production' (thesis) slowly changes, producing its opposite (antithesis)

(b) A clash ensues. A revolution takes place. A synthesis between thesis and antithesis takes place. A new thesis (or power of production) is born.

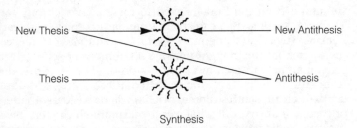

Synthesis

Conflict in both Hegel and Marx is the root cause of the dynamism of the system. In Marx's system, this dynamism stems from class struggle.

Class Struggle and History: Conflict in Marx's dialectical system stems from the struggle between groups of humans, classes, to control the power of production. As G.D.H. Cole outlines it,[20] 'the process of production advances men's knowledge and command over the forces of nature increase, but in this advance there appears no necessary element of conflict ... The conflict that Marx is thinking of is between men, not mankind and nature.'

Marx applied dialectical materialism to history. The outcome, *historical materialism*, divides man's history into epochs each based upon a mode of production which is dominated by a certain ruling class. Each epoch reaches its apogee under this social class. Then, however, the relations of production, part of the *superstructure* of legalities, customs, values, etc., and representing property relations or the mode of ownership of property, comes slowly into conflict with the subtly changing material world beneath its feet, the material forces of production or *substructure*.

Next comes the period of revolution. With the change in the economic foundation, the entire immense superstructure is 'more or less rapidly transformed', but 'no social order ever disappears before all the productive forces for which there is room in it have been developed, and new higher relations of production never appear before the material conditions of their existence have matured in the womb of the old society'.[21]

The opposing class, brought out dialectically during the ruling class's epoch of glory, moves into a position of challenge. As old dominant classes, such as feudal lords, decline, they are challenged not only politically by this new confident antithetical class (such as merchants) but also socially, by the new class ideology. This will provide the new superstructure or value perspectives underlying the new material age. It will provide the new 'illusion of the epoch':

> Gradually conditions change, and, gradually but surely the classes of society are re-arranged, amid turmoil and anguish, the division of wealth is altered. And thus history is a pageant of ceaseless struggle between classes to partition social wealth. For as long as the technics of society change (due to the existence of private property), no existing division of wealth is immune from attack.[22]

What is interesting about this quote, if accurate, is that the 'old society' of the communist USSR has given way, not to a reaction back to a Soviet capitalist class but to a new class of democrats with a political rather than an economic basis. The power of the organised working class (e.g. Solidarity in Poland) is still the determinant social force.

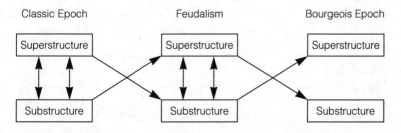

Classic Epoch	Feudalism	Bourgeois Epoch
Superstructure	Superstructure	Superstructure
Substructure	Substructure	Substructure

Each ruling class thus produces its own gravedigger. Countless revolutions, fusions and violent interactions mark the progress of this model. In feudal times, for instance, it was the aristocratic system versus the rising merchant class, culminating in the English, American and French Revolutions, along with countless other uprisings, insurrections and (in some cases) peaceful social adjustments.

The capitalist bourgeoisie have been dominant for nearly 200 years. Even though the capitalist system is unevenly spread over the earth, it has already produced its opposite in the proletariat. Already, according to Marxists, there have been revolutionary proletarian advances in countries with weak capitalist systems such as Russia and China. History is on the march. Many non-Marxists, in opposition, might point out, of course, that such countries were closer to feudalism than capitalism and their communist revolutions was more modernising movements than socialist revolutions as per Marx's timetable. This is indeed a pertinent criticism in such countries as the former USSR. Here the Communist party took over the historical role of the capitalist in forcing industrialisation. As the 'industrialising' class of 'bosses' they have, as the Mensheviks warned in 1917, reaped the odium of the present democratic forces.

Capitalism in its heartland still, however, shows tremendous vitality. Marx had to provide a critique of this enormously energetic system in order to equip his chosen historical vehicle, the working class, with knowledge of its dialectical enemy as it set out on its mission to overcome universal alienation.

Critique of Capitalism: In Volumes 1–3 of his great work, *Das Kapital*, Marx attempted to find the laws that governed the prevailing mode of production, capitalism. With such insights, he thought, one could predict the future of the system.

The two basic classes involved in the capitalist mode of production are the bourgeoisie and proletariat. There has been much criticism of Marx as to the composition of these two classes but essentially one class, the bourgeoisie, controls the mode of production via its control of capital. The other class, the proletariat, is ultimately dependent upon the decisions of the bourgeoisie on how this capital will be spent.

The dynamic nature of the system emerges from the drive by the bourgeoisie to accumulate capital: a voracious, Social Darwinist 'survival of the fittest' process. 'Small and inefficient producers, merchants, craftsmen or peasants were bound to succumb sooner or later to the competition of their larger, more efficient capitalist competitors.'[23] The endless thrust of the bourgeiosie was to get big or go under, driving capitalists to every corner of the world and into every element of society in search of a profit. Nothing was sacred and everything was reduced to money values.

Similarly, while an inexorable polarisation was taking place, with more and more classes falling into the proletariat, a dynamic based upon the search for security spurred some non-capitalists towards survival in this system. Hard work and access to new technology or land speculation etc. might create some new capitalists or a small capitalist class (the *petit bourgeoisie*). This small capitalist class was forever insecure, between possible capital absorption and proletarianisation.

At the basis of the dynamic capitalist drive towards accumulation and/or security lay capital itself. People needed capital for accumulation, and hence security. 'But if all things were equal in economic society, and one man's loss was another man's gain, how did capital accumulate?'

Profit: To Marx, capital accumulated by the expropriation by the capitalist of the extra output of the worker, over and above his subsistence wage. During his working day, the average worker, Marx posited (borrowing from earlier economists like Ricardo), produced far more than he was actually paid. The more hours of work per worker and/or the lower the rate per hour paid by the capitalist to the worker, the more profit, or expropriation of *surplus value*, would take place. This is possible because the average worker becomes alienated from the means of production: that is, he is only a cog in the wheel of the capitalist system. He has no decision over his hours of work or rate of pay. He can only take what he can get.

Unlike the medieval craftsman or small farmer, the new proletariat has no property, so he or she is reduced to a factor of production of a commodity, with only labour power to sell. A small group of capitalists dominates the property relations of the system. The value of the labour power to the capitalist is based not on whether the proletariat is musically talented or of noble lineage or can speak five languages. Unlike feudal lords, there are no links of patronage and responsibility between capitalist and worker: what is important is whether a profit can be made. In the reigning state of capitalist competition with his peers, the only question is, can the capitalist extract enough surplus value from the workers to accumulate capital faster than his fellow businessmen? The capitalist himself is on his own treadmill.

New machinery and new techniques may give a temporary advantage in this perennial pursuit of profit. But ultimately, profit stems from the cheapness and/or productivity of the workforce and the availability of surplus value.

Contradictions. Ultimately the system lurches from crisis to crisis due to the contradiction between 'the *social* nature of its production, affecting millions, and the *private* nature of its dynamism'.[24] The system becomes dependent upon the whims of fewer and fewer people in control of production decisions and capital outlay. No social plan but the private desire for accumulation, dominates the system. The capitalist is blind to everything but his capital, and repeats again and again his mistakes in dealing with the proletariat, something that leads to repeated crisis.

If workers manage to achieve a higher rate of wages, capital's answer is to increase mechanisation. This initially means lower costs for the capitalist. But his competitors soon follow. As prices fall for the new mechanised output, the cost of machinery grows faster than wages. The rate of profit declines. At the same time, the capitalist has caused unemployment, by his introduction of mechanisation. A 'reserve army of the unemployed' has been created, and they face beggary or at the least, a dual labour economy.

As competition increases, profit margins further erode as prices fall and capital further replaces labour with machines. The paradox emerges that production increases while, with increasing unemployment, consumption decreases. Stockpiles abound. Marginal firms increasingly go bankrupt. A depression or similar crisis ensues. To later Leninists, and other neo-Marxists, war or imperial ventures may alleviate or delay these crises, but never stop them.

Crisis succeeds crisis with historical regularity. Fewer and fewer firms will survive, increasing in size over time. New capitalist firms may enter on the backs of new technologies but ultimately they too must undergo this cyclic survival test. However, the system must go on with closer and closer crisis and polarisation, until, finally there will be an apocalyptic crisis caused by the exhaustion of nature and the proletariat. The system of social production and 'the conditions of bourgeois society are too narrow to comprise the wealth created by them'.[25]

The productive forces capitalism has released are too powerful for capitalism's ruling class, the bourgeoisie, to handle because of its limited view of the world. Production for social need is not on the agenda. At this juncture, the proletariat will enter the stage of history and take over. With its wider, more collectivist and democratic view of the world, it will be able to handle the new forces of production.

But how was the proletariat to come onto the stage of history? To most nineteenth century observers, the proletariat in Europe was losing its combativeness. Under social democratic leaders, it seemed quite happy to come to terms with capitalism, to accept its values and to defer to the leadership of the bourgeoisie. *Marxism/Leninism*. Lenin wrote:[26] 'We are Jacobins tied up with the working class.' Throughout the nineteenth century, events did not unfold as Marx predicted. Fewer and fewer European parties based their practical policies upon a Marxist development which seemed further and further from reality. Indeed, as modern social democracy grew, it tended away from Marxist orthodoxy towards revisionism, such as that outlined by Edward Bernstein (1850–1932). This attacked the labour theory of value and especially denied that capital was concentrating in fewer and fewer hands. The class struggle was declining proportionately.

Marxism became more and more the ideology of the radical wing of the socialist movement. They attempted to rescue it theoretically by asserting that capitalism was saved temporarily by colonialism which gave it new markets (see *Rosa Luxemburg*). Eventually, however, it was thought, this must lead to world war.

Others, like Lenin, saw Marxism's primary aim as *revolutionary* theory. The whole point to its existence was to provide theoretical background to the revolutionary act. Unlike Kautsky and Martov and other Mensheviks, who had reduced Marxism to an inevitable process of history, where the proletariat could sit back and wait for the collapse of bourgeois society through history itself (Quietism), Lenin stressed the need for a revolutionary instrument to implement revolutionary theory. For Lenin, the aim was revolution, and history needed prodding along by an act of will (Voluntarism). The best political means to express this act of revolutionary will was via a party dedicated to this act.[27]

Lenin had already stressed the need to adapt Marxism to national conditions in his studies of Russian national capitalism. Now, with Russian conditions of Tsarist oppression in mind, he proposed a new party structure which would achieve the revolution, given the correct objective circumstances.

The role of the Jacobin club in its revolutionary zeal and its dedication to the expansion of the French Revolution was not lost upon Lenin. In 1902, in his book *What is to be done?* Lenin proposed the basic principles of Bolshevism: The new Bolshevik Party, later the Communist Party, was to be a party of professional revolutionaries. Party discipline was to be developed by adopting a 'common line' of correct theory which was itself flexible and adapted to the times. The achievement of revolution was the primary task, as the mass of the proletariat was only capable of insurrection, or, at the worst, trade union activities. A dedicated band of Bolsheviks with a clear-minded approach to theoretical problems would act as the drive motor or catalyst that would take the proletariat across the Rubicon of the political revolution. Many of the proletariat were in fact frightened to cross the divide between the old and new societies. What was needed was a disciplined group of professionals who had already achieved the social revolution in their own souls, and had thrown off bourgeois morality. These people were outsiders, tightly organised and loyal only to the party which would act in the best interest of the working class, which, if conscious of itself as a class, would approve the actions taken. They would be the 'vanguard' of the new proletarian world.

Structure. Lenin's greatest achievement for communism lay in the theory and practice underlying the Leninist-style Communist Party. Basically, the party was a *group of professional revolutionaries* whose primary duty lay in being ready 'to provide the spark'[28] which would lead to the proletariat becoming aware of itself in any crisis or class conflict. It was an officer corps always in training for the revolution.

Training was by praxis. Members had to be involved in social organisations not just in theoretical discussion. *Democratic centralism* controlled the policy outcome of theoretical discussion. Policies and theory could be freely discussed at all levels of the party. However, once a decision had been made, it became binding upon all members as the party line.

As Rosa Luxemburg warned quite early,[29] such a party structure, particularly after the banning of factions in 1921, could lead only to the domination of the party by its central committee and finally by the party secretary. Bureaucracy was inevitable.

The Party was the *vanguard of the proletariat (State and Revolution,* 1917). By virtue of its political consciousness, the party was the guard of the proletarian state even after the revolution. In Russia's case, many writers assert that the party had to become the state after the Russian Revolution, as the small proletariat had been destroyed after the Civil War.[30]

To many critics of Leninism, the party created a new state and become indistinguishable from it. Unassailable behind the vanguard theory, which transforms critics into counter-revolutionaires, neither the state nor the party withered away; instead, democracy did. This bears little resemblance to the original Marxist vision.

Essentially, Leninism was a method of practical revolution with Marxism as its rationale. The outcome, however, has been a one-party state. This has made it difficult to foster alternative Marxist interpretations of policy until the recent collapse of the Soviet Union. Marxism as a living ideology fell into disrepute as it became the hallmark of a totalitarian party, particularly under Joseph Stalin, (1879–1953), Lenin's successor.

The fight for domination of the Russian Communist Party by Stalin and Leon Trotsky (1879–1940) was a classic struggle between the managerial faction and the ideological one. As Tylecote and Lonsdale-Brown argue, Stalin's victory within the party was a victory for the state technocrats who were more interested in the USSR as a state power than a socialist society. Therefore modernisation and industrialisation came first in order that the international game of states could be played. The party became transformed into a modernising machine of experts.

The rationale of the revolution had, however, been Marxism. The desire for the socialist spirit and utopia still had to be fed. Stalinism therefore transformed Marxism via the party line into a form of international and internal discipline. The party became dedicated to Stalin's view that 'objective factors in the mode of production' were foremost in changing man, not a praxis of subjective spirit and objective factors. Obedience and industrialisation preceded democracy.

The party became not a catalyst for raising mass consciousness, but an instrument for managing society. This is the process of Stalinism that Gorbachev hoped to reverse with *perestroika* and *glasnost*. Humankind would follow material changes. Under Stalin, via purges of the old Bolsheviks, the party was transformed from a revolutionary to a bureaucratic managerial system. Material change itself was the *telos*. This reduced socialism to measured norms of output rather than human emancipation:[31] 'Growth' was the mystique. Somehow, this process of growth would cause material plenty to transmute into human happiness without the need for individual decision making in the process. 'Such crude materialism still bedevils much communist thinking in many communist systems.'

Stalinism showed the basic problem inherent in Marxism/Leninism that Rosa Luxemburg had prophesied. It could so easily be transformed from a tool for mass revolutionary consciousness into a self-perpetuating oligarchy of technocrats, justified by a distorted Marxism that no-one dared dispute for fear of being labelled counter-revolutionary.

Summarising the Trotsky/Stalin conflict over this problem, Martin points out that Trotsky had disputed this party role with Stalin, emphasising the need for an open party with factions.[32] (a similar factionalised open party idea was encouraged by the Gorbachev reforms of 1985–91). These would oppose centralised bureaucracy. The party would be host to all revolutionary socialists, not an empire controlled by one group. The Soviets, as well, should rule, as proletarian democracy, not a shadowy apparatus of an élite chosen by list (*nomenklatura*).

In 1927, Stalin ousted Trotsky over the issues of 'proletarian democracy' and 'permanent revolution'. Stalin's bureaucracy opposed the first issue and the war-weary Russian people the second. 'Socialism in one country' promised peace and modernisation. Outmanouevred, Trotsky was exiled to Mexico where he was assassinated in 1940.

The first clash between technocrats and democrats within a Marxist-Leninist state had ended in the triumph of the former. But the tension between the two tendencies is continuous, adding to the insecurity of the ruling élite and the need for total control.

Marx and technocracy sit ill with each other.

A Summary of Communist Theory

The Theory of the State

(a) The state is the executive of the ruling class. It is not neutral in the bourgeois/proletariat context. The state will act to use force against the workers.

(b) The bourgeois state should be overthrown and replaced by a state dominated by the dictatorship of the proletariat. After a period of time, a decentralised democracy will emerge dispensing with the role of the traditional hierarchical state.

(c) The state's roles will diminish or 'wither away'.

The Theory of Society

(a) Society is a product of the prevailing mode of production.

(b) This mode of production produces two elements, a substructure and superstructure, which can interact with one another.

(c) Society changes incrementally and dialectically with change initiating from subtle shifts in the mode of production.

The Theory of Progress

(a) Progress is implicit in material change in production. Mankind actualises itself by producing more leisure and thus more ability to overcome alienation.

(b) Progress is caused by the tension between contradictions building up in the class structure due to natural change in the powers of production. Eventually, a revolution in political, social or combined terms takes place.

(c) History is the progress of man's mode of production, producing more and more which cannot be contained by the old order, rather than idealist factors such as Hegel's spirit pervading history with man as instrument. Man and his production are alone in a world, which has no other meaning.

Contemporary Communism

Contemporary Communism is no longer the monolithic movement envisaged in Stalin's time with its international discipline.

Indeed the entire Soviet Union as the centre of communism has disintegrated under the pressure of internal nationalist forces and the crisis of Russian overlordship initiated by Gorbachev's variety of 'liberal communism'. For the foreseeable future, the former USSR and Eastern Europe will follow an interesting path of capitalist and democratic socialist experiment.

While the USSR existed however as a Leninist state (1917–1991), there had been a trend from communist monolithism to polycentrism, to the present crisis of the ideology and ruling class and the removal of bureaucratic communism to a rump ideology, both in the former USSR and in the remaining communist states of China, Cuba, Vietnam, North Korea.

The trend from monolithic ideological unity was always present due to a desire for national adaptation of Marxism even though such 'national deviationists' were heretics in Stalin's period. Since Stalin's death in 1953, there has been a trend towards polycentrism or national/regional interpretation of policy and tactics, first enunciated and accepted by the Italian Communist leader Togliatti in 1956. This policy was further underlined by Gorbachev (1985–91), resulting in East European independence and finally the logical disintegration of the last European Empire — the USSR.

Gorbachev's doctrine of 'national decision re the path to socialism' completely overturned Breshnev's doctrine of 1968. This doctrine was used to justify the Soviet invasion of Czechoslovakia in 1968 on the grounds that the USSR was the guardian of communism and thus had the right to protect that creed in other communist states.

The major reason for polycentrism, however, was the Sino-Soviet split of 1962, a further reflection of the inner party tension between revolutionary and technocrat. Both Russia and China fell out over international policy. Nikita Khruschev's Russia, having come perilously close to atomic war with the USA over Cuba and the presence of Russian missiles on the island (1961) had redefined communist ideology to include the notion of 'peaceful coexistence' with the capitalist powers. Maoist China objected to this decline in revolutionary commitment, 'The East wind was prevailing over the West' or history was on the side of revolution against the colonial European powers.

This split over revolutionary policy was matched by other factors. China felt no need to defer to Russian communism as the only correct mode. China had successfully made her own revolution. Mao had reconstructed Marxism-Leninism to emphasise the peasant over the worker, and the war of liberation over the sudden urban coup of 1917. The peasant commune as envisaged in the wartime 'Yenan Way' was seen as an alternative to the Russian managerial party and society.

Mao's writings were accepted as original additions to Marxism, alongside those of Lenin and Stalin. While Stalin was alive, the Chinese could listen respectfully to this original Bolshevik. However, they were not about to obey his successors.

For the Russian part, there were elements of traditional nationalism and 'Yellow Peril' racism in their attitude to China. In the words of Dostoevsky 'In Europe we were Asiatics, whereas in Asia, we too, are Europeans.'[33] The Russians were ambivalent about the dominance of the East over the West wind.

The Sino/Soviet split had several effects upon contemporary communism .

It made possible more *flexibility* and *polycentrism* in communist movements. This was particularly so after the Chinese rejected 'the theory of two camps' which implicitly gave the USSR leadership in any confrontation with the USA.[34] China developed from 1964 the 'theory of the three worlds'.[35] Here the Third World countries, including China, stood in between the two superpowers and were in a position to exploit differences between the two. Great power hegemony, it was believed, should be fought.

The ensuing splits between communist partners meant *a decline in the effectiveness* of communism as an instrument of Soviet policy and/or radical change.

Nevertheless, with varying differences on tactics, and with different emphases upon worker, peasant, radical nationalist or coalitions of forces as the source of change, most communist theorists tended to agree that contemporary capitalism was reaching a post-World War II crisis. What were the essentials of this claimed crisis?

The Crisis of Capitalism

Communist analysis using Marxist theory has constantly identified 'crises' in capitalism. Time and again, capitalism has survived this doom-saying and gone on to greater productivity and expansion.

Yet, as Heilbronner says,[36] it must be remembered that Marx's model in *Das Kapital* was built upon 'pure' capitalism which, like 'pure' socialism, existed only as an ideal type. A crisis leading to the total collapse of real world capitalism would be unlikely: the process would be piecemeal and selective.

Capitalism has broken down periodically in the nineteenth and twentieth centuries. It broke down partly because it developed the instability Marx predicted: 'a succession of business crises (or cycles), compounded by a plague of wars, destroyed the faith of the lower and middle classes in the system.'

But these material factors of business cycles were only the initial bases or breakdown. Capitalism failed also for *social* reasons.[37]

There was allegedly a crisis of belief in the existing social values and political system. These values were often weaker in Third World countries, where polarities in wealth were more obvious, and where both foreign ownership and local co-operation with this ownership was more blatant and poverty more widespread. Communism was often more successful in such countries where the social values of capitalism were less embedded or hegemonic.

Marx predicted that in order to rescue the system of capitalist values 'the government would have to rise above the interests of one class alone'[38] and this would be 'socially impossible' in the long run.

It is based upon this belief in the inevitable crisis in capitalism that contemporary communism approaches the business 'crisis' of the late twentieth century.

Arguments for the Crisis: Radical analysis stresses the role of 'long waves' in capitalist economic growth. Long wave theory argues that capitalism is stimulated initially by a new market (e.g. housing) or technological breakthrough (e.g. the steam engine, motor car or computer) or a combination of both into a massive spurt of growth. Various countries lead these developments (e.g. nineteenth-century Britain with steam and twentieth century USA with the car).

Other countries are drawn into this spurt of growth as commodity sources, second level manufacturing countries or markets. There emerges a world hierarchy of core, semi-periphery and periphery countries. Even enclaves and regions within countries emerge, dominated by the world system rather than the national government. Eventually, the initial spurt, due to technology, fades. Profit diminishes and, in the pure capitalist system, crisis and depression sets in.

While long wave theory is contentious, the theory has been the major basis for Kondratieff cycles,[39] named after the Russian economist of the early 1920s who, using historical data, argued that capitalism went through long wave movements of growth and decline approximately every fifty years. The theory has grown in acceptability. Many capitalist firms employ statisticians known as 'chartists' to follow such long waves.

There is some unity of opinion among many such 'chartists', to the effect that we are at the end of the post-World War II long wave.[40] A business crisis is inevitable, according to these sources.

The second argument for this crisis in capitalism stems from the communist analysis of the decline of the welfare state and social democracy. According to this argument, capitalism in the West was saved after the 1929–40 Great Depression and World War II by the rise of Social Democracy and Welfare Liberalism. This ensured policies that mitigated the worst effects of capitalism, stoked employment by government planning and kept consumption high by fiscal egalitarian policies, public works, and transfer payments in the form of unemployment benefits, etc. Class warfare was numbed by government intervention.

Many communist analysts, therefore, agree with some Western scholars[41] that the Keynesian episode in the post-war 'First World' countries (in particular France, Britain etc.) was an aberrant period. Revolution however was not prevented in the weaker capitalist Third World countries, particularly as they had to bear the burden of the transfer of wealth by poor terms of trade to support high living standards in First and Second World countries, or had to fight against direct colonial exploitation of this wealth, as in Vietnam.

The 'pure' capitalism depicted by Marx did not collapse according to these theorists because it did not exist. First and Second World capitalist governments were able to come out of crises because imperialism gave them colonies to exploit; social democracy allowed some distribution of mitigating wealth and Keynesian policies gave them indirect tools of redistribution. This was enough to pacify the class struggle in such countries.

Third world capitalist countries such as Brazil had no such leeway and surplus to spend. They often had to resort to internal force and National Security states to maintain themselves. There was only enough in this world system of surplus extraction for the Third World élites to benefit, not the masses. They thus became the tools and agents of the world system, not 'their own nation'.

Now, to communist analysts, the world capitalist system has risen above this post-war three-tier world system. Driven by its inexorable desire for more, and faced with a business crisis and a decline in profits, the First and Second World welfare state is now too expensive for capitalism to maintain. Based generally upon Lenin's theory of uneven development, this argument indicates there will be:

(a) a *transfer of industry* to cheaper labour countries by international capitalism;

(b) a *decline in welfarism* in First and Second World countries, due to a middle class tax revolt and the decline of the nation state to a local administrative body for world capitalism. Government will become less concerned with equity and more with management;

(c) all this is made possible, by the growth of *a dual labour economy* and social acceptance of this division. The working class becomes divided between skilled, highly paid labour with firm tenure and high wages, and semi-skilled and unskilled labour floating in and out of contract part-time and casual labour.

This is exacerbated in First and Second World economies by the quickening substitution of machinery for labour and the arrival of a 'Third Wave' post industrial consciousness[42] de-emphasising the factory, blue collar image of the worker and pushing a highly individualistic and alienating 'post-modernist' philosophy which argues that reality is confined to the individual alone. The working class becomes defined as those who possess jobs, and who are increasingly conservative in practice.

Eventually, this division has an impact on the *union movement* itself. Recognising full employment as a mirage, more and more unions turn to co-operation with management to maintain the hierarchy of labour and its wage levels. This is aided by a world-wide turn to the American-style company enterprise union,[43] encouraging a wider focus upon their enterprise productivity alone, rather than a nation-wide concept of a basic wage for all.

In these circumstances, a 'class' awareness declines amongst the employed, with consciousness tied immediately to the firm or self. Disciplining the workforce is easy and wild variations in living standards emerge and are accepted. Andre Gorz's 'South Africanisation' of Western economies emerges with a 'knowledge' class, on top and a 'serf' class serving them.[44]

On the other hand, radicalisation increases amongst the marginalised and disaffected workers, while social democracy, in these circumstances, declines as an option in the First and Second World countries. The crisis impacting upon these countries simply deepens the already existing contradictions. Communism moves forward.

But how true is this communist prognosis of capitalist crisis, particularly in the light of the demise of the USSR and the subsequent prestige of communism as an ideology? As Martin points out,[45] many elements stand in contradiction to the communist thesis:

(a) The First and Second World working class is not powerless in this scenario. The extension of the franchise has made it difficult if not suicidal for politicians to implement the exclusionary and selective policies as outlined above.

(b) If the power of the franchise is true, then it is unlikely that mass or even partial immiseration is the future for the Western working class. There may instead be reconstruction of the meaning of work, work sharing and massive re-education, along with movements towards workers' control of their employment.

The expansion of the boundaries of democratic action is limited only by a failure of the imagination.

Response to the challenge of industrial change may indeed be more possible in the Western systems than the communist with their one-party states — a challenge with which many communists have only just begun to grapple following the collapse of Soviet power.

Communism in Power: The Problem of the Party

Communists have always claimed that of all the socialist and anarchist movements of the Left, only the Marxist-Leninist have been successful in snatching power and creating 'really existing' socialist societies.

While there would be much argument amongst socialists as to what constitutes the true doctrine, and whether communism has simply created different nationally attuned forms of state capitalism, there is undeniably truth in the historical role of Marxist-Leninists in 'snatching power'.

The major reason for this success has been the role of the party as a revolutionary tool. In this, it has been highly efficient. The major problem that follows a communist revolution has been, however, the continuing monopoly of political power by the party, particularly by its inner oligarchy. The whole problem reduces to organisation. When should the militants be organised and when should they be disbanded and the mass socialist movement be trusted to take over (an initiative tried with disastrous results — at least for old-fashioned communism — by Gorbachev)?

As Milibrand points out:

> organisation is created by revolution but creates problems for (continuing) revolution ... if an organization has state power, there tends to emerge a privileged stratum in the party and in state structures who develop interests that are not identical with those who are direct producers.[46]

As Friedman points out, the whole problem of organisation has bedevilled the socialist movement since the debates of the First and Second Internationals. In the First International, or meeting of world-wide Left organisations, the Marxists defeated the Anarchists and stressed the role of an organised party in achieving the revolution. In the Second International, the debate was largely between Mensheviks and Bolsheviks. Lenin carried the day for the narrowly organised, professional band of revolutionaries rather than the Menshevik desire for a mass party that anyone could join.[47]

The Bolshevik model of party had two specific purposes: first, the achievement of a revolution leading to world socialism, and, second, a peculiar response to the radical nationalist state demands of pre-World War I Russia.

The second factor won most adherents, even though the initial drive to join the party may have been the call of socialist ideology. The radical nationalist state path explains the triumph of Stalin over Trotsky after Lenin's death. However, for further elaboration of how important this factor is in turning the party from socialism or mass democracy onto the path of state capitalism, Wallerstein's 'world systems' core/periphery theory and the arguments of Lonsdale Brown and Tylecote will be utilised.[48]

The essence of core/periphery theory is that the world system of political states is in constant motion, ascending to or descending from First, Second or Third World status. These stages are referred to as core, semi-periphery (or semi-core) and periphery nations. All such states compete or co-operate for position, and aim for the core, or dominant stage, where they are finally secure.

Dominant positioning can come two ways: by economic dominance (economic empire) or by political dominance (military empire).

Some countries, such as the USA, are core economic nations. Others, such as Britain, have slipped historically and economically to secondary core positions. Others lie along a spectrum of semi-periphery (partly developed) to peripheral countries, dependent on raw commodities, often in monoculture (such as Sri Lankas' tea). Other countries, such as South Korea are on the rise. Others achieve only 'political' empire (the former USSR), and depend on their armed forces and a tightly disciplined state for their position in the international hierarchy of states. They are, however, economically uncompetitive compared with a 'core' economic empire such as the USA. In terms of an attractive consumer society, political empires cannot gain much prestige, as they depend on force and a closed society to keep their population's discontent at manageable levels.

Most of the capitalist world is integrated in the twentieth century into this world capitalist system. The only way to rise for these nations, as long as they are capitalist, is to co-operate with, and accept integration. But this also means the reduction of the national government to a quasi-independence.[49]

According to this scenario, as the national ruling groups collaborate with the demands of international capital, the nation's economy becomes dominated by comprador (agent) capitalists stressing free trade over protection; foreign market oriented farmers and a privileged export commodity trade workforce. Other groups become marginalised and/or excluded. The nation's government becomes an executive for world capital. Its political decisions are judged by capital in the core countries by a fall or rise in its currency price, stock market fluctuations, and investment policy and ratings.

Lonsdale-Brown and Tylecote argue that a socialist revolution[50] breaks this nexus with world capitalism. The political revolution releases forces that give back independence to an internal radical national élite. But this new élite is forced to play the world state game and socialism is relegated to a secondary position. The social revolution that follows is mainly shaped to fit the demands of this international power game.

Essentially this is what happened in Russia in 1917. Tsarist Russia between 1880–1914 was slowly being integrated into European capitalism as a semi–periphery country with some industry. However, it was mainly a raw commodity exporter (e.g. Ukrainian wheat).

World War I alienated the peasantry and workers from the Tsarist ruling groups of merchants, aristocracy and bureaucrats, and the new Bolshevik élite, stressing both socialism and nationalism, swept to power.

But nationalism exacts its own price. The new Marxist/Leninist state became a 'bureaucratic nationalised' one, not a mass democratic socialist society. The very act of entering the international state structure, which cannot be ignored for the sake of survival, reacts back upon the ensuing social revolution.

Economic power becomes linked to the attainment of 'core' status, or some autarchic position. The state becomes strengthened in its role as manager, political motivator and organiser of the political process.

This communist state may approach 'political' empire but it cannot achieve 'economic' empire. To achieve 'economic' empire would require the release of the full productivity of the working class and peasants. To achieve this by a reversion to the capitalist system would be opposed by the Left-wing of the party, and probably the workers themselves. Certainly it would be difficult to sell in the teeth of widespread Marxist teachings.

The other way to achieve full productivity would be for the emergence of workers' control in industry and large-scale rural production. This would be bitterly opposed by the technocratic/ managerial element within the party or the new neo-liberal elite in the new democracies, wedded as it is to bureaucratic management and a suspicion of 'proletarian' democracy. Between these groups are the party members, fearful of such 'Right' and 'Left' experiments in a world divided between two camps, the capitalist and socialist. Experiments like these, diminishing party control, would simply invite military intervention from the capitalist world as in Russia in 1919–22. No change launched by the party can therefore go far enough. A peculiar stagnation ensues.

The party is in a dilemma. It sees itself as the shield of socialism. In a core/periphery world, however, it must build up the power of the state to compete with and neutralise powerful capitalist states. The party thus becomes integrated with the state. Rather than dismantling it, it strengthens it. It becomes as committed to growth, as Bahro indicates, as any capitalist system. It will also 'violently resist attempts to transform (the system) in a socialist direction'.[51]

The older the regime becomes the less likely it will be to fulfil its original socialist promise, as the new generation of bureaucracy has been brought up to regard Marxism as a smokescreen to justify privileged élite rule,[52] whose aim is state strength. This is not lost on the masses who often become alienated from the whole system.

The demands of the managerial hierarchical state are always in contradiction with the ideology of Marxism, with its broad demcratic thrust. Using the justification of the demands of the Cold War and capitalist intervention, the socialist future is postponed.

But the party is always faced with tension and further dilemma because of this position. Instead of post-capitalist history being a test of socialist democracy and the existence of Marxist theory, interacting with practice, motivated by the aim of emancipating the people,[53] the aim becomes identified with the good of the party. The working class is identified with government decisions.[54] 'Once one loses sight of that telos [aim] then one may use any criterion one likes for judging practice.'[55]

The dilemma deepens, however, as the ideology is the justification for the system. The party must use Marxism as the catechism and rationale for power. Yet this same catechism preaches ultimate worker control and equality. It supplies the very ideas of equality that have been used against it (e.g. Poland in 1981).[56] Yet the ideas of worker equality cannot be fulfilled in an internationally competitive state system. The party is thus caught between duty to its national state role and duty to its socialist role.

The deterministic power of the core-periphery world of states has thus far dictated the dominance of the national state.[57] However, the internal tensions, with a restive working class which has been promised the future, are enormous. 'As libertarian and left communists of the 1920s/30s predicted, anti-bureaucratic movements would be endemic in a Party which was leader focused and not responsive to the masses.'[58]

With this dilemma in mind — how much to build the state in its pursuit of safety as a 'core' nation, and how much to fulfil internal hopes for (true) socialism and freedom for its working class — the erratic governing path of communist parties can be traced. As Friedman indicates, some bought off internal dissatisfaction by increasing internal capitalism and consumerism (former Communist Hungary). Others have allowed levels of workers' control and industrial democracy to integrate the regime with the people (former Communist Yugoslavia). Others have released worker tension with the regime by unleashing massive criticism of bureaucratic tendencies within the party (e.g. China, during The Great Proletarian Cultural Revolution of 1966–76). The collapse of the Stalinist communist states in Eastern Europe and the Soviet Union itself (1989–91) has introduced new contending elements such as a revival of capitalism and nationalism. These two streams also raise dilemmas for the remaining communist movements. Should the party join the nationalist upsurge as in present-day Serbia in order to preserve the socialist structure? If so, what then of the internationalism of the working class? Will this not lead to national socialism and racism as observed under Hitler? Will the capitalist be long in manipulating such disunity? If the capitalist system is reintroduced (as in China, Russia, Poland) is not the party introducing a class enemy, a viper in its bosom? Some point to the Tienanmen Square confrontation (1990) as an outcome of this policy. The capitalist road should be abandoned. Others argue the necessity for capitalism to re-emerge. The party will benefit from the marginal economic efficiency of small entrepreneurial firms. It will also benefit as workers and peasants feel the arrogance and power of capitalist bosses and private property at all levels. This will be reflected in a resurge of support for a new democratic communist party e.g. Polish electors in 1991. (This last position is a revival of the 1918 Menshevik position).

A short case study of China will exemplify this pull between the needs of the state and the need to achieve socialism, showing their effects on the course of the Chinese Communist Party.

China: A Case Study

The Chinese Communist Party was formed in Shanghai in 1922. At first it was urban, based upon a new coalition of classes that had been in formulation since the May 4th Movement of 1919. This stemmed largely from the student population of China. Beginning in Peking as a reaction to demands made upon the nation by the Japanese in 1915, and the craven reaction of the Chinese warlords to these demands, the May 4th Movement was a massive nationalist reaction of the alienated intelligentsia. This intelligentsia had rejected the previously dominant ideology of Confucianism and was searching for a new Chinese cultural and political synthesis which would incorporate concepts of Western progress, give China independence and dignity in the world of nations, and at the same time be free of the domination of Western ideas. Marxism-Leninism was judged the ideal creed.

Because it was of Western origin, it fostered notions of Western progress. It was also acceptable to the Chinese as it was rejected and feared by the Western core countries themselves. It also provided concepts that could unite the intelligentsia and the masses. Since it was anti-colonial and anti-capitalist, it united both the nationalist and the social rebel.[59] But most of all it promised a way forward for a state that had reached the bottom of the core-periphery ladder.[60]

China in the late nineteenth and early twentieth centuries was in the process of dismemberment by European and Japanese colonialists. Spheres of interest had been carved out by various powers. These enclaves were developed by the foreign powers in partnership with collaborating classes of warlords and comprador (foreign agent) city merchants, particularly in the port cities.

A helpless imperial government presided over this dismemberment. The burden of loan debts, foreign extortions and court upkeep fell increasingly upon a peasantry already racked by landlordism.

The old ruling coalition of China, the Confucian scholar gentry, the warrior class and the landlords, were increasingly rendered obsolete by this imperialism. No new coalitions seeking to retain Chinese independence had yet emerged. What was needed was a cultural revolution, which the May 1st Movement provided:

> The majority of people had reached such a rock bottom of misery that they had nowhere to go but up. The release of this mighty energy of raw human hope could only occur if the people could recognize their own misery. A worn out culture gave them no such transcendental power and illiteracy no such instrument. The first mission of the May 4th Movement (radicals) came clear to them. It was to hold up to the people a mirror of their own misery and to clear the cobwebs of 4,000 years by showing them they could remake their own existence.[61]

In core/periphery theory, the Chinese revolution was caused by the desire of radical nationalists to reformulate an independent minded coalition of forces so that China could regain her rightful place in the world pantheon of states. The old wornout class of imperialist collaborators had to be swept away.

To other social theorists, however, the Chinese revolution was a cultural one. The political and social revolution occurred together, unlike during the Russian Revolution.

The Chinese Revolution was quite early taken out of the hands of the traditional intelligentsia and the Russian-model communists, with the smashing of urban-based communism in 1926 by the

Kuomintang nationalist armies. Under Chiang Kaishek, the Kuomintang, based upon the urban merchant class and country landlords, turned upon their erstwhile anti-Japanese and anti-warlord communist allies.

Communism survived only in the mountains under Mao Tse-tung. The subsequent period of peasant communism saw ideology centre upon the role of peasant in the revolution. The party had to motivate the peasant rather than the urban worker. The peasant was community based, not state orientated. The state was seen traditionally as something alien and oppressive belonging to the useless cities and urban civilisation.

The success of the Revolution of 1949 brought to power a party based largely upon the writing of Mao Tse-tung, who stressed the role of the revolutionary will, of men against machines, and of the individuals who made up society, rather than the primacy of the state.

The success of the Revolution, however, thrust the party, at the helm of the Chinese state, into the tough world of competitive states.

The 'two line'[62] struggle began immediately between the modernisers, and those forces advocating Chinese socialism based upon peasant experience, the Yenan Way.

During the 1950s, the 'New Democracy' period of mixed private/socialised property and a market plan economy was followed by a copy of the Russian Stalinist model of a centrally planned economy. This was found to be ill suited to Chinese conditions[63] because it emphasised heavy industry at the expense of agriculture which had little surplus to give. The Maoist Left of the Chinese Communist Party was convinced that a Russian-style urban exploitation of its own countryside was at hand. They were convinced that urban classes, including the new expert technocrats, the bureaucracy and party Right-wing 'capitalist roaders' were prepared to sacrifice the peasant in order to play the international states game.

The consequences for society due to this 'Right' adjustment of the Stalinist model[64] (1957, 1961–65) would be the reemergence of class stratification and privilege. This convinced Mao and the Left that they faced not merely a difference in development strategy, but a profound political struggle over the future shape of Chinese society.[65]

The Stalinist model was subjected to a 'Left' adjustment in 1958–60 and particularly during the Great Proletarian Cultural Revolution (1966–76). This 'adjustment' closed China to most foreign technology and influences (including those from the USSR). It moved China away from 'growth' *per se*, with a commitment to industrialism, towards a system emphasising peasant consumers self-sufficient in both industry and agriculture. This was the no-market, no-plan egalitarian solution of the Maoist Left.[66]

But the world system of contending states does not allow for a nation to opt out of the system of trade or to stand still in a world of fearsome military technological growth.

In 1976, Mao died. Soon after his death, the state was taken over by the 'modernisers' under Deng Xioping. Dedicated to a 'core' great power China, this faction turned towards the 'capitalist road' so execrated by Mao.

As Prybyla goes on to indicate, between 1978–86, the commune system was largely dismantled and industrialisation became the major aim of the regime. Private ownership of the land was partly restored, causing the decline of collective property such as irrigation systems, soil improvement schemes and even the health of the peasants themselves. Beggars and rich peasants have re-emerged in China.

The problem for the party engaged in this socialism and modernisation mission is, of course, how far to go in the dismantling of both the Maoist and underlying Stalinist system without reducing China to new foreign dependence on investment and 'becoming simply another modernising technocracy without a guiding socialist vision'.

How can the party on the 'capitalist road' avoid demands for concomitant 'bourgeois liberalism' from rising market capitalists? If these are acceded to, how can the party avoid criticism from the poor worker and peasant, and perhaps a future revolution? How can it avoid demands for worker's control against the very capitalists who are being resurrected? Marxism and the egalitarianism of the Cultural Revolution have bitten too deep for the party to purge society of egalitarian sentiment. The Left still exists.

The problem for the party is that it cannot gain 'core' nation or superpower status by following the capitalist road unless it frees the market of its political controls. If it does this, it must use the state to hold down resulting worker and poor peasant unrest. It must be prepared to face unrest also within its own ideological ranks. It may in fact have to face the abdication of power to a Western-style democracy, perhaps dominated politically by a rising rich peasant/capitalist class. This would be unacceptable to the party's vision of itself.

On the other hand to continue Maoist policies or any such socialist egalitarian policies such as the 'iron pot', whereby all workers have egalitarian wages and virtually life tenure on jobs, would hold back Chinese development and productivity. A secure socialist-based workforce is unlikely to work overhard without the fear of unemployment. Such policies would mean Chinese failure in the superpower economic stakes. The party would similarly be a hindrance to worker's control anarcho/ syndicalist developments. Either way, the party represents a hindrance to development on either the Left or the Right.

Australian Communism

As Marx wrote in the 'Eighteenth Brumaire of Louis Bonaparte,' 'Men make their own history but they do not make it just as they please ... but under circumstances directly encountered, given and transmitted from the past'. Australian Communism has been no exception to the order of things 'transmitted from the past'. Australian communism emerged within a peculiar society. This was a society, as McQueen outlines,[67] where

(a) derivativeness and dependence were unavoidable;
(b) the content of this unavoidable dependence was loaded with racism and materialism;
(c) society was closed to non-mainstream dependency ideas.

The 'working man's paradise' ideal[68] has dominated the mainstream of Australian political culture throughout the nineteenth and twentieth centuries. Alternative ideals were depicted as alien, un-Australian and destabilising.

Australian communism, therefore, has emerged as a marginalised creed. This was largely due to the 'ease of the success of Australian capitalism' producing a Second World economy within a secure, dependent Deakinite system. The political economy of Australia as a Second World country meant a First World standard of living for most (with significant exceptions, e.g. Aboriginals) within an economy based upon Third World dependence upon commodities such as minerals.

'The practical success of Australian capitalism [was largely painless] because of [Australia's] special position within the world capitalist system.'[69] This success rested upon the four foundations of the Deakinite state — racism; arbitration/wage indexation; protection and dependency. The key factor in this state's stability, where centre politics dominated 'stressing enlightened middle class liberalism and moderate labour [walking] hand in hand with the President of the Conciliation and Arbitration Court ...'[70] was the dependency factor. This determined the style of historical development in several periods of Australian history to which the state builders of the particular period responded and reacted, whether they came from Left or Right.[71]

Politicians in Australian history openly stressed the desirability of a close foreign relationship with a core country so that 'for almost the entire period of [Australian] existence as a European settlement, Australia has been the privileged [client] of the world's leading capitalist nation'. This factor has led directly to the rise and security of the Deakinite state. This state is thus primarily a product of '... the class structure of [international] monopoly capitalism and not merely an [outcome] of the internal class structure'.[72]

The existence of such a dependency has led to the success of Deakinism. The success over eighty years of such a state in ordering and satisfying society (with merely some lapses) has had three major effects on the development of communism and other Left radicalism in Australia:

(a) there has been great difficulty in communism *breaking out of a vanguard position*. Contact with the mass working class has been discontinuous from the earliest development of radical, non-Labor Party thought in the last century.[73] Labourism has dominated working class loyalty, which has reflected one side of the dominant ideological mixture of fused liberalism and social democracy which has been the major value out-growth of Deakinism;

(b) only in periods of *great external traumas* like World War I, the Great Depression or the Vietnam War has this closed Deakinism been disturbed. But until now — the age of the Pacific Basin restructuring — it has never been dismantled.[74]

Alternative radical thought in these periods has been able to penetrate some way into the consciousness of the Australian working class and the radical middle class on the backs of anti-conscription, radical economic nationalism and anti-imperialism. This point can be exemplified by a quote from Lloyd Ross[75] in V. Burgmann's *Revolutionaries and Racists*:

Labor's leaders were stunned by World War I (for example) as they lacked an intellectual basis for an independent attitude in foreign affairs. And the unions ... were absorbed in daily routine, saturated with craft outlooks which kept apart the different unions and were full of satisfaction ... because of recent social reforms.

(c) Thus Australian communism has oscillated between *liquidationism*, or the frustrated belief that the party should disband and join the ALP to strengthen its Left wing due to worker satisfaction with the existing system and apathy or antipathy to the communist creed, and *mass party building*.[76] There have been periods when communist party popularity has risen due to its image of patriotism or its positive image in the light of some external trauma (e.g. World War II, and the popularity then of the USSR.), but usually the party has been marginalised and ineffective.

A middle position for Australian communism has been to see itself as the Left 'think tank'. Its influence has been believed by many of its members to be greater than its electoral impact due to the dearth of theory in Labor Party circles and the ease with which alternative communist programs appear to have become the program of the ALP Left. This Trojan horse self-image has not proved satisfying for many of its members desirous of effective political power, rather than existence as a pressure group.

The future of Marxism in Australia, if not Marxism-Leninism, as typified by the Communist Party is linked intrinsically to the type of change that may occur in the Deakinite state. Changes in this state may be happening due to world capital change, Pacific Basin restructuring and any concomitant working class dissatisfaction, and may open society to alternative creeds both from Marxism, the New Right and other hitherto radical ideologies, such as the Greens.

The Australian state has always been the key to society, as uniquely 'from 1788 onwards there has been a strong control administration whose function it has been to fashion a society around it'.[77] The state has serviced the 'closed' society it has created under Deakinism. But as the contemporary state of the late twentieth century is forced to change, society will follow. The instincts of traditional Labor and Liberal parties is to search for another dependency — as in the present emphasis upon Asian Studies generally and Japan in particular — to maintain the centrist hegemony. If this is not forthcoming with the same sureties of the Deakinite era, then Australia may be facing a new and different era where 'true' capitalism not Deakinism creates the same classic capitalist two nations of a core/periphery (underclass) society so reflective of societies such as the USA. In this situation, with the Australian historical legacy of unionism and radicalism, new alliances of left socialist thought could re-emerge — this time (with the absence of Deakinism) as an effective political force.

A new world order is emerging in response to contemporary forces just as in 1917. A new world order was predicated on the forces unleashed by the Russian Revolution. The Australian Communist Party was a response to that historical conjuncture of forces.

Communist Party Development in Australia

The Australian Communist Party was formed in 1920. Many of its original numbers came from a background of anarcho/syndicalism, groups such as the International Workers of the

World (IWW) plus small Marxist groups, especially the Socialist Labor Party and the Australian Socialist Party. Such groups already had Marxist theory as a large part of their background. Others joined with a Fabian social democrat background.

The first difficulty facing Australian communism, therefore, was the formation of a tightly-organised Bolshevik (Leninist)-style party according to the principles of Marxist-Leninist ideology and organisation. By 1925, this was achieved largely by the Communist Party directing its work to the trade unions, and by expelling those who would not conform to democratic centralism,[78] or who still retained anarcho/syndicalist and social democratic ideas.

The post-World War I period saw a downturn in radical politics. The impact of the 1890s Depression and the conscription issues of World War I had declined. Australia in the 1920s was prosperous. With this prosperity came the cyclic problem for radical alternatives, as the Deakinite state started to mollify and reward the working class upon which communism based its hopes.

Nevertheless, the indirect influence of the Communist Party via its ideas and its popular trade union leaders built its pressure group power in this period far beyond the actual numbers of its members. Communism became marked as a symbolic threat to the reigning social ideology of a loyal 'working man's paradise', for the first time. Both Labor and conservatives politicians reacted to this new phenomenon.

In 1924, communists were banned from holding dual membership in the Labor Party. Indeed, such leading Labor politicians as J. Lang were to wage war on them with equal, if not more, virulence, than they were to wage it against conservatives.

During the late 1920s,[79] the Conservative Bruce-Page government constantly raised the spectre of the Red Menace. Legislation was passed under the guise of fighting Bolshevism which sought to abolish the Commonwealth Arbitration Court. The conservatives, however, had over-reacted and attacked one of he bases of the Deakinite state, and the Bruce-Page Government fell in the election of 1929.

Communism as a radical ideology could survive within Australian society as long as it stayed within the boundaries of the Deakinite state. This limitation was to be a source of frustration for the future of communism, forcing it more and more into the role of a trade union-based pressure group party dependent upon a number of hard-working union leaders, rather than a wide mass party with support from all social strata.

The external traumas of the Depression of 1929–40 and World War II greatly aided the expansion of Communist Party membership, which stood at 20,000 in 1943, but they did nothing to enhance its electoral success. Some communists were elected (e.g. Fred

Patterson for Bowen, Qld), largely for local reasons. Working class loyalty was still given to the ALP led by Curtin and Chifley during the war and in the immediate postwar period.

Communism in the World War II period was seen by the mass of Australians as loyal to the Australian state,[80] as they were wholeheartedly behind the fight against Fascism. Communism followed a United Front policy, which stressed the alliance of the Communist Party with the Left wing of the ALP. By following a policy of 'unity from below' it was hoped to align the militant members of the ALP with the Communist Party. With time, the initiative of leadership would pass to communists, along with the spread of class consciousness and Marxism-Leninism. The ALP leadership could then be bypassed.

The period from 1945–65 in Australia was, in fact, disastrous for Australian communism. The rise of Catholic Social Movement opposition to communism within the Labor Party confronted the 'unity from below' program within the trade unions, ALP branches and other working class organisations. This was ultimately to precipitate the great Labor Party Split of 1954–55 which led to the birth of the Democratic Labor Party. The DLP was able to gain enough electoral support to be prominent in excluding Labor from Federal power until 1972.

One major reason for communist decline was the return of Deakinite stability to Australia, helped along with the new Keynesian economic tools and the rise of the welfare state. The Menzies era of 1949–65 reflected the high point of the success of internal Deakinism helped by the new external hegemony of American Pacific domination and the return of Japanese economic demand in the 1960s for Australian commodities.

For Australian communism, the objective factors of the Menzies era were allied to the rise of the first 'Cold War' (1951–65). Australian communism lost its wartime image as a loyal assistant and was increasingly depicted as a disloyal enemy of the Australian suburban way of life. This followed similar 'Cold War' ideological attacks throughout the West, aimed at marginalising not just communism, but all socialisms.

The battle was largely a battle of symbols and ideals. The Australian way of life was depicted as fused liberal conservatism, built around the nuclear family. Australia was 'congratulated for lacking a revolutionary heritage'.[81]

Communism for its part fought back in the battle of images by stressing an alternative radical image of Australia, built around the rebelliousness of the Eureka diggers and Ned Kelly. 'The bushman was given a specific socialist heritage.'[82]

For a time, this emphasis on working class rebellion provided a lusty, but ultimately sterile and sexist image, which had already been obsolescent in largely urban Australia by the 1920s. With massive post-war migration, a massive cultural emphasis on Henry Lawson was also in danger of becoming Anglo-chauvinist.

In 1951, the Menzies government felt the rejection of communism had become widespread enough to ask for a referendum to ban the party after the High Court had rejected ordinary legislation attempting bans. Like the Bruce-Page government of 1928, however, they had over-reached themselves.

Vigorous propaganda by the Communist Party and by the Labor Party marginally convinced the Australian voter that this action overstepped the boundaries of the Deakinite state, and would eventually be aimed at the worker's broad movement.

The Menzies referendum was defeated. Communism would stay. But increasingly it was confined to the position of a trade union pressure group.

The Australian Communist Party, like other communist parties in advanced capitalist countries, began a slow decline in the Keynesian era from 1956–85. Apart from the existence of a long Western war boom and Keynesian governmentalism stimulating prosperity, the Australian party was faced with internal problems linked to its internationalism, a Left wing dependency problem unique to Communist parties.

Khruschev's denunciation of Stalin's crimes and the Russian invasion of Hungary in 1956 caused a crisis of faith for many members. Russian imperialism seemed little different to that of the West. Hungary seemed a case of national communism wishing to follow a neutral road in its development outside the NATO/ Warsaw Pact 'Great Power' confrontation. The Russian army crushed this phenomenon brutally.

But the denunciation of Stalin had the greatest impact on membership, bringing with it a crisis of faith in Stalinism itself as a mode of Marxist-Leninst ideology.

Although the Australian Communist Party took a leading role in the anti-Vietnam War movement of 1965–75, much of the increasing radicalisation of youth in this period was bled off into New Left movements, rather than into increased membership for the party. Many of the Vietnam period radicals, were significantly middle class. They reflected Australia's cultural dependency (this time on the Left) in their almost slavish reproduction of American New Left issues, attitudes and tactics. To them the Communist Party was old-fashioned, undemocratic and riddled with bureaucratism.

The Vietnam radicals were largely steeped in notions of participatory democracy and direct action, reflecting similarities to pre-communist radicals such as the anarcho/syndicalist IWW (International Workers of the World).

Like those earlier anarcho syndicalists of the IWW,[83] the New Left drew dependently on American radicalism rather than the Russian model of the Communist Party. The Cold War thus polarised even modes of protest, while the ALP remained steadfastedly Australian, at least in the minds of its mass following.

The 1968 invasion of Czechoslovakia by the Russians, however, was to produce the deepest split. The Communist Party of Australia condemned the invasion. The USSR was accused of great power chauvinism. It had again interfered in a socialist bloc country, this time (unlike in Hungary in 1956) rather bloodlessly to put down national communist and 'liberal' developments.

Under Party secretary Dubcek, the Czechoslovak Communist Party tried to develop 'socialism with a human face'. This action program contained an attack on bureaucracy and other 'distortions' which the increasingly 'liberal' Australian Communist Party supported.

This development was opposed as disloyalty to the USSR and communist internationalism by a minority of members. In 1971, these broke away to form the pro-Moscow Socialist Party of Australia.

An earlier smaller split had occurred at the time of the Sino-Soviet dispute, in 1962. A small Maoist party, the Communist Party of Australia (Marxist-Leninist) was formed by breakaway members of the party.

By 1975, therefore, three communist parties existed, as well as various Trotskyite sects. Sectarian marginalisation seemed to be the common future of all these parties and sects. Even though one of the greatest radical periods in Australian history had occurred due to the external trauma of the Vietnam War, the electoral and membership benefits of this were largely of benefit to a resurgent ALP.

The Deakinite state was still intact except for its 'white Australia' policies. Under its protection, the Australian working class was still content with centre politics and home-grown parties of moderate liberal/social democrat radicalism.

Like the American New Left, the Australian New Left remained based largely on students and the middle class. The blue collar worker was not interested in radical change. Radicalism barely penetrated a class rendered, according to Marcuse[84] 'quiescent by a lack of repression and drained of any remaining revolutionary propensity by the prevailing sexual license'. Radical politics thus barely penetrated trade unions steeped in anti-theoretical craft unionism and inured to their role as part of the management of the Deakinite state.

Australian communism in the 1970s began to reject its Stalinist past. Euro-communist ideas, stressing a more social democratic/

pluralist base rather than the traditional working class, which was increasingly difficult to define, began to influence theory. Emphasis upon ex-consensus groups such as Aboriginals, on feminist issues, on gay liberation and environmentalism, emerged. None of these policy changes reversed, however, the decline in the party influence or membership.

Australian communism has failed to take root either as a major ideology or a party with electoral power. This had led to frustration and fragmentation within it, particularly in the long post-war boom, from approximately 1950–75. The collapse of the USSR was a final push leading to the demise of the CPA which, in 1990, formally closed down.

Under the Deakinite state, Australia has emerged as a 'closed society'. The working class, at whom the Communist Party aimed its programs, has been largely dominated by labourism and seems content with the boundaries of the Deakinite system.

However, as McQueen states, 'Australian society has been largely built around its state not *vice versa.*' This is extremely unusual as it is generally the changing nature of society that brings forth a state.[85] The Australian state produced Deakinism. The state was mainly needed to provide services for a largely suburban nation.[86] Now, due to external pressure, the state which created the original closed Deakinite society eighty years ago, is changing the foundations again under the ALP.

In the 1980s, Australian economy and society is restructuring towards the Pacific Basin.[87] The foundation of Deakinism — protectionism, arbitration/wage indexation, racist policies — are all undergoing change. These changes will also mean a parallel change in the Australian political system and/or traditional values. The emergence of the 'New Right' has already borne this out.

For the remnants of Australian communism, like the rest of the Australian traditional Left, the danger is that they may be locked into defending a disappearing Deakinite system, thus losing both the theoretical and political initiative.

Suter points out three factors influencing contemporary politics (taking his lead from Alvin Toffler's book, *The Third Wave* (1980) which argues that the industrialism which bred both capitalism and communism is over).[88] These factors are:

(a) the decline of the role of the nation state;
(b) the rise of transnational capitalism;
(c) the proliferation of people's power, non-governmental social movements at local levels in particular, built about 'issues' rather than 'classes'.

For communism in Australia these changes mean several options:

(a) Australian communism(s) can cling to their historical radical sectarian positions. This will mean slow decline. However, they may still have some influence on ideas and programs in their traditional role as 'think tank' to the Labor Left. This position will involve a defence of a disappearing historical phase, Deakinism, and the Keynesian welfare state. The position is, therefore, essentially conservative and defensive.

(b) Conversely, Australian communism may follow the former Soviet exhortation for all parties to adapt to national analyses.

This entails 'liquidationism'. This would mean the disbandment of the party and the dispersal of members and funds into other radical parties or into the ALP.

(c) As the New Right presses for a new conservative party to the Right of the present Liberal Party, many Left observers[89] argue for a similar development. A radical party should be formed to occupy the Left position on the political spectrum being vacated by an increasingly conservative Labor Party.

Both Labor and coalition governments (so the argument runs) are dismantling the Deakinite state. In so doing, they are exposed as state liberal, free trade parties. (As Suter argues,[90] this is unavoidable as the nation state is declining in power and must conform to the demands of world capitalism.)

However, the traditional working class vote will be alienated by this change in its traditional party. For the first time since 1920, Australian radical ideology, if not necessarily Marxism or Marxism/Leninism, may have a real chance to penetrate as an alternative ideology.

For, unlike the Great Depression or World War 11, the anchor of solid dependent links to a core country on which to base social democrat or state liberal policy, offering the junior partner trading and security treatment, does not exist.

Many radicals believe increasing sections of the Australian community face exclusion and radicalisation as Keynesianism and Australian Deakinism decline as economic and historically viable tools. The New Right (its critics say) has no answer to this but vague pre-Keynesian market economies. This can scarcely prevent a growth of radicalism.

Whether the best instrument for this is a new radical party, a broad Left coalition or a Rainbow movement, is left open. Whatever occurs, many Australian communists believe a unique historical opportunity[91] has arrived for communism or radical Left action to break out of its marginalisation.

Notes

1. Kaplan, Morton, A. (ed.) *The Many Faces of Communism*. NY, Free Press 1978, p. 23.
2. Duverger, M. *Political Parties* Third Edition. London, Methuen, 1978.
3. Bullock, A. and Stallybrass, O. *The Fontana Dictionary of Modern Thought*. UK, Fontana/Collins, 1977, p. 117.
4. Heilbronner, R. *The Worldly Philosophers*. UK, Penguin, 1980, p. 118.
5. Brugger, B. *Practice, Praxos and Pragmatism*: On the Correct, Handling of Maos 'On Practice', Australasian Political Studies Association Conference, Brisbane, Australia, August 1986, p. 8.
6. Heilbronner, p. 108.
7. Chiou, L. *Maoism in Action: The Cultural Revolution*. Queensland, University of Queensland Press, 1974.
8. Martin, J. *A Guide to Marxism*. NY, St Martin's Press, 1980, p. 141.
9. Marx, K. *Theses on Feuerbach* in Feuer, L.S. *Marx & Engels*: Basic Writings on Philosophy & Politics. p. 286.
10. Cole, G.D.H. *The Meaning of Marxism*. Michigan, University of Michigan, 1964, p. 152.
11. Engels, F. *Socialism: Utopian and Scientific* in Feuer, L.S. Marx and Engels: Basic Writings on Philosoply and Politics. NY, Doubleday, 1959, p. 127.
12. Marx, K. *Theses on Feuerbach* in Feuer, p. 283.
13. Engels, R. *On Historical Materialism* in Feuer, p. 90.
14. Sargent, L.T. *Contemporary Political Ideologies* Fifth Edition. Illinois, Dorsey Press, 1969, p. 29.
15. Marx, K. *Critique of Political Economy* in Feuer, p. 84.
16. Heilbronner, p. 111.
17. Cole, p. 272.
18. Ibid.
19. Cole, p. 273.
20. Cole, p. 274.
21. Marx, K. *Critique of Political Economy* in Feuer, p. 85.
22. Heilbronner, p. 113.
23. Groth, A.J. *Major Ideologies*. NY, John Wiley, 1971, pp. 74–75.
24. Ibid.
25. Marx, K. *Manifesto of the Communist Party* in Feuer, p. 55.
26. Bullock, and Stallybrass, p. 325.
27. Frolich, P. *Rosa Luxemburg*. Frankfurt, Europaische Verlagsunstalt, 1967, p. 108.
28. Sargent, p. 47.
29. Frolich, pp. 104–05.
30. Deutscher, I. *The Unfinished Revolution*: Russia 1917–67. NY, Oxford University Press, 1967.
31. Brugger, p. 17.
32. Martin, p. 79.
33. Roberts, J.M. *The Trimph of the West*, London, BBC Publications, 1985, p. 170.
34. Kaplan, p. 342.
35. Kaplan, p. 346.
36. Heilbronner, pp. 126–130.
37. Ibid.
38. Ibid.
39. Samuelson, P.A. *Economics* Sixth Edition. NY, McGraw-Hill, 1964, p. 255.
40. 'Big Depression on Way' *Courier Mail*, Queensland, 12 December 1986.
41. Gough, J. *The Political Economy of the Welfare State*. London, Macmillan, 1979.
42. Suter, K. 'A New International Order' *New Leaves* 78, December 1986, Queensland, pp. 15–18.

43. Blandy, R. 'How we can make this country work better with enterprise unions' *National Times on Sunday* 19 January 1987.
44. Gorz, A. *Paths to Paradise*. London, Pluto Press, 1985.
45. Martin, pp. 130–44.
46. Milibrand, R. in Friedman, E. (ed.) *Ascent and Decline in the World System* Vol. 5. London, Sage, 1986, p. 294.
47. Milibrand, p. 290.
48. Friedman, pp. 255–72.
49. See Suter.
50. Friedman, E. (ed.) *Ascent and Decline in the World System*. London, Sage, 1986, pp. 255–72.
51. Westoby, A. *Communism Since World War II*. UK, Harvester, 1981, p. XI.
52. Kaplan, p. 24.
53. Brugger, p. 14.
54. Kaplan, p. 24.
55. Martin, p. 110.
56. Laba, R. 'Worker Roots of Solidarity' in *Problems of Communism* July-August 1986, p. 67.
57. Friedman, pp. 255–72.
58. Westoby, p. Xl.
59. Bianco, L. *Origins of the Chinese Revolution*. USA, Stanford University Press, 1967, p. 46.
60. Friedman, pp. 255–72.
61. Leach, R.H. '*The Concept of Struggle in Maoism*', Master of Social Science (Hons) Thesis, University of New England, Australia, 1976, p. 118.
62. Maxwell, N. 'To Get Rich is Glorious' *The Listener* 11 November 1986, pp. 6–7.
63. Prybyla, J.S. 'China's Economic Experiment: From Mao to Market' *Problems of Communism* January-February 1986, p. 21.
64. Ibid.
65. Maxwell, p. 6.
66. Prybyla, p. 25.
67. McQueen, H. 'What's Wrong with Australia?' in Mayer, H. and Nelson, H. (eds) *Australian Politics: A Reader* Fifth Edition. Melbourne, Longman Cheshire, 1980, pp. 74–75.
68. White, R. *Inventing Australia: Images and Identity 1688–1980*. Sydney, Allen and Unwin, 1981.
69. McQueen, p. 74.
70. Fitzpatrick, R. 'The British Empire in Australia' quoted in *Australian Heritage* Vol. 9. Sydney, Lansdowne, p. 1,556.
71. Leach, R. 'The Balkanization of Australia' in *Dyason House Papers* Autumn 1978.
72. McQueen, pp. 73, 75.
73. Burgman, V. 'Revolutionaries and Racists: Australian Socialism and the Problem of Racism 1887–1917', Phd Thesis, ANU, Canberra, 1980, p. 245.
74. Leach, R. 'Right Wing Labor' *Arena* 76, 1986.
75. Ross, Lloyd 'The Role of Labor' in Gruttan, C. Hartley (ed.) *Australia*. University of California Press, 1947, quoted in Burgmann, p. 245.
76. Sharkey, L.L. *An Outline History of the Australian Communist Party*. Sydney, Australian Communist Party, 1944.
77. McQueen, p. 72.
78. Sharkey, pp. 17–19.
79. Maddox, G. *Australian Democracy: Theory and Practice*. Melbourne, Longman Cheshire, 1985, p. 278.
80. Ibid.
81. White, p. 159.
82. White, p. 157.
83. Burgmann, pp. 205–08.

84. Christenson, R.M. *et al. ideologies and Modern Politics* London, Nelson, 1972, p. 293.
85. McQueen, p. 72.
86. Chaples, E. *et al. The Wran Model. Electoral Politics in NSW 1981–1984.* Melbourne, Oxford University Press, 1985.
87. See Leach.
88. Suter, p. 15.
89. McKnight, D. (ed.) *Moving Left.* Sydney, Pluto Press, 1986.
90. Suter, pp. 15–17.
91. Boswell, N. and Hirst, D. 'The Rise of the New Left' *The Australian* 15–16 November 1986.

References

Bianco, L. *Origins of the Chinese Revolution.* USA, Stanford University Press, 1967.
Blandy, R. 'How we can make this country work better with enterprise unions' *National Times on Sunday,* 19 January 1987.
Boswell, N. and Hirst, D. 'The Rise of the New Left' *The Australian* 15–16 November 1986.
Brown, W.J. *The Communist Movement and Australia: An Historical Outline 1890–1980.* Australia, Australian Labor Movement Publications, 1986.
Brugger, B. *Practice, Praxis and Pragmatism: On the Correct Handling of Mao's 'On Practice'* Australian Political Studies Association Conference, Brisbane, Australia, August 1986.
Bullock, A. and Stallybrass, O., *The Fontana Dictionary of Modern Thought,* London, Fontanal Collins, 1977.
Burgmann, V. *'Revolutionaries and Racists:* Australian Socialism and the Problem of Racism 1887–1917', PhD Thesis, ANU, 1980.
Byrne, C. *Communism and Us.* Melbourne, Hawthorn Press, 1964.
Chaples, E. *et al. The Wran Model. Electoral Politics in NSW 1981–1984.* Melbourne, Oxford University Press, 1985.
Christenson, R.M. *et al. Ideologies and Modern Politics.* London, Nelson, 1972.
Chiou, L. *Maoism in Action: The Cultural Revolution.* Queensland, University of Queensland Press, 1974.
Cole, G.D.H. *The Meaning of Marxism.* Michigan, University of Michigan, 1964.
Deutscher, I. *The Unfinished Revolution: Russia 1917–67.* NY, Oxford University Press, 1967.
Duverger, M. *Political Parties* Third Edition. London, Methuen, 1978.
Feuer, L.S. *Marx and Engles: Basic Writings on Philosophy and Politics.* NY, Doubleday, 1959.
Friedman, E. (ed.) *Ascent and Decline in the World System* Vol. 5. London, Sage, 1986.
Frolich, P. *Rosa Luxemburg: Ideas in Action.* Frankfurt, Europaische Verlagsunstalt, 1967.
Gorz, A. *Paths to Paradise.* London, Pluto Press, 1985.
Gough, J. *The Political Economy of the Welfare State.* London, Macmillan, 1979.
Groth, A.J. *Major Ideologies.* NY, John Wiley, 1971.
Heilbronner, R. *The Worldly Philosophers.* UK, Penguin, 1980.
Kaplan, Morton, A. (ed.) *The Many Faces of Communism.* NY, Free Press, 1978.
Laba, R. 'Worker Roots of Solidarity', *Problems of Communism* July-August 1986.
Leach, R.H. 'The Balkanization of Australia' in *Dyson House Papers* Autumn 1978.
Leach, R.H. 'Right Wing Labor *Arena'* 76, 1986.
Leach, R.H. 'The Concept of Struggle in Maoism' Master of Social Science (Hons) Thesis, University of New England, Australia, 1976.

Maddox, G., *Australian Democracy: Theory and Practice*. Australia, Longman Cheshire, 1985.

Martin, J. A *Guide to Marxism*. NY, St Martin's Press, 1980.

Maxwell, N. 'To get rich is glorious' *The Listener*, 11 Nomvember 1986.

McQueen, H. in Mayer, H. and Nelson, H. (eds), *Australian Politics: A Reader* Fifth Edition. Australia, Longman Cheshire, 1980.

McKnight, D. (ed.) *Moving Left*. Sydney, Pluto Press, 1986.

Prybyla, J.S. 'China's economic experiment. From Mao to Market' *Problems of Communism*, January-February 1986.

Roberts, J.M., *The Triumph of the West*. London, BBC Publications, 1985.

Sargent, L.T. *Contemporary Political Ideologies* Fifth Edition. Illinois, Dorsey Press, 1969.

Samuelson, P.A. *Economics* Sixth Edition. NY, McGraw-Hill, 1964.

Sharkey, L.L. *An Outline History of the Australian Communist Party*. Sydney, Australian Communist Party, 1944.

Suter, K. 'A New International Order' *New Leaves* 7, December 1986.

White, R. *Inventing Australia: Images and Identity 1688–1980*. Sydney, Allen and Unwin, 1981.

Australia's Heritage Vol. 9. Sydney, Lansdowne.

'Big Depression on the Way', *The Courier Mail*, Queensland, 12 December 1986.

Recommended Reading

Rius *Marx for Beginners, Lenin for Beginners, Mao for Beginners, Cuba for Beginners*, all Sydney, Unwin Paperbacks, 1985.

Martin, J. A *Guide to Marxism*. NY, St Martin's Press, 1980.

Feuer, L.S. *Marx and Engels: Basic Writings on Philosophy* and Politics. NY, Doubleday, 1959.

McKnight, D. (ed.) *Moving Left*. Sydney, Pluto Press, 1986.

Barratt Brown, M. *Models in Political Economy*. UK, Penguin, 1984.

Winthrop, N. (ed.) *Liberal Democratic Theory and its Critics*. Sydney, Croom Helm, 1985.

Boswell, N., Hirst, D. 'The Rise of the New Left' *The Australian* 15–16 November 1986.

6

Anarchism

> The modern state ... is nothing but a conspiracy to exploit, but most of all to demoralise its citizens ... I understand moral and religious laws, not compulsory for everyone, but leading forward and promising a more harmonious future. I feel the laws of art which always bring happiness. But political laws seem to me such prodigious lies that I fail to see how one among them can be better or worse than any of the others ... Henceforth I shall never serve any government anywhere.
>
> (Tolstoy as quoted in Woodcock *Anarchism*, p. 209)

Anarchism in the public mind conjures up an image of the bomber or terrorist under a black flag. The reality is that the term 'anarchism', meaning 'no government', covers several belief systems and modes of action besides this violent stereotype.

All anarchist systems of belief, whether violent or non-violent, agree on several basic themes. Amongst these are

(a) *The primacy of the individual*[1] in the political culture;
(b) The need for a lifestyle of *'voluntary simplicity'*. Or a standard of living which is an adequate sufficiency, 'poverty but not destitution'. An anarchist despises the pursuit of consumerism as it is linked to mindless industrial growth.
(c) An *anti-industrial* ethos which stresses that the machine should serve humanity, not vice versa.
(d) *The state* and its accepted hierarchical system is the true enemy.

In the last theme, anarchists stress that 'class did not create the state, and hence the imbalance of economic wealth. Indeed it was the reverse.'[2] The state was created by those who controlled force. This monopoly of force led to the creation of an imbalance of wealth, and thus classes. The state is the villain of history, not necessarily capital, as stressed by Marx.

Anarchists believe that without the state, hierarchy could not be enforced. Bullies would not be granted legitimacy. The essential fairness of ordinary people acting spontaneously and collectively if organised upon a small community basis would prevent the accumulation of wealth and power in a few hands.

Thus the revolution to overthrow privilege would not come from just workers alone, as Marx stressed, but from all people. Indeed, *workerism*, or the emphasis upon the working class as the main tool of historical change, would backfire. The workers would simply create another hierarchical state, even though it was called a 'workers' state', and, another élite resting upon state power would emerge.

For the pure anarchist, there are no laws of history or historical materialism which ensure that new classes dominate each stage of history. There is simply a repeat of state oppression under the new illusions of that epoch.

Anarchism detects a certain continuity in human history— an idealist motivation in contradistinction to Marxist materialism. Anarchists see the 'will to action' in history motivated by a blind desire to unify material and ethical life. To do this, each generation is driven by the urge to be free.[3]

However, men and women commit the cardinal mistake of recreating the state instead of destroying it. Thus they recreate their chains by creating a new élite with new ideological class favourites.

Thus anarchy stresses the need for societal not state change. Unlike the Marxists and social democrats of the Left who believe that the state is a vital instrument for mass societal change, anarchists believe that change from the top down can never succeed. The state will always attempt the easy way and use coercion. This in turn will always cause alienation and obstinate resistance.

The major purpose of anarchist thought and action is thus 'the survival of the libertarian spirit against the relentless demands and tyrannies of the state'. Anarchism, consequently, receives attacks from both the Right and the state-based Left of the political spectrum.

As Woodcock points out, pure anarchism is therefore an intensely moral movement[4] with a simple belief in the primacy of ethical action as the basis of human life. People are not caught up in historical laws of history, or the market, but are the sum total of their acts of ethical will, and their urge 'to authenticity or self realisation'.

This emphasis upon moral action in community distinguishes anarchism from Right libertarianism, which stresses individuality, but in a near Social Darwinist mode. The market becomes the arbiter of all action and *laissez-faire* applies even to morality. Self-centredness is raised to a given principle of nature.

The collective aspect of the pure anarchist emphasis upon morality, on the other hand, places it on the Left side of the political spectrum.

Ultimately, anarchism stresses the paradox of individuality being discovered in freely given moral collective action. Personal authenticity can only emerge if people cherish each other as individuals, to be won over by reason and consensus rather than by force, or even majority vote. As Proudhon wrote, 'Universal suffrage is counter revolution.'[5]

Implicit in pure anarchism is a pre-industrial attitude to the machine and its social impacts. Thus anarchism is essentially anti-industrial. All forms of anarchism see the conventional Left and Right as totally caught up in the politics of industrial growth. They deplore the emphasis on possession in the industrial state to the detriment of the human spirit. Both Left and Right are, they believe, in fact variations of technocracy. They are rhetorically, but not realistically, ideological enemies.

Erich Fromm's words in *The Art of Loving* (London, Allen and Unwin, 1975) reflect some of these Left libertarian or near anarchist sentiments:

> Modern capitalism needs people who cooperate smoothly and in large numbers; who want to consume more and more; and whose tastes are standardized and can be easily influenced and anticipated. It needs people who feel free and independent, not subject to any authority or principle or conscience — yet willing to be commanded, to do what is expected of them; to fit into the social machine without function; who can be guided without force; led without leaders; prompted without aim, except the one to make good, to be on the move, to function, to go ahead.
>
> What is the outcome? Modern man is alienated from himself, from his fellow man and from nature.

Some anarchists, such as the anarcho-syndicalists, accept industrialism, but only on the basis of workers' control of the productive process. The socialist 'nationalisation' of industry is rejected as managerial rights are preserved by the imposition of state-selected managers. The workers still remain powerless and are not consulted.

Both economic styles of organisation — the *privatisation* of industry by the capitalist and *nationalisation* by the state — are opposed. They produce class domination or bureaucratic domination respectively. The anarcho-syndicalist prefers *collectivisation* or the collective ownership of the workplace vested in those who labour there. Management should not be imposed but elected by the employees themselves. Workers' control will produce freedom at the very base of industrial society, the productive arena. All other freedoms will flow from this fact.

But pure anarchism rejects concentration upon the worker class alone. All citizens can be free. There is no hierarchy of classes. All people possess the potential to act in their own interest.

To achieve this consciousness, anarchism[6] stresses the tactics of constant *propaganda of enlightenment* outlining a society of equals based upon *direct,* not representative democracy: *spontaneous revolutionary awareness* whereby each individual can identify the enemies of freedom and if necessary, the methods of *direct action* (as action radicalises the individual far more than theory). It is the meaning of 'direct action' that divides anarchists historically.

Direct action can mean the 'insurrectionary act of terror' (Enrico Malatesta — 1850–1932). The act of terror, such as an assassination, is explained as 'the propaganda of the deed'. The deed puts fear into the hearts of the oppressors who find they do not have a monopoly of violence. It is propaganda, as it shows the masses it is necessary to act, and thus it is a trigger to a mass uprising. In many ways it is based on the Robin Hood syndrome found in most societies, where the rich and powerful cannot escape some 'hero of the people', even if of bandit background.

This aspect of direct action has often led historical anarchism into an ideological flirtation with the criminal class, and a rationalisation of criminal action as blind resistance to oppression.

Alternatively, direct action is explained as the direct non-violent action of a Gandhi. Authority is challenged by passive resistance, boycotts, sit-down strikes or civil disobedience. Such actions are designed to appeal to the morality and humanity of both the oppressor and oppressed in seeking a reasonable solution to a problem.

It is the violent stereotype of 'the propaganda of the deed' which has haunted the anarchist image. Many anarchists argue 'the state imposed [this] definition of anarchism on the public [in the late nineteenth century]. Despite all evidence to the contrary, governments and the press only too willingly equated anarchism with violence and destruction. Anarchists were described as 'filthy', 'mad', 'evil' and — just to add a touch of xenophobia — 'foreigners'.[7]

This stereotype has continued with the rise of the terrorism of the 1970s–80s. Largely European groups, such as the Red Brigades of Italy, have pursued an ideology with elements both of Marxism and notions of anarchist direct action.

This contemporary anarchist image, however, was also paralleled by another stereotype emerging from the counter-culture of the 1960s. This movement stressed the alternative life style seeker, the 'flower power' hippie image and the pursuit of 'personal politics' in the non-violent, participatory democracy of the commune.

It is necessary to outline a short history of the origins and development of both these anarchist images in order to show how anarchism has often been misinterpreted and/or underestimated in the extent of its influence upon contemporary culture.

Origins

Anarchism has three major historical streams: *individual anarchism; anarcho-syndicalism* and *anarcho-communism.*[8]

Individual anarchism has a long history in Western religion and culture, while anarcho-syndicalism and anarcho-communism are ideologies stemming from the nineteenth century interaction with socialism and organised labour.

The roots of anarchism are sometimes said to be found in early Christian movements which stressed other-worldliness, simplicity of living and personal conscience over orthodox and hierarchical church direction. Such Christian streams can be found in early Gnosticism,[9] Egyptian anchoritism, and especially the Protestant sects of the Reformation which rejected state secular power for the directions of inner conscience.

However, anarchism of the nineteenth and twentieth centuries probably owes more to the humanism of the Renaissance than religious thought. True anarchism is eternally concerned with humanist aims such as can only be developed in a secular society based on individual liberty, free of religious and state tyranny.

Religious-based anarchism certainly stimulated much of the teaching of Gerard Winstanley (1609–50) and William Godwin, (1756–1836) in the English anarchist tradition. Winstanley emerged during the English Revolution (1642–50) as the leader of a small sect of radicals known as the Diggers who stressed that land should be owned collectively and that the power of the state was the foundation of oppression.

However, both Winstanley, and later Godwin, used religious-based 'natural law' to underwrite their political case. Godwin had immense influence on the basically liberal Anglo-Saxon culture. He stressed consensual decision making and the role of property in destroying spiritual purity, stressing 'virtuous simplicity' and spontaneous communitarianism.

The individualist anarchism of Godwin, was of a non-violent, world-weary 'liberalism writ large'. It never denied liberalism's stress on the individual.

The collectivism of later Anglo-Saxon socialism was to fall upon largely stony ground until it came to terms with these liberal foundations of Anglo-Saxon society. Then, it adopted the managerial outline of technocratic state liberalism or moved to a libertarian socialist position with Godwinite anarchist overtones. Thus elements of anarchism or even anarcho-syndicalism would probably come easier to an Anglo-Saxon society, should radicalism prevail, than the grey hierarchy of a Marxist-Leninist society.

Despite the description of the Enragés, an extreme group of French revolutionary Sansculottes, as 'anarchists intent upon the destruction of law and order', by their conservative opponents in the Republican National Assembly, the first noted anarchist of the nineteenth century to propose solutions to social problems via a new collectivity was Proudhon (1809–65). He laid the philosophical foundations for continental European anarchism. His ideas were in the tradition of individual anarchism, but he realised the necessity of outlining a new society based upon the free association of individuals, in which direct action would supplant constitutional democracy.

Proudhon, in his most famous statement, declared that 'all property is theft'. He recognised the inequality that ownership of property imposed on society and the need for the reform of this situation. He did not outline, however, an alternative communist society. Instead he envisaged intermeshing communities where workers, artisans and farmers controlled the means of production. Small private ownership would flourish on the land, while workers would control the factories via their unions. A system of 'mutualism' and 'federalism' would replace the state. This anarchist society would be a structure of local communities linked together by mutual interest and federated in a loose system of communes.

Proudhon's system gave priority to the local community. As a man of peasant stock himself, he reflected the peasants' suspicion of urban civilisation and their deep sense of the uselessness of the state and the administrative class.

In anarchist thought, Proudhon stands as the architect of the anarchist social utopia. Later thinkers were to develop his basic themes. Later thinkers were to include men such as Mikhail Bakunin, Peter Kropotkin, Leo Tolstoy and Enrico Malatesta. These nineteenth century thinkers and activists were to add to Proudhon's foundations, elaborate on the violent and non-violent tactics of anarchism and contest the hegemony of Left political thought with Marx.

Mikhail Bakunin (1814–76), a Russian noble and ex-army officer, was a contemporary of Proudhon and one of the fathers of anarcho-communism and later anarcho-syndicalism. Bakunin supported 'mutualism' but wished for communal property to replace the small freeholds of Proudhon. Implicit in such small freeholdings, to Bakunin, was the capitalist road, and the selfishness which he despised.

Bakunin was involved in a drawn-out struggle with Karl Marx to dominate the First International[10] over whether anarchism or Marxism would lead the world-wide movement of the working class. Bakunin set out to capture the working class for anarchism by endorsing collective property:

> With Bakunin there appeared two new tendencies in anarchist theory. The doctrine shifted from abstract speculation on the use and abuse of political power to a theory of political action. At the same time anarchism ceased to be the political philosophy of the most radical wing of the petty bourgeoisie and become a political doctrine which looked for the mass of its adherents among ... the proletariat, although its central cadres continued to be recruited from amongst the intelligentsia. Without Bakunin, anarcho-syndicalism ... is unthinkable.[11]

Collective property and spontaneous violent revolutionary acts against the old society, were Bakunin's major contributions to anarchist thought.

In the struggle with Marxism, anarchism proposed spontaneous action compared with the structure and discipline of the Marxist party. This spontaneity was not nihilism, or mindless destruction, but a recognition that the capitalist class would not easily be forced from the stage of history and would fight its ground if necessary. In so doing, however, it would cause each individual worker to lose his or her illusions about the morality of the system. Therefore the 'propaganda of the deed' as propounded by Enrico Malatesta (1850–1932) would trigger mass destruction or repression by the bourgeoisie or the state. This savage reaction would bring worker revulsion and spontaneous mass action, whether a revolution or the general strike. The workers would learn from their own spontaneous actions their power. They would 'morally regenerate the world'.[12]

Peter Kropotkin (1842–1921) was also one of the major architects of anarcho-communism.[12] Kropotkin built upon Proudhon's mutualism but suggested a further system of distribution which would equalise the standards of poor and rich locales. He agreed with Fourier's emphasis on the need for attractive work. This would encourage a free society, as a feeling of useful achievement overcomes alienation and would, he believed, be the driving force behind a willingness to work.[13]

Kropotkin foresaw the ultimate problem of centralised socialism — the inability of a state socialist political system to provide a decision making apparatus complex enough to cope with the myriad of small and local economic demands.

Capitalism had this ability in its structure of thousands of small entrepreneurs, all making market decisions. Its productive efficiency would therefore surpass that of state socialism, with a resultant loss of prestige in the eyes of the masses. This was despite the fact that decentralised democratic (or anarcho-communist) socialism offered a solution to social needs which capitalism could not solve because of its wealth concentration; its tendency to boom and bust; its impulse to monopolisation; and its class power base narrowness. Kropotkin sadly predicted that socialism would lose the ideological struggle unless it democratised and decentralised its system along anarcho-syndicalist-communist lines. The capitalist could never meet the challenge of 'worker's control' or local decision making because his system of property ownership and managerial rights were essentially feudal.

The decentralisation of decision making in socialist states appears to be a lesson beginning to be learnt. China under Deng Xioping has moved to free up the state socialist system, (although along more capitalist lines than anarcho-communists would approve). The timid democratisation proposals of the former Soviet communist leader, Gorbachev, reflected a closer approximation of Kropotkin's decentralised system than China's. However, it would seem that Gorbachev's neo-liberal successors are more interested in the capitalist road than Kropotkin's 'worker' control. In the West, social democracy's rising interest in such concepts as the 'enabling state' reflect Kropotkin's directions.

Kropotkin wrote the following on the Russian Revolution in 'Letter to the Workers of the World' (1920):[14]

> The immense constructive work that is required from a social revolution ... cannot be accomplished by a central government ... It requires the knowledge, the brains, and the willing collaboration of a mass of local and specialized forces which alone can cope with the diversity of economic problems in their local aspects. To sweep away that collaboration and to trust to the genius of party dictators is to destroy all independent nuclei (such as trade unions) turning them into bureaucratic organs of the Party. But this is the way not to accomplish the revolution ...

The period of Kropotkin's writings was paralleled by the rise of Italian and Spanish 'propagandists of the deed'. This had little link with Kropotkin's views of mass movements of free sovereign individuals. It was to have reflections in twentieth century terrorism and in the *foco* theory espoused by Che Guevara, which stressed the trigger role of a small band of guerrillas in setting off a revolution. At the same time, the non-violent anti-industrial stream of anarchism was to be influenced by one of its most important contributors.

Count Leo Tolstoy (1828–1910) His beliefs, which can be classified as anarchistic, had a basic religious foundation stressing a rebirth of a society similar to the early Christian communities of the Bible, and as described by Roman historians and church history.

Tolstoy's tactics to achieve this society were to recommend 'a moral rather than a political system'[15] based upon individual spiritual change due to exposure to superior moral and rational community. Gandhian methods were later to reflect many of Tolstoy's ideas.

Tolstoyan anarchism stressed universal common humanity over the nationalism supported by the state. Patriotism was 'badly flawed',[16] as a means for bettering human spiritual life. Similarly, the myth of scientific progress was a materialistic cul-de-sac for the human spirit.

The Tolstoyan vision of common humanity was thus based on an anti-scientific vision of a society built upon 'virtuous simplicity'. This unified Christian principles and a communistic approach to property, with pacifism as an integral component. As well as deeply influencing Gandhism, these ideas were integrated into Christian anarchism in the West.

Tolstoy's non-violent anarchism was to re-emerge in the post-World War II Indian independence struggles against the British and amongst the counter-culture of the 1960s. But on the whole, anarchism between 1900–40 was to lose the struggle for influence over the Left to Marxism. The impact of the Russian Revolution of 1917 gave Marxism-Leninism preeminence as an ideology amongst revolutionary socialists. Anarchists of all kinds were dismissed as confused and preproletarian in their ideology, as well as being downright counter-revolutionary in their belief in (often armed) resistance to Bolshevism.

Tolstoyans in particular were dismissed as cult folk who would throw away the benefits of industrialism for workers, or, alternatively, as dangerous idealists who would attempt to persuade workers to reason gently with Cossacks as they were being ridden down. The workers were rendered helpless by such tactics.

Differences over the nature of action are still intensely divisive for anarchism, and in Marxist/anarchist historical rivalry.

In the Russian Revolution of 1917, anarchists and libertarian socialists were among the first to be arrested or exiled by Lenin's government. (A continuation of the struggle between Marx and Bakunin at the First International.)

Ukrainian anarchists under Nestor Makhno did attempt to set up a movement during the Russian Civil War. They fought both Whites and Reds, as a third force. Eventually, they were overcome by the Red Army.

At the end of the nineteenth century through to the beginning of the Depression of 1929, anarchism gave birth to several ideological streams. There existed:

(a) *violent anarchism* — the doctrine of 'the propaganda of the deed'.

(b) *Non-violent and religious-based anarchistic styles*, such as the primitive Christianity beliefs of Tolstoy, and

(c) *cultural anarchism*, with its stress on the anti-hero such as the tramp, the outlaw, the swagman or the bohemian.

One of the major influences of anarchism upon the labour movement was via the pre-World War I anarcho-syndicalist movement in the USA and also, to some extent, in British Commonwealth countries such as Australia.

Anarcho-syndicalism

Anarcho-syndicalism stressed the concepts of the 'One Big Union', class interests before nationalism and the action of the general strike. It spread throughout the Western union movement, especially in unions for semi-skilled and unskilled workers before World War I.

Anarcho-syndicalism in the pre-World War I period stressed that traditional craft unionism was not enough. These unions had to escape their narrow trade bases, and become organised regionally or on an industry basis. They also needed anti-capitalist policies, anti-racism, class universalism and pacificism.[17]

Through the Industrial Workers of the World (IWW), anarcho-syndicalism gained some support amongst American workers and some influence in other English-speaking countries. IWW influence was extremely high in 'direct action' against World War I recruitment, particularly in Australia. The war was regarded as a trade and anti-working class one, and the anti-conscription campaigns in Australia of 1916–17 allowed an avenue for dissemination of their ideas.

Many anarcho-syndicalists moved over into the post-war communist parties. However, their commitment to libertarian socialism and anti-bureaucratic tactics made it difficult for them to operate successfully within Marxism-Leninism. In several cases, purges were made to rid communist parties of anarcho-syndicalist ideas.[18]

During the Spanish Civil War of 1936–39, anarchist influences were extremely strong in the Republican forces. Anarchist militia, based upon their anarcho-syndicalist-style union (CNT/FAI) were instrumental in resisting the uprising of the Spanish Army against the Republic and in organising the ensuing popular land reform and worker control in industry. In-fighting between anarchist forces, socialist majority forces and small communist forces who controlled Russian arms and aid was one of the major reasons for the eventual Republican defeat.

The ideological gulf between the Marxist emphasis upon the use of the state first to change society, and the anarchist belief in the uselessness of top-down change and the priority for changes in people's hearts, seems unable to be bridged.

Contemporary Anarchism

The effect of contemporary anarchism is felt more as an influence on life and political thought than as a movement.

The anarchist movement had left its mark within the socialist camp in the tenets of libertarian socialism, including anti-bureaucratic policies, the stress on spontaneity; the emphasis on equality and democracy within the productive arenas exemplified in the continuing drive in socialism for 'worker's control' of the factory, and equal wage levels and 'participatory democracy' in the state and community.

In cultural life in general, the effect of anarchist emphases upon 'personal politics' has been continuous, especially since the 1960s. Its 'personal politics'[19] involves the concept of 'voluntary simplicity' and the necessity of changing personal behaviour at a community level, rather than attempting change through the state.

The alternative lifestyle movements of the 1960s reflect much of this cultural heritage of anarchism. Criticism of this style of 'alternative' lifestyle has come from both Marxist and conservative commentators.

According to them, alternative lifestyles are:

(a) a product of welfare statism and illusions about the continuity of affluence. With the downturn in affluence, such people are condemned to a life of poor landless agricultural subsistence. Welfare handouts are essential to their existence because without state-controlled economic infrastructure, most alternatives are not self-sustaining.

(b) a style of life devoid of many of the opportunities their parents possessed. Especially in rural areas, these people have condemned their children to a return to poverty, further flawed by a 'degenerate' system of *laissez-faire* morality.

Against these critics, anarchists point with some pride[20] to the fact that in some communist countries where worker movements spontaneously break out against party control, the intuitive movement is towards libertarian socialist structures with anarchist overtones, and rarely towards a renewal of capitalism. For instance, the Worker Council movements in the Hungarian uprising of 1956 are stressed as models of libertarian Soviets seeking the Great Republic.[21] Poland in 1956, 1970–71 and the Polish Solidarity movement of 1980–82, stressed self-management and the general strike. These events were held to be highly influenced by the tradition of anarchist thought.

In the West, however, anarchist thought has served a different purpose. It has provided radicalism with a third way or critique free of Stalinist bloody-handedness, and the capitalist anti-worker tradition. As Apter writes, 'the virtue of anarchism as a doctrine is that it employs a socialist critique of capitalism and a liberal critique of socialism'.[22]

In the West, particularly with the New Left movement of the 1960s, anarchism lost much of its quaint nineteenth century stereotyping. Instead

anarchism today is a form of liberalism which rejects capitalism. As a doctrine of individualism ... it has relevance despite some of the flamboyance and gesticulations of its practitioners.[23]

This particular usage of anarchism — the third way — was useful to the student movement of 1968 and the Vietnam War period. A dissent from capitalism was sought, but one not associated with the old Leninist Left and the working class.[24]

On the other hand, the worker stress of Polish Solidarity was originally in the tradition of the old anarchist emphasis from Bakunin upon the worker movement as central to the achievement of the Great Republic.

Since the 1960s, the Western stress upon the third way has left the workers' movement largely ignored. Indeed, many anarchists, especially those who have moved to ecological 'Green' positions, regard much of the traditional working class as part of the industrial problem. These traditional elements of the working class are pro-growth and anti-conservation, it is believed, and totally locked into the hierarchical industrial structure.[25]

The third way, with its anarchist overtones, has built itself around cores of peace, ecology, alternative lifestyles and social justice. It has attracted a new, radical, largely middle class, support group which has, however, repudiated class as a basis for politics. Instead, the anarchist universalist stress on moral action and ethical policies is espoused. This stresses the 'citizen' in the tradition of liberalism, not the 'worker' in the tradition of Marxism.

This movement argues its relevance because of the exhaustion of Leninism in the West and the decline of social democracy into an alternative technocratic management system. The resulting radical vacuum will be filled, it is argued, by a combination of 'anarchism as a form of liberalism that rejects capitalism' and a rebirth of anarcho-syndicalist libertarian socialism.

As Gorz points out,[26] contemporary Western society has seen the end of traditional industrialism, with its heavy manufacturing, which is now moving into Third World countries with their cheap labour.

The state itself within these developed countries, according to Suter, is rapidly becoming linked to a new world system[27] of transnational capitalism. The traditional roles of the state are being transcended as its controlling hierarchical élite is being transformed into a local executive for outside interests.

In such a scenario, a dual labour economy with a permanently or semi-permanently unemployed sector is unavoidable. This transition will be accompanied by the collapse of national state-based economic theories such as Keynesianism and monetarism.[28] To combat these sudden changes the world needs new ways of thought, new paradigms, or ways of thinking about the human condition.

Socialism was such a new paradigm in the nineteenth century. However, it attempted to maintain industrialism, simply removing the capitalist class. As Hutton and Connors outline in describing the ideas of a modern anarchist, Murray Bookchin, a new paradigm is needed to meet the coming ecological crisis, requiring a radical new way of living one's life based upon the acceptance of 'virtuous simplicity' and reinterpreting values along non-hierarchical lines of language and consensus.[29]

The emerging Green movement has seen the rebirth and re-direction of much anarchist and counter-cultural thought into the creation of this new paradigm. Anarchism, resurrected as a new form of radical liberalism, has re-emerged on the ideological stage.

Anarchism in Australia

The heritage of anarchism in Australia has, like that of the West in general, been largely cultural and in terms of political ideas rather than as an organised movement.

Anarchism, like socialism of Marxist or libertarian origins, was marginalised in the formation of the Australian political culture of the nineteenth century by the predominance of state liberalism as a common Left/Right ideology in the formation of the Deakinite state. This demanded a technocratic, managerial code of state and hierarchical politics that precluded anarchism because of its basic premise of anti-statism. As the peculiarity of the Australian political culture was that 'the state formed society and not vice versa',[30] nineteenth-century anarchism seemed to have little to offer except as an ideological curiosity and a doctrine for eccentrics.

Nevertheless, the ideology of anarchism did take root in Australia. One major initiative was the founding of the Anarchist Club in Melbourne in 1886. Anarchists were active in the subsequent labour turmoil and the rise of the labour movement of the 1890s. But the principal outcome of their presence in this turbulent period was to aid the state to categorise and stereotype labour action within the European tradition of the violent anarchist 'propagandists of the deed'. As James[31] indicates, the state was perfectly willing to use the anarchist 'bomber' bogey to frighten the public, and to distort the nature of the worker movement. This allowed it to pass severe legislation such as Henry Parkes Treason Felony Act in NSW. The state was aided in this by the emerging picture of Australia as a haven of peace, distant from European and American political excesses. The state was there to protect society against distant thunder and its malevolent trouble makers emigrating to Australian shores. The absurdity of the Egon Kisch case of the 1930s and the controversies over the vetting of Vietnamese and Chilean migrants in the 1980s still reflect this 'purified continent' attitude.

Anarcho-syndicalists ideas rather than pure anarchism had a larger impact upon the labour movement in its period of formation between 1880–1917.

Anarcho-syndicalism made its entry into Australian labour politics via the International Workers of the World and their American sources in Detroit and Chicago.[32] The IWW stressed industrial over craft unions on the basis that craft unionism led to a hierarchy of labour aristocracy, and eventual reformism. They were persistently anti-racist, stressing universal brotherhood in an age in Australia when the 'Yellow Peril' and White Australia policy were an integral part of the founding Deakinite state.

Most importantly, the IWW was consistently opposed to reformist unionism and socialism. Their view of the world was that of class above nation or race. Nothing permanent, in the eyes of the IWW, could be done to ameliorate the condition of the working class by increasing national prosperity or assuming racial superiority. Ultimately, capitalism would make adjustments that would require sacrifices by the working class. Thus the IWW never confused the poor with the working class.

With this view, the IWW were bound to come into conflict with the central tenet of British/Australian style social democracy, i.e. the abolition of poverty rather than the abolition of capitalism itself.[33] Despite their constantly reiterated warnings that labourism, the move to include trade unions in the tripartite state, and the continuation of craft unionism would simply lead to a new labour hierarchy wishing to preserve and manage the existing state, eventually even accepting the existing poor, the IWW were marginalised within the labour movement.

The real impact of IWW and other anarchist ideas came within one of the most traumatic periods in Australian history. (Trauma theory argues that so tightly cocooned has Australia been within its Deakinite state structure and so culturally exclusive, that only a massive trauma such as a world war or a depression can break into the dominant ideology and its complacency,[34] with new explanations and paradigms.) This trauma was World War I.

As Burgmann outlines,[35] so complacent and committed to utilitarianism were Australian union leaders that few had the ideological means to cope with either the Depression of the 1890s or the subsequent anti-conscription movements of World War I. The influence of marginalised groups such as the IWW began to grow in these anti-war and conscription campaigns around the themes that World War I was a trade war between capitalist nations, and a class war which the workers were fighting for their masters.

As Hutton points out,[36] the impact of the anti-conscription campaigns of the period 1916–17 was to leave the imprint of anarcho-syndicalist pacifism and anti-militarism upon the labour movement forever. Of all the issues adopted by the labour movement and the ALP, the issue of conscription is one of the most divisive and idealistic in a party and movement which has often elevated pragmatism to an art form. As such, 'anti-conscription' has entered, along with 'suspicion of the money power'; 'internal discipline' and 'the pursuit of equality', into the 'language of laborism'.[37] Few labour leaders can approach this issue in a non-traditional manner without massive membership upheaval.

After World War I, many anarcho-syndicalists joined the fledgling communist party. In the late 1920s, a purge of such non-Leninist thinkers took place. The Australian Communist Party became a staunchly Leninist one until the great splits of the 1960s. Anarcho-syndicalism declined as a viable working class movement as both Leninism and labourism came to dominate the radical position under the Deakinite state.

As in the USA, the rebirth of anarchism in Australia coincided with the external trauma of the Vietnam War and the rise of New Left student politics in the period 1964–75. As Gordon points out,[38] the New Left movement in Australia was dominated by an ethos of libertarian socialism and anarcho-liberalism similar to the American New Left movement.

The ALP and, to a lesser degree, the labour movement, were influenced by some ideas of the New Left. The Left wing of the Labor Party raised some libertarian socialist ideas such as participatory democracy,[39] but hierarchical labourism still remained the major *raison d'être* of the ALP.

Ideas of workers' control were discussed by radical unions in this period, but, ultimately, the prosperity of the period was too great to inspire workers to make radical changes in their existence. Major changes inspired by anarchist thought were to occur outside the industrial arena.

Alternative lifestyles and the necessity of 'personal politics' were a vital element in the counter-culture inspired by the New Left. From the early 1970s, alternative lifestyles especially along rural commune lines, spread throughout Australia.

The alternative lifestyle movement stresses the need to break out of the Australian mainstream lifestyle with its emphasis on unending consumerism and narrow competition. These materialist anti-cultural ambitions, as alternative lifestyle enthusiasts argued, were alienating recipes for spiritual dissatisfaction. Unfortunately this *petit bourgeois* mentality was the foundation of Australian culture and permeated all values and approaches to problems. Therefore, they argued, 'the break with the *petit bourgeois* consciousness can only be done by resorting to classic anarchist "virtuous simplicity"'.[40] Only in such a manner could Australian society be regenerated to face the anti-growth challenges of post-industrialism.

Many commentators argue that the eighty-year-old Deakinite state which gave middle Australia its secure foundation for the Lucky Country is breaking up.

New political formations, it is argued, will follow this sea change in Australian economics, as Pacific Basin restructuring and integration takes place. The social democratic/state liberal common platform that formed the traditional middle ground will have to be readjusted.[41]

In this scenario, a new conservative party may emerge around the New Right and other Right-wing elements, on the basis of Free Trade and monetarist economies. Large elements of the existing National and Liberal parties may break off to form the new conservative party. The residue of the existing National/Liberal parties, comprising the old ideologues of Deakinite state liberalism will retain a diminished role in Australian politics, or will join the Right-ward moving ALP.

The ALP will become a liberal democratic rather than a social democratic party. In this process, to absorb the Deakinite liberals, it must shake off its socialist Left wing. The vacuum on the Left caused by the ALP move to the centre must be filled.

Commentators such as Camilleri[42] argue that this could not be filled by a Left Marxist-Leninist party. The traditional cultural image of such a party as totalitarian will militate against it. Only a libertarian socialist-anarcho-syndicalist and anarcho-liberal coalition based upon a credible Australian analysis could possibly fill the predicted radical vaccum.

Notes

1. Woodcock, G. *Anarchism*. USA, Penguin, 1962, p. 23.
2. Burgmann, V. 'One Hundred Years of Anarchism' *Arena* 74, 1986, pp. 108–09.
3. Maximoff, G. *The Political Philosophy of Bakunin*: Scientific Anarchism. NY, Free, Press, 1953, pp. 60–68.
4. Woodcock, p. 25.
5. Taylor, A.J.P. in Marx, K. and Engels, F. *The Communist Manifesto*. UK, Penguin, 1967, p. 26.
6. Libertarian Socialist Organisation, *Revolution Re-Assessed*. Brisbane, Australia, Planet Press, 1982. pp. 3–52.
7. Stafford, J. 'Anarchism and Australian Labor History' *Tribune* 15 October 1986, p. 11.
8. Sargent, L.T. *Contemporary Political Ideologies* Fifth Edition. Illinois, Dorsey Press, 1969, pp. 159–75.
9. Pagels, Elaine. *The Gnostic Gospels*. UK, Penguin, 1985.
10. Tylecott, A. and Lonsdale-Brown in Friedmann, E. (ed.) *Ascent and Descent in the World System*. Vol. 5. USA, Sage, 1982, p. 290.
11. Maximoff, p. 13.
12. Woodcock, p. 23.
13. Woodcock, p. 192.
14. Woodcock, pp. 204–05.
15. Woodcock, p. 217.
16. Woodcock, pp. 214–16.
17. Burgmann, V. 'Racists and Revolutionaries: Australian Socialism and the Problem of Racism 1887–1917' PhD Thesis, ANU, Canberra, 1980.
18. Sharkey, L.L. *An Outline History of the Australian Communist Party*. Sydney, Australian Communist Party, 1944.
19. Hood, N. 'Dreams or Pioneers' *Australian Society* January 1987, p. 39.
20. Hutton, D. and George, G. 'Anarchy or Chaos' *Social Alternatives* 2 (3) 1982, p. 5.
21. Feher, F. and Heller, A. 'Are there prospects for change in the USSR and Eastern Europe?' *Praxis International* 5 (3) 1985, pp. 323–32.
22. Apter, D. and Joll, J. *Anarchism Today* Studies in Comparative Politics. UK, Macmillan, 1971, pp. 1–2.
23. Ibid.
24. Gordon, R. (ed.) *The Australian New Left*. Australia, Heinemann, 1970, pp. 3–43, 66–95.
25. Gorz, A. *Farewell to the Working Class: An Essay on Post-industrial socialism*. London, Pluto, 1982.
26. Ibid.
27. Suter, K. 'A New International Order' *New Leaves*, 7, December 1986; Friedmann, E. (ed.) *Ascent and Descent in the World System* Vol. 5. Sage, 1982.
28. 'The crisis of the dismal science' *Guardian* 12–13–14. January 1982.
29. Hutton, D. and Connors, L. 'Bookchin: Ecology of Freedom' *New Leaves* 2, April 1986, p. 28.
30. McQueen, H. 'Whats wrong with Australia?' in Mayer, H. and Nelson, H. (eds) *Australian Politics A Fifth Reader*. Melbourne, Longman Cheshire, 1980.
31. James, B. *Anarchism and State Violence in Sydney and Melbourne*. James, B. Libertarian Resources, 10 Church St, Newcastle, 1986, as referred to in *Tribune* 15 October 1986, p. 11.
32. Burgmann, V. 'Racists and Revolutionaries: Australian Socialism and the Problem of Racism 1887–1917', PhD Thesis, ANU, Canberra, 1980.
33. Hinton, J. *Labour and Socialism: British Labour History 1867–1914*. UK, Wheatsheaf, 1983, p. 30.

34. Leach, R. 'Right Wing Labor' *Arena* 76, 1986.
35. See Burgmann.
36. Hutton, D. and George, G. 'Anarchy or Chaos' *Social Alternatives* 12 (31) 1982, p. 5.
37. Beilharz, P. and Watts, R. 'The Discourse of Laborism' *Arena* 77, 1986 pp. 66–95.
38. Gordon pp. 3–43.
39. Summy, G. 'Jim Cairns' Revolutionary Democracy' *Politics* VII, 1 May 1972, pp. 55–67.
40 See Hood.
41. Camilleri, J. 'After Social Democracy' *Arena* 77, 1986.
42. See Camilleri.

References

'Anarchy or Chaos' *Social Alternatives* 2 (3) February, 1982.
Apter, D. and Joll, J. *Anarchism Today* Studies in Comparative Politics. UK, Macmillan, 1972.
Beilharz, P. and Watts, R. 'The Discourse of Laborism' *Arena* 77, 1986.
Burgmann, V. 'One Hundred Years of Anarchism' Arena 74, 1986.
Burgmann, V. *'Racists and Revolutionaries: Australian Socialism and the Problem of Racism 1887–1917'*, PhD Thesis, ANU Canberra, 1980.
Camilleri, J. 'After Social Democracy' *Arena* 77, 1986.
Carter, A. *The Political Theory of Anarchism*. London, Routledge and Kegan Paul, 1971.
Friedmann, E. (ed.) *Ascent and Descent in the World System*. Vol. 5. USA, Sage, 1982.
Feher, F. and Heller, A. 'Are there prospects for change in the USSR and Eastern Europe?' *Praxis International* 5 (3) 1985.
Gordon, R. (ed.) *The Australian New Left: Critical Essays and Strategies*. Australia, Heinemann, 1970.
Gorz, A. *Farewell to the Working Class*. London, Pluto, 1982.
Hinton, J. *Labour and Socialism: British Labour History 1867–1914*. UK, Wheatsheaf, 1983.
Hood, N. 'Dreaming or Pioneers' *Australian Society* January 1987.
Horowitz, I.L. *The Anarchists*. NY, Dell, 1964.
Hutton, D. and George, G. 'Anarchy or Chaos' *Social Alternatives* 2 (3) 1982.
Hutton, D. and Connors, L. 'Bookchin: Ecology of Freedom' *New Leaves* 2, April 1986.
Joll, J. *The Anarchists* Second Edition. London, Methuen, 1975.
Leach, R. 'Right Wing Labor' *Arena* 76, 1986.
Libertarian Socialist Organisation *Revolution Re-Assessed*. Brisbane, Australia, Planet Press, 1982.
Marx, K. and Engels, F. *The Communist Manifesto*. UK, Penguin, 1967.
Maximoff, G.P. *The Political Philosophy of Bakunin: Scientific Anarchism*. NY, Free Press, 1953.
McQueen, H. 'What's wrong with Australia?' in Mayer. H. and Nelson, H. (eds) *Australian Politics* A Fifth Reader. Melbourne, Longman Cheshire, 1980.
Miller, M. (ed.) *Peter Kropotkin: Selected Writings on Anarchism and Revolution*. USA, MIT Press, 1973.
Munro Clark, M. *Communes in Rural Australia*. Australia, Hale and Ironmonger, 1986.
Pagels, Elaine. *The Gnostic Gospels*. UK, Penguin, 1985.
Ritter, M. *Anarchism: A Theoretical Analysis*. UK, Cambridge University Press, 1980.
Sargent, L.T. *Contemporary Political Ideologies* Fifth Edition. Illinois, Dorsey Press, 1969.
Sharkey, L.L. *An Outline History of the Australian Communist Party*. Sydney, Australian Communist Party, 1944.

Skillen, A. *Ruling Illusions: Philosophy and the Social Order.* UK, Harvester Press, 1977.
Stafford, J. 'Anarchism and Australian Labor History, *Tribune* 15 October 1986.
Summy, G. 'Jim Cairns' Revolutionary Democracy' *Politics* VII, May 1, 1972, pp. 55–67.
Suter, K. 'A New International Order' *New Leaves* 7, December 1986.
Vaizey, J. *Revolutions of Our Time: Social Democracy.* UK, Weidenfeld and Nicholson, 1971.
Woodcock, G. *Anarchism.* USA, Penguin, 1962.
Woodcock, G. (ed.) *The Anarchist Reader.* UK, Harvester, 1977.

Recommended Reading/Viewing

Woodcock, G. *Anarchism.* USA, Penguin, 1962.
Apter, D. and Joll, J. *Anarchism Today* Studies in Comparative Politics. UK, Macmillan, 1972.
Burgmann, V. 'One Hundred Years of Anarchism' *Arena* 74, 1986.
Carter, A. *The Political Theory of Anarchism*, London, Routledge and Kegan Paul, 1971.
Matewan (video movie) — I.W.W. influence on the US coalfields — an adaptation of a true story.
Sammy & Rosie get laid (video movie) — English anarchism in a declining city area (1990–FICTION).

7

Cross-Spectrum Ideologies

This chapter will deal briefly with four selected contemporary political doctrines whose elements can be found in the Left and Right ideologies indicated in the previous chapters. Alternatively, these doctrines can be self-defined and stand alone.

The four selected doctrines imperialism, racism, feminism and Green environmentalism, are pervasive in modern political thought, either for their historical influences, their growing political power, or for the perspectives they have brought to mainstream ideologies. It is for these reasons that a short outline of their specific origins and basic aims is necessary for the conclusion of this book.

Imperialism

The ideology, though not the practice, of Imperialism was largely an outcome of the European 'New Imperialism' period of 1870–1914. Imperialism may be defined as the domination of one state over another and the subjugation of the latter's inhabitants to alien rule. Such rule is usually imposed by force, with subsequent exploitation. This process is an ancient phenomenon.[1]

However, the term imperialism itself (derived from the word 'empire') did not come into political use until the 1890s[2] in Britain. The British politician Joseph Chamberlain and his followers used the word to typify the program of colonial expansion to solve domestic problems of unemployment, restricted markets, low production and falling profits. Chamberlain's opponents, the 'Little Englanders', wished to expand production and consumption at home. Investment abroad was a cost to the nation. Chamberlain's term 'imperialism' thus came to typify an ideology of racial exclusion, mercantilist economies, closed conservative nationalism, and a labour aristocracy (or sharing the benefits of empire with the home nation's working class). These various ideas, however, had been promulgated as rationales for empire since the inception of European colonial expansion in the sixteenth century. Nineteenth century Imperialist ideology merely drew them together into a coherent whole.

Two broad types of nineteenth century rationales for imperialism emerged — the *economic doctrines* and the *idealist ones*. However, it is important to remember the social utility of the doctrines of Imperialism at the particular historical time from 1870 to 1914. Imperialism was a useful tool for social coherence and cross-class loyalty at a time when socialism was challenging the old order of Europe.

What caused the 'New Imperialism' period (1870–1914), rather than earlier centuries, to be one of articulated imperialist ideology? The answer probably lies in the increasingly competitive nature of imperial expansion in the nineteenth century, paralleled by the rise of liberal and socialist criticisms at home. Behaviours (such as slavery) that had been acceptable in the eighteenth century were becoming a focus for criticism with the rising consciousness of oppression in the nineteenth century, and rationales were needed to deflect such feelings.

This section will deal with some of the main idealist and economic doctrines advanced as a defence of imperialism in this period.

Idealist Doctrines

If there were functional economic reasons forming the basis of European expansion, as Hobson and Lenin would have us believe, there were also sociological and state political reasons for this expansion as outlined by Schumpeter and Wallerstein. Imperialism was as eagerly accepted by social classes such as the English gentry as by English capitalists and statesmen.

The colonies provided a field of paternalist employment for entire generations of officials drawn from the gentry and upper urban middle class of the metropolitan powers. In the words of a nineteenth-century Liberal politican, the British Empire was 'a system of outdoor relief for the upper classes'.[3]

At the same time the dominant social ethos of the times was aggressive.

We must find new lands from which we can easily obtain raw materials and at the same time exploit the cheap slave labour that is available from the natives of the colonies, the colonies would also provide a dumping ground for the surplus goods produced in our factories. The Empire, as I have always said, is a bread and butter question.

If we want to avoid class struggle in the United Kingdom, we must become imperialists.[4]

As Cecil Rhodes wrote, Imperialism stressed national chauvinism, gender hierarchy and racial differences. The majority of the middle and working classes, whether of the Left or Right, were as pro-imperialist within these hegemonic values as the ruling élites. Social Darwinism had imposed these imperialist values upon the mass of the people via education, the media, etc.

In this complex situation, a number of doctrines had arisen that coalesced into the intricate ideology of imperialism that permeated the New Imperialist period.

The Doctrine of Religion: From the sixteenth century, much of the rationale for imperial conquest rested upon a missionary spirit involving bringing the light of Christianity to the heathen. This rationale was particularly true of the sixteenth century Spanish and Portuguese *conquistadors* who had recently crusaded against the Moors in their native lands in the Iberian Peninsula.

Protestant imperial powers put less emphasis upon the doctrine of religion. This was partly due to the 'exclusivist' nature of Calvinist-based Protestantism, such as that of the Dutch in South Africa. Such religious beliefs postulated an elect group or race superior to the lost souls of other groups or races.

Catholicism, on the other hand, was 'inclusionary'.[5] Spanish Catholicism had taken up the philosophical question of the spiritual nature and common humanity of the colonised native with complete seriousness. In the sixteenth century, under the influence of Father Bernardo de Las Casas, the American Indian had been elevated at least to spiritual, if not quite legal, equality with the Spaniard. This required a repudiation of the separate origins (or polygenic) theory of man's origins (that is, only the whites were the children of Adam (Paracelsus 1520)).[6]

Polygenic theory was an early explanation for native 'primitivism' encountered in European expansion. Protestant nations, although encouraging mission work, were far more inclined to exercise imperialism under the doctrine of civilisation.

The Doctrine of Civilisation became an important and enduring factor in the ideology of Imperialism until well into the twentieth century, almost completely overshadowing the doctrine of religion.

The rise of the European Enlightenment in the seventeenth and eighteenth centuries was a major influence on this doctrine. It posited a civilising mission for Europeans, especially the 'Nordics', who would bring virtue, order and technology to 'primitive' races. Unlike the doctrine of religion which would bring spiritual progress, the doctrine of civilisation was humanist, and measured its success in terms of secular advancement and the conquest of savagery, disease and ignorance.

The Enlightenment was an offspring of the European Renaissance. It stressed secular advancement, where the major purpose of government was the emancipation of the people. In the metropolitan country, this became a mission of tutoring the savage, ignorant working class in the manners, virtues and values of the middle class. In the colonies, emancipation meant first of all civilisation. In all these endeavours, the actions of the ruling class would be governed by reason and self-sacrifice, not superstition.

On the one hand, the Enlightenment admired the unspoilt Rousseauian nature of 'primitive' peoples. This culminated in the 'noble savage' stereotype of eighteenth and nineteenth-century Romantic literature. In the case of advanced 'native' societies such as China, the Enlightenment stressed the depth of ancient wisdom present, and the respect to be shown, as a result, to such societies.

On the other hand, as Van den Berghe indicates, in *Race and Racism*, the driving economic pressure to exploit new lands and to rationalise such trades as slavery led the Enlightenment into constant contradictory and hypocritical rationalisation. As the prevalent mercantilism of the eighteenth century grew, stressing the fact that colonies should benefit the home country by becoming sources of staples, such as sugar, and in return being organised as closed markets for home goods, so did logical problems with the doctrine of civilisation.

The Doctrine of Profit: By the mid-nineteenth century, the prevailing Enlightenment Doctrine of Civilisation began to be replaced or paralleled by the Doctrine of Profit, based upon the rising ideology of Social Darwinism.

Social Darwinism was the mid-nineteenth century adaptation of Charles Darwin's theories of nature's 'survival of the fittest' dictum as applied to European imperialism and its attendant racism. As enunciated by such theorists as Herbert Spencer (1920–1903), it excused imperial exploitation as a natural scientific outcome of the biological 'superiority' of the European races.

Social Darwinism expressed the need for scientific explanations and utilitarian rationales for actions common in the Victorian era. Colonies had to be useful and to pay their way. Profitable exploitation was not only necessary for imperialism to be acceptable to the home taxpayer, but it also reflected the 'Manchester school' values of the rising European industrial entrepreneur.[7] This social class, particularly in Britain, had values at variance with the old landed gentry, who remained supposedly steeped in the values of the Enlightenment. In the British case, the struggle between these two ideological bases of imperialism — the Enlightenment and Social Darwinism — roughly reflects the nineteenth century struggle for political dominance between the industrialist and the landed gentry in English politics.[8]

Social Darwinism penetrated deeply into European 'low' culture, its attitudes, literature and politics. Working class social values were highly influenced by the 'fear' aspects of subsequent racism, reinforcing national chauvinism, pressures for conformity, the assimilation of migrants and 'competitive' racism (the worker racism caused by fear of cheaper labour drawn from other ethnic sources competing for jobs).

Social Darwinist rationales for imperialism were to greatly influence its corollary of racism. Influenced by the 'scientific' writings of nineteenth-century race 'specialists' such as H.S. Chamberlain and the Comte de Gobineau, white imperialism, with its stress on racial hierarchy, was to culminate in the Aryan dementia of Nazism.

The Doctrine of Settlement: A common doctrinal source for imperialism from the sixteenth to the nineteenth centuries was the doctrine of settlement.

The doctrine of settlement has receded as a rationale for Imperialism. In its eighteenth and nineteenth century heyday, however, it rested on a number of requirements:

(a) The need to have an outlet for excess home population. (This was a safety valve against class warfare.)
(b) A large colony of expatriates brought both prosperity and security to empty strategic lands. (This was linked with the policy of mercantilism where colonies existed to provide needed staples for the mother country.)
(c) Settlement by home colonists brought civilisation faster to those lands where native races were numerous.

British imperialism had even developed rationales[9] in law to differentiate the legal rights of both colonists and conquered peoples in various types of imperial ventures.

The notion of *terra nullius*, derived from earlier British colonial experiments in Ireland (particularly the plantations of Northern Ireland), applied to 'savage' lands such as Australia, where no civilisation was held to exist. British law, custom and civilisation, therefore, were held to be dominant, and were transferred *en masse*. Any existing tribes or 'primitive' cultures would have to conform to such law and custom, as they possessed no 'state' or political entity.

On the other hand, native cultures with a recognised state and political structure, such as India, were regarded as being held in trust, where native law could be partially recognised, especially in the remaining tribal or princely states.

Thus various types of British colony appeared.

In the British Imperial cases, the doctrine of settlement was best enunciated by Edward Gibbon Wakefield (1796–1862), with his 1829 plan[10] for colonial settlements paying for themselves by the controlled sale of land. Wakefield argued that land prices should be kept high enough to stop the labouring class from too easily acquiring land. At the same time, they should be kept low enough so that labourers could always see a possibility of becoming landowners. Constant expansion on the frontier would provide more land, and the government revenue from land sales could be used to finance the voyage of more and more labourers from England.

Outlining this self-financing scheme in his book *A Letter from Sydney* in 1829, Wakefield aroused great interest. The British government provided support for the idea since it was cheap and promised to replicate 'New Britannias' in lands such as Australia.

Influential statesmen such as Lord Ripon[11] saw the scheme as vital for creating safety values for the British population, as a source of mercantilist profit, and, especially, as a vital aspect of the doctrine of strategy. Such settlements would replace colonies Britain had lost in the USA. In the coming struggles with European powers and with the USA itself, Ripon was aware that the empire would be held only by home industrial growth; staple producing colonies; and naval power and secure strategical bases for its use. Britain's position as a core or dominant state would depend in the last instance on its geopolitical position.

The Doctrine of Strategy: Of all the rationales for political imperialism, the doctrine of strategy still exerts most pressure on states. Great powers such as the former USSR and the USA in the mid-twentieth century, still undertake political imperialist adventures based upon 'strategy' even though economic imperialism has fundamentally changed and is no longer necessarily a partner of military power.[12]

Geopolitics,[13] or the belief that state power rests upon control of certain geographical points, resources, states and populations, still exert their fascination upon governments. The most recent geopolitical 'doctrine of strategy' theory was the 'domino' theory.

In the 1950–60s, it was believed after the communist takeover of China and North Korea, the rest of Asia would fall like a pack of dominoes to the communists if the West did not intervene. The place chosen to stop the dominoes and communist geopolitical hegemony in Asia was Vietnam, especially during the Second Vietnam War of 1965–75. This indicates the continuing strength of the doctrine of strategy in spurring actions by dominant states involved in the world system's 'balance of power' struggle.

While the doctrine of strategy is an ancient reason for the expansion of state political and military power, the 'New Imperialism' period was the period of its major use.

The quasi-science of geopolitics emerged in the period 1890–1920, under the auspices of Karl Haushofer, a German geographer and nationalist.[14] Geopolitics assigned certain destinies and importance to various nations and geographic points throughout the world, outlining a scenario where states were in eternal struggle for domination of the world. Due to racial, industrial or organisational factors, some states were better equipped in this struggle than others.

Under the doctrine, Germany, for instance, was fated to dominate middle Europe because of its position, population, racial strength and organisation. Britain was fated to dominate nineteenth-century world trade and to be the world's core country, as it controlled India and possessed what Admiral Fisher of the Battle of Jutland (1916) described as the five keys that locked up the world. These 'keys' were Dover, controlling the English channel; Gibraltar, controlling the Mediterranean; Cape Town, controlling the route around Africa; Suez, controlling the Red Sea Route, and Singapore, the key to the Indian Ocean. These bases dominated the middle ocean, the Indian Ocean, across which all trade between Europe and Asia had to travel. If the trade went around South America, it was also controlled by Britain from her base in the Falkland Islands. The world was secured in *Pax Brittanica* by the British Navy.

In geopolitics, the 'middle ocean' was matched strategically by the 'middle land'. This Asian land mass, or 'heartland', was controlled by the Russian Empire. Only Russia could match Britain's control of the Europe/Asia water route by her route across Siberia. According to geopolitics, Russia was bound for greatness. Britain, on the other hand, was fated to decline if her naval power faltered in the Indian Ocean.

Weakened by two world wars and the rising nationalism of her colonies, Britain had retreated by 1972 to her other strategic option, 'Little England'. A new nation filled the core national vacuum abandoned by her. From 1945, the USA became the hegemonic power. Her interpretation of the doctrine of strategy ruled Western military and economic decision making in a different manner, with greater emphasis upon Pacific and Latin American strategic bases and commitments.

Doctrines of strategy remain the major arguments whereby governments can achieve public endorsement for imperialist action as the USSR in Afghanistan (1980–89) and the USA in Vietnam (1961–75).

Economic Doctrines of Imperialism

These doctrines receive far less public support than in their eighteenth and nineteenth-century heydays. Then, economic imperialism was widely held to be beneficial to the home country under various forms of the doctrine of profit. One such doctrine was mercantilism.

Mercantilism was a widely held belief, originating in the seventeenth century, that colonies were important as sources of raw materials and as closed markets for home goods. The power of the home nation, the core, depended upon the number and wealth of its colonial possessions (the periphery). This included both internal regions within the home country (e.g. Wales, Scotland and Ireland in Britain) and outside colonies.

The state would be strongly interventionist[15] in these colonies, banning colonial manufacturing or foreign goods by the use of tariffs, excise, shipping monopolies and taxation policy. Stockpiles of bullion gained from mercantile colonial policies would measure the home nation's wealth and ascendency in the world system.

Immanuel Wallerstein, in his 'world systems' theory,[16] argues that the expansion of Europe from the sixteenth century onwards, triggered European mercantilism. Mercantilism hid the fact that European states, with their ruling élites, were co-opting other classes such as workers and merchants into agreement with imperialist ventures. Workers were subtly subject to social imperialism, or colonised by state élite values. This meant that workers often became some of the strongest supporters of imperialism under the belief that imperialism was beneficial to their standard of living. Merchants saw similar coincidence of their ambitions with the dream of vast imperial markets. Many of them also saw mercantilist protection rather than free trade as the proper policy for governments to follow in order to preserve prosperity and jobs.

Paralleling the end of the long European boom of 1848–76, the 'New Imperialism' was, not surprisingly, matched by an adherence to mercantilist philosophy. Mercantilist protectionism involved imperialists searching for new closed imperial markets which could absorb both spare investment and excess population. In the colonies themselves, merchants and statesmen developed a sub-mercantilism to create strong new nations by import substitution, in countries as diverse as Australia and Latin America. Conservatives also were eager to counter the appeal of socialism with mercantilist prosperity for all classes based upon colonial exploitation.

Criticisms of mercantilism and imperialist ventures quickly emerged from humanist liberals, Marxist socialists and, in the twentieth century, from dependency theorists.

The Liberal Critique: John A. Hobson, 1858–1940

Hobson formulated a critique of Imperialism which he related back to the underlying economic system of capitalism itself. As Heilbroner points out,[17] Hobson suggested in his book *Imperialism* (1902) that capitalism suffered from 'a self imposed dilemma — it constantly oversaved'. Capitalism's pursuit of profit was endless. In increasing such profits, it put constant pressure on wages to diminish as a part of costs. At the same time, labour was pressured to work harder and increase productivity. Production increased, but the ability of home labour to consume this production declined as wages declined or stagnated. Capitalism was therefore faced with the problems of overproduction, oversaving and under-consumption. Instead of investing the savings from profits in home industry, and, by increasing home wages lifting consumption and hence longterm profits and living standards, capitalism saw its way out of the dilemma of oversaving through imperialism.

Imperialism created new markets, new demands, new consumers. But, as Hobson pointed out, it also created new wars, for imperialism was competitive. Indeed, it was an unholy scramble. 'Marx had merely said that capitalism would destroy itself. Hobson suggested that (via imperialism) it might destroy the world.'[18]

The Marxist Critique: V.I. Lenin, 1870–1924

Hobson's economic critique of imperialism was taken up and developed along Marxist lines by Lenin, in his treatise *Imperialism, the Highest Stage of Capitalism* (1915).

Lenin agreed with Hobson that capitalism found its way out of the dilemma of oversaving and profit maintenance by turning to imperialism. Falling profit occurred in the home country due to Hobson's overproductionist and underconsumption tendencies. Lenin pointed out that capitalism turned to monopoly production at home to protect high profits. But this solution was only temporary, as eventually the home market was saturated with products and the various monopolies became big enough to withstand most takeover bids from one another. This was a stalemate. The only way out for capital's insatiable drive for growth and profit was to turn to overseas investment.

Such investment toned down class war in the home country as surplus was extracted from colonies (and quasi-colonies, such as the pre-1956 dependent Republic of Cuba) and transported to the home country, where some of it trickled down to the home country's working class. This class became a world labour aristocracy whose sense of universal class brotherhood was muted by the racism and privilege fomented by the imperialist and racist sentiment, colonial booty and extractions of the metropolitan upper class.

The process of imperialism, however, worked to create revolutions in the colonised countries as well as war between competing imperialist powers. The process was also uneven in its development of the colonies, with some colonies able to develop industry and advanced living standards.[19] This might be due to special relationships with the colonising power, as in the case of the white British dominions of Australia, New Zealand and Canada.

Here, common white racial origins and the doctrine of settlement mitigated the impact of imperialism. Other colonies were reduced to, or maintained at, a Third World economic level, with little political ability to break out of this impasse. An example is the sugar monoculture of the West Indies.

This theory of 'uneven development' argued that revolution would arrive back in the imperialist nations only after the various colonies made their way to independence at their various uneven paces. Local political independence and the nationalisation of firms would eventually curtail the transfer of profits by imperialist monopolies. With the curtailment of this colonial extraction of profits, there would be little left to trickle down to the home country working class, which would become radicalised once more by a fall in living standards and opportunity. Imperialism thus created its own destruction dialectically. All this of course implied that such anti-imperialist countries would opt out of the capitalist world system and join the Soviet bloc. With the collapse of the USSR, this scenario seems dubious as the world system seems to be at a pre-Leninist 1917 situation once again.

This tidy analysis of imperialism was challenged by such writers as Joseph Schumpeter in *Capitalism Socialism and Democracy*, 1950. He argued that imperialism was largely a phenomenon of historical values and emotions, such as collective aggression and fear.

Dependency theorists

Dependency theorists went further, however, and stressed the role of the state rather than economic systems, class and psychology.

They and the related World Systems theorists argued that imperialism had to be understood as a state action. The state might be occupied by powerful élites and dominated by values emanating from powerful sociological groups such as the Junkers in nineteenth-century Germany and the landed gentry in early to mid-nineteenth-century Britain[20] rather than the merchant class. Thus state power and economic power might have different origins and programs.

The state had to survive in a vicious Hobbesian world where there was no rule of law, only force. In such a situation, there was a constant historical ascent and descent of dominant core nations, and varying dependent relationships of weaker periphery nations, the stronger manipulating and influencing the weaker nations' internal class and value systems. This imperial relationship between core and periphery nations was *realpolitik*, the 'politics of reality' based upon amoral power.

In this flux of changing core-periphery relations, no-one could lower their guard. *Realpolitik* made mockery of professed ideologies, causing liberal nations such as Britain to embark on imperialist ventures that struck at the very essence of liberal humanity and equality of opportunity. Similarly, it was a cause of the Stalinist abandonment of socialist experimentation after 1928[21] and the subsequent Soviet stress upon industrialism and Russian state modernisation as the essence of Marxism-Leninism.

These 'reasons of state' occurred either with the co-operation of other classes, e.g. merchants in the capitalist system, or in their absence, e.g. Russian communist imperialism, which had no capitalist rationale.

Western imperialism, in the direct colonial form of the nineteenth century, has now virtually disappeared. In its place a new form of imperialism is said to exist.

Neo-imperialism

Neo-imperialism is held to be a phenomenon that is a result of the arrival of the transnational economic firm in the bipolar political world of the great powers.

According to this analysis, capitalism has transcended the narrow national market and the single state-dominated empires of the nineteenth century. Capital is increasingly international, with conglomerate firms forming with German, English, Japanese, and so on, partnerships. This has been specially aided by the rise of new technology such as satellite communications, container shipping and computerisation, which have speeded up regional and world economies of scale. Secondly, there has been increasing development of trade between 'developed' countries, rather than from 'developed' to 'underdeveloped'.[22]

There have always been transnational companies, such as the Hudson Bay Company and the East India Company. But these were linked to, and protected by, a core nation state. The new transnationals are diversified. They exploit the world's division of labour and often possess bases in several countries, as well as being able to diversify funds in a manner that is beyond the reach of any one state.

States, particularly the small weak peripheral ones, find that the terms of trade for their raw commodity trades have mostly declined. The huge transnational companies can make or break such governments by their buying decisions or investment plans.

The state in this situation often becomes the executive of transnational companies,[23] following free trade policies that benefit the trade plans of the companies. Neo-imperialism is complete when the governing national élite identifies closely with these companies, embracing their cultural and political values. This national élite, together with its comprador merchants, may benefit from such collaboration, even though many others in the nation may be marginalised or even exploited, (see the National Security State, in the chapter on fascism).

In such countries, the identification with neo-imperialist ideas forms the basis of the ruling ideology. The country divides between ruling comprador groups defining themselves in Western cultural and political terms against a pro-socialist group and an even larger nationalist group, dismayed by its puppet government. The revolution which may follow will be basically nationalist. Eventually, however, the revolution seeks the socialist path as the only alternative to the domination of world economies by the transnational companies and as an act of defiance towards the hegemonic neo-imperialist power. This was the recent pattern of historical development in such countries as Cuba and Nicaragua.

Racism

A general definition of racism can be found in this statement by Van der Berghe:

> Racism is any set of beliefs that organic, genetically transmitted differences (whether real or imagined) between human groups are intrinsically, associated with the presence or absence of certain socially relevant abilities or characteristics ... It is not the presence of objective physical differences between groups that creates races, but the social recognition of such differences as socially significant or relevant.[24]

Essentially, therefore, racism is a cultural phenomenon not confined to the period of late nineteenth-century European New Imperialism. Racism can be found in all societies, particularly those in a position of dominance over a 'lesser breed' something usually achieved by conquest. The New Imperialism period from 1870–1914 was, however, unique in that it developed racism into ideology. It was based upon pseudoscientific rationales allegedly derived from anthropology and genetics. The period used a political ideology of racism which could be, and was, translated via channels of law, urban design, etc. into racist practices structuring and condoning imperialist systems of racial hierarchy and privilege. Thus if racism was the ideology, racism became the practice via structures of segregation and discrimination.

The period of European expansion created different types of colonies and racial groups, an uneven structure affecting the forms of ideological racism and the practices adopted. In some colonies, a small number of expatriate Europeans controlled vast numbers of 'natives', as in India. In this type of society, a strictly differentiated structure of conduct evolved, with rigid positioning of 'servants' and 'masters', a situation maintained by the different possibilities for social mobility of the superior/ inferior races; by the use of language to delineate social position; and by the domination of economic and political power by the official ruling strata. In some cases such as South Africa, this ruling strata was, in fact, a large white settler group with few expatriate links. Apartheid was thus a form of internal colonialism.

Minority rule racism means an imperial minority holding down a colonised majority by military force, and also by the constant reinforcement of the majority's self-image of inferiority. 'Natives' were locked into a world where language, law, literature, custom and expectation endlessly reinforced their lowliness.[25] Rebellion was averted largely by their psychological internalisation of the conquerors' view. (Similar theories of the psychological internalisation of 'self-portraits' by the dominated that use the perceptions of the dominant, have been advanced to explain class servility and sexism.)

In some cases (e.g. black Americans), a large minority racial group has existed side by side with the majority white group. In some areas (e.g. the Southern United States), an attempt was made to continue total domination similar to that of the days of slavery, producing many of the aspects of minority rule (or colonising) racism. Black Americans were subjected to discrimination and segregational practices in law, language and custom even after the American Civil War in which the anti-slavery Northerners were victorious. As long as they were willing to conform to these practices and internalise the ruling race's view of their inferiority, few problems emerged. Any deviation, however, was met with violence such as lynching, particularly from lower class whites who felt their position in society threatened by this non-conformity to the rigid order of things.

In other areas without a history of slavery, such as the northern United States, the existence of such a large unassimilable minority group was viewed as a threat to traditional culture, and also to jobs. Like other areas with a fear of Asian or any foreign migration that might threaten the standard of living and wages (e.g. Australia with its Asian 'Yellow Peril' fear) a virulent form of *labour racism* often emerged as part of working class politics. The New Imperialism period was marked by a rise in labour racism linked to exclusivist, or closed, nationalism, which narrowly defined the 'proper' citizen in both cultural and biological terms. In an era when imperialism was creating a labour aristocracy at home and an economic autarchy abroad, such racism was an attempt to preserve the economic privileges of the emerging 'labour aristocracy' at home.

Socialism and democracy were narrowly confined to this working class aristocracy in the core nation. Other non-national workers were excluded biologically or ethnically. Humanity was defined not in the universalist terms of the Enlightenment, but through the pseudo-scientific anthropological and genetic theories of nineteenth century racist ideologies based upon Social Darwinism. *Herrenvolk*[26] or 'master race' societies were a logical extension of this labour aristocracy thinking, even in a liberal democratic context such as Britain. The racist basis of contemporary British National Front politics and European neo-fascism are in many ways residuals of the 'closed' nationalist period of the New Imperialism.

Nineteenth-Century Ideologies of Race

Racist ideologies had largely rationalised themselves prior to the advent of nineteenth-century Social Darwinism, through religious justification. This referred in particular to the Old Testament and the 'children of Ham' (read black people), who were condemned to the 'hewing of wood and the drawing of water'. Similarly, the view was widespread amongst colonising nations that the American Indian belonged to a race that existed before Adam and was not of humankind.[27]

The eighteenth century, under the influence of the Enlightenment, had resorted to a more scientific approach to the question of race, since religious superstition did not suit the ideal type of eighteenth-century rational gentleman.

Eighteenth-century anthropology outlined the monogenic and polygenic theories of mankind. The monogenic theory stressed the common origin of all humankind. The polygenic theory stressed the different origins and species of the separate races.[28] Until then, racism did not have the firm scientific basis and prestige to become acceptable ideology amongst exponents of imperialism who thought of themselves as belonging to the 'high' culture. The various rationales for racism, whether derived from religion or anthropology, were already providing a firm basis for future popular justification for exclusionism. Already, biologism was providing a justification for social theory.

As Greta Jones indicates,[29] the works of Charles Darwin completed this slow historical process of unifying social theory with biologism and providing a scientific rationale for racial domination coinciding with the needs of the age. Darwin himself initiated the idea of 'natural selection' and the 'survival of the fittest' as it related to the animal world in his book *Origin of the Species* (1859). Others, however, created *Social Darwinism*, relating his theories to human society. Racial superiority was regarded as natural. It was 'nature's way of evolving superior man, superior nations and superior races'.[30] Social Darwinism managed above all to salve the conscience of imperialism.

The foremost proponent of Social Darwinism was Herbert Spencer (1820–1903). He outlined a theory of an organic society evolving over time through struggle which killed off the inferior in warfare. Economic competition was another version of struggle, in which the weak fell by the wayside. Nations rose or fell according to the strength of their business or military élite. (In historiography, R. Tawney's 'tired élites' theory of history reflected something of this Social Darwinist position. Nations rose and fell as the ruling élites' strength decayed through self-indulgence.) Thus Social Darwinism could justify not only the New Imperialism but élitist capitalist education and, eventually, the entire class system, on the basis of 'struggle' and 'biologism'.

European racist ideologies such as Arthur de Gobineau's (*Essays on the Inequality of the Human Races*; 1853) and H.S. Chamberlain's (*The Foundations of the Nineteenth Century*, 1911) reflected the Social Darwinism of Spencer. They also dovetailed with the economic liberalism of *laissez-faire* prevalent at the time and the 'organicist' theory of 'closed nationalism', under which all classes were unified in the one living national organism that was struggling with other national organisms to survive in a vicious world. Added to this was the notion of the Aryan origins of European Nordics, the Aryan race allegedly being the source of all Nordics in ancient times. By intermingling with 'lower' Latin or Celtic or Slav races, the Aryans had lost their biological purity and also their mission — to dominate and civilise the world. In Europe, in countries such as Germany, this ideological soup was flavoured by the romantic nationalism of Herder, with its Germanic national 'mission', and the philosophy of Nietzsche which predicted the rise of supermen leading the 'master race' to undreamt-of destinies after the overthrow of the slave religion of Christianity.

As Van Den Berghe writes,[31] racism cannot be accounted for purely as a consequence of slavery, colonialism or as a derivative of an autarchic capitalist system of production. The rise of racist theory was congruent with a number of factors based upon the competitiveness of nationalism and imperialism.

Racism served as a rationale for 'closed' conservative nationalism and as a means of pushing back 'universalist' socialism. At the same time, it offered the workers of the racially superior nation a special psychological position in a hierarchical world. If equality could not be achieved at home, at least superiority over other races was part of the racist 'social contract'.

Racist theory was and is functional as political theory as it restricts the definition of a human being. It justifies democracy for the master race, but guarantees tyranny for 'lesser' races. Injustice is excused and practised towards such 'out' groups, even in basically liberal countries such as Australia and the USA on the basis of biology. Biology and social theory are one, just as they are in the following feminist critique of women's oppression.

Feminism

A definition of feminism reads[32] that '[it is] the advocacy of the rights and equality of women in social, political and economic spheres and a commitment to the fundamental alteration of women's role in society.'

Thus the thrust of feminist ideology has always been in two directions, one emphasising normal civic equality (e.g., 'the right to vote' for women) and another stating that such actions, while useful, are ultimately inadequate. The whole of society 'is permeated by a sexism which structures and maintains the oppression [of women] in psychological and biological terms'.[33]

The ultimate aim of this second, more contemporary form of feminism is 'women's liberation' from social roles which reflect the pervasive dominance of patriarchy, or the domination of the male. Such roles are claimed to be internalised by legions of women, thus creating a second-class, submissive citizen whose mental and spiritual self-castration has led to her existence as a 'Female Eunuch'.[34]

This section will outline feminist arguments, some historical feminism and also some of the contemporary positions within the women's movement.

Contemporary radical feminism seeks to combat the 'biologism' which underlines the basic perspectives of patriarchal society. Patriarchal society, that built around the notions of male dominance and pre-eminence within the family, community structures and power relationships, has argued that 'biological "natural" differences between the sexes are a source of natural inequality'.[35] As in racism, biology and social theory have united to rationalise the dominance of males, and this sexism has penetrated even into the political ideologies of the political spectrum.

While most feminists agree[36] that the ideology of feminism stems from *liberalism* in its insistence on individual liberty and justice, they argue that most liberal political thinkers, including Locke and Rousseau, refused to allow liberal thought to reach its logical extension — its application to the basic assumptions of patriarchal society. With the possible exception of J.S. Mill, most liberal thinkers did not allow liberal thought to extend to and corrode the assumptions of patriarchal society. Mill did regard patriarchy and the political subordination of women as a 'gross violation of liberty and justice', but like all male philosophers, he was limited in extending his logic to attack the very structure of male power in society.[37]

Some non-liberal male ideologues, such as Friedrich Engels in *The Origin of the Family, Private Property and the State*, applied *Marxist materialist analysis* to the position of women in society. Engels attempted to explain women's subordinate position in terms of the evolution of capitalism, surplus value and the disposal of women as property. This materialist argument lies at the basis of the contemporary divisions in radical feminism, between the liberal and the socialist streams of analysis. These analyses agree that the differences between male and female are socially constructed and are the source of women's oppression. The difference lies in the actions to be undertaken to combat this oppression. Should liberal society simply be adapted to include women within the promise of liberalism or should capitalist society be overturned, to free both men and women from economic exploitation and oppressive social roles?

A third contemporary stream of feminist thought, *biologism*, claims the superiority of female sex differences. Women's biologism, the way of life, ethics and attitudes allegedly dictated by biology, is superior to the male, being more loving and tolerant and less aggressive. This woman-centredness[38] argues for the imposition of 'women's values' on the entire world. Such 'essentialism', arguing that gender is the source of morality, would be the source of a moral revolution. Other biologism exponents argue for 'separatism' or a women's way of life that is 'not hostage to the male's approval'.[39] This may extend to radical lesbianism.

All three contemporary streams agree that prior to the post-World War II New Left movement, feminism did not attempt to combat cultural oppression. Instead, it attempted simply to carve out women's position within the dominant ideologies, using a political language that was not uniquely feminist. Consequently, it is argued, the great liberal and social revolutions of the last two centuries have failed, because they did not address the needs of a substantial number of the population. Eventually conservatives have inherited these revolutions and stopped them short of their promise, or reversed them. However, no matter who won, half of the world's population couldn't have cared, as their burdens remained the same whether the patriarchs were liberal or conservative men. The women's revolution is aimed at the very basis of society, its 'given' social roles, and so it will make for fundamental cultural change. Women's liberation presents an irreversible revolution to conservatives. All new revolutions which include a fundamental feminist component will go further than conservatism is able to contain.

Feminism, it is argued, must go beyond the historical 'inclusivist' battle to the 'cultural revolution'. 'Inclusivism' consisted of women's early battle to be included within the ordinary realm of political actors and citizens. While it aimed at the logical extension of democratic rights to women (as to blacks and other minorities), it always had an undertone of cultural bias against women, resting upon the psychological, sexual and other misogynic sources of Western culture. The identification and labelling of these sources had to await the language of late twentieth-century sexism, the extension of political science to include sociology and psychology, and the escape from the Victorian 'illusion of reason'.

Women had to battle against the sexism of historical leaders in political thought whose eminence gave a false sanctity to their sexist references. An example is Edmund Burke's 'A woman is but an animal and not an animal of the highest order.'

The early 'inclusivist' wave of feminist thought and action became a powerful movement in the nineteenth century. Earlier, seminal writers such as Mary Wollstonecraft *Vindication of the Rights of Women* (1791) laid the foundations of nineteenth-century feminist thought which applied the liberalism of both the American and French Revolutions to the position of women and used the liberal language of citizenship and the vote or suffrage.

As Allen points out,[40] however, 'the Victorian women's movement's focus on "inclusivism" through the equal electoral suffrage movement, should not be stressed too far.' This movement encompassed *private sphere feminism*, which rejected the subjection and inequality suffered by women in their domestic situation; and *public sphere feminism*, which refused to accept sex-divided public spheres. *Expediency feminism* simply united the followers of the first two around women's suffrage, as the key to the door of liberation.

Echoes of contemporary feminism can be found in the nineteenth-century rise of *evangelical feminism*, stressing in biologism, women's intrinsic moral superiority, and *socialist feminism*, with its libertarian critique of marriage and sexual relationships.[41]

With the extension of the suffrage to women in the early part of the twentieth century, the radical impulse in feminism tended to decline between 1920–65. Several reasons have been advanced for this decline:

(a) the failure of libertarian socialism, with its stress upon human emancipation due to the rise after 1928 in the USSR of Stalinist Marxism stressing industrial production over human possibility;

(b) the increasingly effective Hollywood role typification of women via movies and mass magazines as family-orientated;

(c)   the rise of 'mumism', depicting the family home as 'the empire of woman' wherein the suburban male and children succumbed to a benevolent despotism. Women's political power was defined as familial and maternal, not social;[42]

(d)   the impact of two world wars, where the socially disturbing after-effects could be avoided by stressing the stability of family life as the major goal for returning soldiers, and for women lately emancipated from traditional roles and ambitions by war factory work or military service.

All these elements led to the overpowering so-called 'feminine mystique'[43] of the 1940s and 50s which Friedan points out was almost total in its limitation of women's options.

Contemporary Feminism:

The New Left movement of the period 1961–75 was based upon opposition to the Vietnam War and, in the USA supported the Black Power movement. The latter stressed the psychological and sociological aspects of oppressive racism. This was particularly important in order to define how racism could exist as an institution in a purportedly liberal society such as the USA.

This mode of analysis was rapidly adopted by the rising feminists, who found that not only were they confronted with a widespread socially accepted 'feminine mystique', which dominated middle class society and was disseminated at every level of the media, but also that they were faced with similar sexism from the males within the so-called 'radical' New Left movement.

It was obvious to many that a real women's movement could only come from women themselves, just as Black Power had come from blacks. It was to be expected that conservative white male society would actively oppose such liberation and radical white male society would trivialise or passively oppose it.

The outcome of rising feminist activism was, as Eisenstein relates,[44] a 'two wave' historical movement. The first wave (or, as Randall calls it, the 'older branch')[45] continued the earlier emphasis upon electoral change. However, allied to this was a central attack upon language; the sexual politics of love which stressed women's subordination, the 'double standard' morality for women forced on them by males, and the social structure of sexism. Anti-sexist community action was undertaken to spread the message of changing one's consciousness within these four areas. This meant the awakening of women to their hidden oppression in language, in love making and throughout the structure of patriarchical society, as well as the 'conscientisation' of males to their inherited and previously unconsidered behaviour to their sisters. Both liberal and socialist feminists, while differing over ultimate aims, stressed the role of rising consciousness against these embedded injustices as central to women's liberation. Socialist feminists in particular operated to correct a critical element in the Marxist model, i.e. the role of women in production.[46] They have pointed to the fact that the struggle of capital against labour has often meant an unjust struggle of labour itself against women, where women have been defined, like 'coloured' labour, as a source of cheap anti-union labour which threatens white male labour. Women were thus boxed in at home or pushed into trivial, usually unskilled jobs that were defined as women's work, in the clothing industry, for instance. So-called 'radical' institutions such as unions have often acted in a most oppressive manner towards women. One of feminists' first jobs was to infiltrate such organisations and raise their consciousness by the constant voting pressure of organised women workers.

The 'second wave' of Eisenstein's model (Randall's 'younger branch') paralleled the older one, but rose to strength in the mid-1970s. They stressed separation. This wave shifted from considering 'gender difference as a source of oppression to one of pride'. The second wave stressed freedom from male domination in a woman-centred ideology where women could be autonomous. Radical lesbianism was the ultimate freedom from patriarchy.

As Eisenstein outlines,[47] this woman-centred ideology or 'metaphysical feminism' divorced feminism both from the socialist and the liberal Left. It therefore opted out of mainstream politics, causing division and confusion within feminist ranks, as the separatists were seen to pursue their own 'sexual apartheid'.

On the other hand, Stacey in *The New Conservative Feminism*,[48] argues that the extremism both of radical separatism and Marxist feminism has led to the emergence of a new 'conservative' feminism, completing feminism's cross-spectrum impact. In the 1980s, Stacey continues to argue, the nuclear family is alive and well. It is not strengthened by equality. Nor has heterosexuality been displaced. Women still feel the pressure of the biological clock, demanding that they reproduce. This 'reproduction' factor will still demand that the social roles of husband/wife/mother/father be performed, something, which can rarely be rejected without damage to the offspring.[49]

The 'nature and nurture' argument underlying radical feminism which stresses the changing of 'nurturing' in order to restructure power relations between the sexes, has now been challenged by the rise of conservative 'nature' arguments linked to the New Conservatism, to the effect that nature demands certain roles of the male and female. These roles cannot be changed.

Nevertheless, the effects of twenty years of feminist consciousness raising and political gains have been widely disseminated in both social consciousness and in institutions throughout the political community. No political ideology today can ignore women's issues in their philosophical frameworks. There is little likelihood of a massive return to a dominant ideology of subservience.

The Green Movement

This movement represents an ecology-based political ideology that stresses the reduction, control or elimination of industrialism. In effect, it argues that the Left/Right political spectrum is battling for control of an industrialism which is itself the real political problem. Industrialism underlying the traditional spectrum is implicitly hierarchical and growth-demanding. Because of this inbuilt hierarchy necessary for production, freedom for the mass is an illusion. The Right produces a capitalist hierarchy and the Left a bureaucratic state one. Revolution is not an answer to the injustice of the industrial system. It produces simply a change of masters. Human emancipation is chained to the chariot of growth. The pursuit of growth will always be chosen at the expense of such emancipation due to the domination of such technocratic values in such an industrial society.

The fundamental disaster awaiting both Left and Right as an outcome of this domination of technocratic culture (nature dominating, machine and science centred), is the destruction of the biosphere. As Bahro points out,[50] this will occur within a hundred years, and the resulting tragedy will not differentiate between regimes of the Left or Right.

What is needed, as Gorz points out,[51] is a new paradigm. This means that, for survival, mankind needs to develop a new approach to the earth based upon 'virtuous simplicity'; alternative modes of technology, energy, work and consumption; and new harmonic social relations based upon social justice. Without this fundamental change in attitude, the earth's delicate ecological system will collapse.

In order to achieve such a turnaround in perspective, the Green movement argues that decision making must be returned to the base of society — to the ordinary people. It must be taken out of the hands of technocratic experts and rich élites who are totally involved in such growth values.

Similarly the work ethic which underlies the growth complex is not wrong, but just distorted. We have been caught in 'work for work's sake', something that fills the void once filled by religion and philosophy (Gorz). We need to question the purpose of work, and its ethical function. This can only occur if workers' power or, more pertinently, citizens' power, is expanded.

History

The Green movement is a direct inheritor of Anarchist thought and goals, and of the single issue social movements dedicated to conservation or anti-nuclear power of the 1950s to the 70s.

The anti-nuclear power movement of the 1950s, the Committee for Nuclear Disarmament, was extremely strong in such countries as Britain, drawing attention to alternative energy and technology and raising the consciousness of citizens concerning the dangers of nuclear power. Despite the Cold War and the accusations that CND was a front for communists, this was one of the few social movements of the time which had tremendous cross-class support in nearly all the European countries where it operated. From these early beginnings, it was obvious that a cross-class radical liberal movement did have a constituency. This existed in most industrialised countries and could be mobilised in the middle of the Cold War, especially around local issues (e.g. river pollution) which were non-ideological.

It was obvious that such an ecologically concerned or radical liberal constituency would not respond to a workerist appeal (i.e. the traditional socialist/Marxist model). They would, however, respond to a transcendentalist or universalist appeal that was non-violent yet still confrontationist. Respectable modes of change were also important, at least in the 1950s.

The impact of the Vietnam War and the student movement of the period saw an upsurge of interest in anarchism and self-management. As Apter pointed out,[52] this was an 'anarchism which wanted liberalism without capitalism'. It saw itself as a third way between state Marxism and capitalism, both of which depended upon a foundation of industrialism.

The oil crisis of the 1970s and the resultant turn to nuclear power revived the anti-nuclear movement, particularly in Europe. Anarchist or self-management groups had already despaired of the workers' movements as forces for change. Not only were workers as committed to economic progress as capitalists, but their élites strengthened the industrially-based state by joining their hierarchy; by pursuing national, not universal interests; and by conniving to substitute consumption for the human emancipation of their followers.

Such anarchist/self management analyses were strengthened by the alternative lifestyle/personal politics movements of the 1960s and 1970s. Ecological harmony in lifestyles and the preservation of natural beauty also became an object of interest to a section of a richer and more mobile middle class which was escaping the basically suburban lifestyles of the 1950s.

A sense of urgency began to prompt the first stirrings in the 1970s of a unified Green movement in Europe as a political force.

This sense of urgency was stimulated by the writings of such men as E.P. Thompson.[53] Thompson felt chilled by the fact that post-industrial society was not in the hands of the feudal lord or even the capitalist; instead, like Veblen, Thompson saw modern society under the control of the cold technocrat. This 'expert' was interested in efficiency and domination of the earth or other firms or nations. Ensconced in the modern state or great bureaucratic capitalist firm, this expert was dedicated to what Thompson called 'exterminism' — the domination of nature and other human beings. Against such a caste of controllers who inhabited both Left and Right societies, it would be necessary to organise a new third force.

Table 7.1

	Dominant Paradigm	**Alternative Economic Paradigm**
Core values	Material (economic growth)	Non-material (self-actualisation)
	Natural environment valued as a resource	Natural environment intrinsically valued
Economy	Domination over nature	Harmony with nature
	Market forces	Public interest
	Risk and reward	Safety
	Differentials	Egalitarian
	Individual self-help	Collective/social provision
Polity	Authoritative structures: experts influential	Participative structures: citizen/worker involvement
	Hierarchical	Non-hierarchical
	Law and order	Liberation
Society	Centralised	Decentralised
	Large-scale	Small-scale
	Associational	Communal
	Ordered	Flexible
Nature	Ample reserves	Earth's resources limited
	Nature hostile/neutral	Nature benign
	Environment controllable	Nature delicately balanced
Knowledge	Confidence in science and technology	Limits to science
	Rationality of means	Rationality of ends
	Separation of fact/value, thought/feeling	Integration of fact/value, thought/feeling

Table 7.2

	ALPHA TECHNOLOGIES (modified)	BETA TECHNOLOGIES ((re-)created)
Food	Reduce trade in food, drop cash crop practices; curtail international agribusiness	Try to restore the old system where the food is grown within the horizon; local autarky
		Patterns of local food preservation and storage
		Collective ground that can be used for food
Clothes	Curtail international textile business	Try to restore patterns of local handicraft for better quality and lasting clothes: symbiosis with food production
Shelter	Curtail international housing business	Try to restore local house building patterns from local materials
	Make houses and habitats less centre-periphery dominated; transfer more work to homes	Collective ground that can be used for housing
Medical care	Better distribution of centres for negative health care; rural clinics; sanitation standards; control of drugs; control of epidemics	Emphasis on life in the beta community as positive health care participation; less distinction between healthy and ill
Schooling	Better distribution of centres for schooling	Emphasis on the community as education, integrating school, work, leisure
Transportation/ Communication	Less centralised, two-way patterns between beta-units; collective means of transport, cars for long distance only	Try to restore patterns of walking, talking — bicycles, wall posters; cars banned inside units; cable TV, local papers
Energy	Better distribution of centres for large-scale energy production	Solar/wind/wave/biogas networks

	ALPHA TECHNOLOGIES (modified)	BETA TECHNOLOGIES ((re-)created)
Defence	Democratised armies, better distribution of commanding positions	Local defence patterns, military (guerrilla groups), non-military (*satyagraha*)
Environment	Recycling, cleaning up technology	Local control and more dependence on smaller economic cycles
Comprehension	Social transparancy, through citizen participation and reporting	Small size units (10^{0-2} and 10^{2-3} for micro and macro units respectively)

This new force should build upon other single issue movements such as CND. It should avoid workerist analyses as too narrow and aim at the universalist citizen; it should combat the dominant paradigm, based upon the creation of material wealth by stating and spreading an alternative paradigm, followed up by political action to enforce these new values. The essence of this Green alternative ideological paradigm can be summed up in Table 7.1.[54]

Political action to achieve much of this new paradigm would take place inside a version of the 'Enabling State' (see Social Democracy chapter).

Here, as J. Galtung indicates[55] an amalgam of Alpha (expertled technologies and political structures) can be paralleled by Beta structures (people-centred and participatory democratic technologies and social organisations). The technocrat can be turned around to aid society, not 'exterminate' it.[56] (See Table 7.2.)

Summary and Criticisms

The Green movement has brought an interesting and timely alternative to the traditional Left/Right industrial-based political spectrum.

The rising support for ecological protection and awareness of the environment has penetrated all mainstream parties in the democracies. The Green vote has taken on a cross-class importance that was preceded by the women's and migrant/racial vote. In some countries such as West Germany a Green Party has arisen which is finding a radical ecological constituency of its own. This may be a peculiarity to West Germany where the radical voice had long been stilled or denied its usual channel (e.g. the Communist Party) due to laws and attitudes peculiar to the West German state and society.

In most other countries, Green ideology is cross-spectrum, although Green parties may be in the process of being launched as Red/Green Coalitions or radical liberal/ecological alternatives with no link with workers' movements. Many Green commentators believe that society is becoming politically triangular rather than the classic Marxist bipolar confrontation of capital versus labor. With the rise of the new public middle class, and the general blurring of the nineteenth century divide between the proletariat and bourgeoisie due to mass culture, consumerism and the control of media by monopolies, the socialist versus capitalist dichotomy is dying.

The new political triangle consists of labor, capital, and the new environmental lobby based largely on the ecologically aware middle class. Neither capital or labor-based parties can win unless they incorporate some of the demands of the ecology group.

This interest group pressure varies, of course, given the level of democracy in each country. National Security States, particularly in the Third World, are renowned for their antagonism to environmental lobbies in their desperate race to industrialise. Such environmental pressures are often regarded by Third World countries as part of the North/South domination inherited from the colonial distortion of the world's wealth during the 16th to 20th centuries. Having achieved high living standards, the North (or developed countries) now have the arrogance to admonish those countries who wish to achieve the same level. But without industrialisation, the Third World will fall into the capitalist debt trap and/or go under with the population explosion.

The Green political answer to this Third World dilemma and intrusion is that the level of debt must be forgiven; the 1st world must transfer huge amounts of wealth and sustainable technology to the Third World on an interest free basis to avoid disaster and the terms of trade must be altered in favour of the Third World. This should be the New International Economic Order.

In the face of the dominant capitalist structure of international finance based on a world system of distortion since the sixteenth century, this Green program[58], to many Third World regimes, is simply utopian. To many Greens, this program also seems utopian. Three trends have appeared in Green politics which have been labelled 'Realos' and 'Fundos' (in Germany) and the Red/Green coalition trend previously mentioned.

The impact of the corporate technocratic state in the West, has seen the interaction and/or co-option of the elite officials of capital and labour organisations around common programs (See corporate state). This process of co-option is also happening to environmental lobby leaders in most of the democratic nations. Thus a consensual program of influence over environmental matters in emerging.

This is part of the process endorsed by the 'Realos'. The 'Fundos' prefer a pure program divorced from compromise politics, based partly on the premise that there is no time for gradualism in the face of ecological disaster. There must be a 'big bang' approach to ecological change and sustainable development. In essence, this continues the 'revolution versus reformism' alternatives of the historical social democratic movement.

Lastly, there is the increasing trend to Red/Green coalition politics. Here the triangular emergence of party politics is taken to be an increasing convergence of democratic socialist groups who have emphasised radical democracy; worker's power and local decision-making over technocratic state socialism (See p. 137) with Greens of a similar social program objective. Such a new alliance falls away from the prevailing notions of elite consensus and capitalist integration. It continues the radical impulse of the French Revolutionary slogans and the dreams of the Great Republic of Equals while coming to grips with the problems of industrialism and a planet in crisis.

All Green movements, because of their radical paradigm face major criticisms. Some of these capitalist and socialist criticisms are:

1   *Eco-fascism*. By what right do Greens intend using the state to hinder the material life of others?
     This is particularly hypocritical if Greens themselves have already achieved middle class affluence but intend cutting others off from reaching this level due to some vague future Armageddon (the capitalist and Third World criticism)

2   *Anti-workerism*: Are Greens in fact aiding the conservative cause by splitting the radical Left vote for aims with which workers cannot identify? Are not Greens taking the bread out of worker's mouths by opposing, on principle, such things as logging and dam building in areas where in fact they may never go? (the Socialist criticism)

The Green response to these criticisms would be to say that the critics have not got the message, that they are locked into the wrong paradigm. As Bahro[59] says with regard to this traditional worker v. capitalist paradigm and their criticisms of the Green's new paradigm:

Q.   [Is this Green paradigm] a much more fundamental project?
Bahro: Yes, more radical. An appeal to human dignity and not to human weakness.
Q.   A project beyond Left and Right?
Bahro: It is the project of another civilisation.

Notes

1. Bullock, A. and Stallybrass, O. (eds) *The Fontana Dictionary of Modern Thought.* London, Fontana, 1977, p. 303.
2. Bullock and Stallybrass, p. 304.
3. Tylecote, A.B. 'German Ascent and British Decline (1870–1890) — The role of upper class structure and values' in Friedman, E. (ed.) *Ascent and Decline in the World System.* Vol. 5, US, Sage, 1984, p. 47; Schumpeter, J. *Capitalism, Socialism and Democracy.* UK Allen and Unwin, 1950.
4. *Development News Digest* March 1977.
5. Gossett, T.F. *Race: The History of an Idea in America.* USA Schocken Press, 1963, pp. 17–32.
6. Gossett, p. 15.
7. Tylecote, pp. 46–48.
8. Ibid.
9. Maddock, K. *Your Land is Our Land.* Australia, Penguin, 1981, pp. 9–32.
10. Phillipp, J. *A Great View of Things.* Melbourne, Nelson, 1971.
11. Ibid.
12. Platt, D. *Past and Present* 'Economic Factors in British Policy during the New Imperialism', Vol. 39, 1965, pp. 120–28.
13. See Bullock and Stallybrass.
14. Ibid.
15. Horrocks, J.W. *A Short History of Mercantilism.* UK, Methuen, 1925, pp. 1–11.
16. Friedman, E. (ed.) *Ascent and Decline in the World System.* US, Sage, 1984, p. 10 and 115–47.
17. Heilbroner, J.R. *The Worldly Philosophers,* Fifth Edition. NY, Simon and Schuster, 1983, pp. 149–53.
18. Ibid.
19. Evans, P. *Dependent Development: The Alliance of Multi-National, State and Local Capital in Brazil.* US, Princeton University Press, 1979.
20. See Tylecote.
21. Callinicos, N. *Is There a Future for Marxism?* UK, Macmillan, 1982, p. 208.
22. Heilbroner, p. 157.
23. Suter, K. 'A New International Order' *Green Leaves* 7, December 1986.
24. Van den Berghe, P. *Race and Racism: A Comparative Perspective.* NY, John Wiley, 1967, p. 11.
25. Fanon, F. *The Wretched of the Earth.* Harmondsworth, Penguin, 1967.
26. Van den Berghe, p. 29.
27. Gossett, T.F., pp. 3–31.
28. Jones, G. *Social Darwinism and English Thought.* UK, Harvester Press, 1980, p. 141.
29. Jones, pp. 10–11.
30. Gossett, p. 145.
31. Van den Berghe, p. 17.
32. Bullock and Stallybrass, p. 231.
33. Ibid.
34. Greer, G. *The Female Eunuch.* London, Macgibbon and Kee, 1970.
35. Clark, L.M. and Lange, L. *The Sexism of Social and Political Theory: Women and Reproduction from Plato to Nietzche.* Toronto, University of Toronto Press, 1979, p. 51.
36. Eisenstein, H. *Contemporary Feminist Thought.* UK, Allen and Unwin, 1984.
37. Okin, S.M. *Women in Western Political Thought.* London, Virago, 1980, p. 230.
38. Eisenstein, pp. 46–47.
39. See Eisenstein.
40. Allen, J. *The Feminism of the Early Women's Movements, 1850–1920* in *Refractory Girl* (Aust.) March, 1979, pp. 10–16.

41. Banks, O. *Faces of Feminism, A Study of Feminism as a Social Movement*. Oxford, Martin Robinson, 1981, p. 7.
42. Conway, R. *The Great Australian Stupor*. Melbourne, Sun Books, 1979.
43. Friedan, B. *The Feminist Mystique*. UK Penguin, 1965, p. 3.
44. See Eisenstein.
45. Randall, V. *Women and Politics*. London, Macmillan, 1982, p. 148.
46. Barratt Brown, M. *Models in Political Economy*. UK, Penguin, 1984, p. 101.
47. Eisenstein, pp. 46–49 and 134.
48. Stacey, J. 'The New Conservative Feminism' *Feminist Studies* 9 (3) Fall 1983, p. 575
49. Stacey, p. 578.
50. Bahro, R. *The Alternative in Eastern Europe*. UK New Left Books, 1979.
51. Gorz, A. *Farewell to the Working Class*. London, Pluto, 1982.
52. Apter, D. and Joll, J. *Anarchism Today* Studies in Comparative Politics. UK Macmillan, 1971, pp. 1–2.
53. Thompson, E.P. (ed.) *Exterminism and the Cold War*. London, Verso, 1982, p. 9.
54. Thompson, p. 16.
55. Galtung, J. 'On the technology of self reliance' *Green Pieces* 3, June 1986, p. 12, 21.
56. Galtung, p. 12.
57. Frankel, B. Offe, C. *Changing the Terms: Green, Post Modern, Social Democratic*. Arena (80) 1987, pp. 115–121.
58. Goldfrank, W.L. (ed.) *The World System of Capitalism: Past and Present*. USA, Sage.
59. Galtung, p. 16.

References

Allen, J. 'The "Feminisms" of the Early Women's Movement 1850–1920' *Refractory Girl*, March 1979, (Aust.), pp. 10–16.
Apter, D. and Joll, J. *Anarchism Today* Studies in Comparative Politics. UK, Macmillan, 1971.
Bahro, R. *The Alternative in Eastern Europe*. UK, New Left Books, 1979.
Banks, O. *Faces of Feminism: A Study of Feminism as a Social Movement*. Oxford, Martin Robinson, 1981.
Barratt Brown, J. *Models in Political Economy*. UK, Penguin, 1984.
Bullock, A. and Stallybrass, O. (eds) *The Fontana Dictionary of Modern Thought*. London, Fontana, 1977.
Callinicos, N. *Is there a future for Marxism*? UK, Macmillan, 1982.
Clark, L.M. and Lange, L. *The Sexism of Social and Political Theory*. Toronto, University of Toronto Press. 1979.
Conway, R. *The Great Australian Stupor*. Melbourne, Sun Books, 1979.
Eisenstein, H. *Contemporary Feminist Thought*. UK Allen and Unwin, 1984.
Evans, P. *Dependent Development: The Alliance of Multi-Nationals, State and Local Capital in Brazil*. US, Princeton Univeristy Press, 1979.
Fanon, F. *The Wretched of the Earth*. UK, Penguin, 1967.
Friedan, B. *The Feminist Mystique*. UK, Penguin, 1965.
Friedman, E. (ed.) *Ascent and Descent in the World System* Vol. 5. US, Sage, 1984.
Gorz, A. *Farewell to the Working Class*. London, Pluto, 1982.
Gossett, R.F. *Race: The History of an Idea in America*. USA, Schocken Press, 1963.
Green Pieces 3, June 1986, Australia.
Green Leaves 7, December 1986, Australia.
Greer, G. *The Female Eunuch*. London, Macgibbon and Kee, 1970.
Frankel, B. Offe, C. *Changing the Terms: Green, Post Modern, Social Democratic*, Arena (80) 1987, pp. 115–121.

Goldfrank, W.L. (ed.) *The World System of Capitalism: Past and Present*. USA, Sage.
Heilbroner, J.R. *The Worldly Philosophers* Fifth Editon. NY, Simon and Schuster, 1983.
Horrocks, J.W. *A Short History of Mercantilism*. UK, Methuen, 1925.
Jones, G. *Social Darwinism and English Thought*. UK, Harvester, 1980.
Maddock, K. *Your Land is Our Land*. Australia, Penguin, 1981.
Okin, S.M. *Women in Western Political Thought*. London, Virago, 1980.
Past and Present Vol. 39, 1965, pp. 120–28.
Philipp, J. *A Great View of Things*. Melbourne, Nelson, 1971.
Randall, V. *Women and Politics*, London, Macmillan, 1982.
Schumpeter, J. *Capitalism, Socialism and Democracy*, UK, Allen and Unwin, 1950.
Stacey, J. 'The New Conservative Feminism' *Feminist Studies* 9. (3) Fall 1983.
Summers, A. *Damned Whores and God's Police*. Australia, Penguin, 1975.
Thompson, E.P. (ed.) *Exterminism and the Cold War*. London, Verso, 1982.
Van den Berghe, P. *Race and Racism: A Comparative Perspective*. NY, John Wiley, 1967.
Zubaida, S. (ed.) *Race and Racialism*. UK, Tavistock, 1970.

Recommended Reading

Imperialism

Friedman, E. (ed.) *Ascent and Decline in the World System*. US, Sage, 1984.
Owen, R. and Sutcliffe, B. (eds.) *Studies in the Theory of Imperialism*. UK, Longman, 1972.
Thornton, A.P. *Doctrines of Imperialism*. NY Wiley, 1965.
Heilbroner, J.R. *The Worldly Philosophers*. NY Simon and Schuster, 1983.

Racism

Zubaida, S. (ed.) *Race and Racialism*. UK, Tavistock, 1970.
Gossett, T.F. *Race: The History of an Idea in America*. US, Schocken Press, 1963.
Van den Berghe, P. *Race and Racism: A Comparative Perspective*. NY, John Wiley, 1967.
Maddock, K. *Your Land is Our Land*. Australia, Penguin, 1981.

Feminism

Eisenstein, H. *Contemporary Feminist Thought*. UK, Allen and Unwin, 1984.
Okin, S.M. *Women in Western Political Thought*. London, Virago, 1980.
Friedan, B. *The Feminist Mystique*. UK, Penguin, 1965.
Summers, A. *Damned Whores and God's Police*. Australia, Penguin, 1975.

Green Movement

Hutton, D. (ed.) *Green Politics in Australia*. Australia, Angus and Robertson, 1987.
Gorz, A. *Farewell to the Working Class*. London, Pluto, 1982.
Barratt Brown, M. *Models in Political Economy*. UK, Penguin, 1984.
Bahro, R. *The Alternative in Eastern Europe*. UK, New Left Books, 1979.

Index

anarchism 3, 13, 99, 118, 128, 174, 195, 199, 207, 234
anarcho/syndicalism 13, 72, 128, 184, 187, 197, 204
anti-Semitism 30, 31
Anzac legend 41
alienation 8, 133, 135, 156, 168, 190, 196, 201, 210
Aryans 31, 39, 228

Benthamism 68, 70, 89, 96, 98, 103, 104, 115
biologism 38, 230
biosphere 234
Bolshevism 31, 38, 122, 165, 174, 185
bourgeoisie 19, 121, 155, 162, 164
bureaucracy 13, 59, 99, 131, 157, 166, 167, 176, 187

Caesarism 27, 88
capitalism 4, 12, 47, 58, 62, 66, 158, 175
Catholic Social Doctrine 70, 74, 127, 186
Centre 1, 13, 182, 188
Chartism 74, 119, 140
Christianity 9, 10, 11, 20, 127, 199, 216
class 26, 38, 155, 156, 160, 173, 196, 215
collectivism 2, 81, 136, 137, 197
colonialism 179, 224
communism 3, 4, 17, 62, 75, 114, 143, 153, 168, 182, 201
consensus 80, 115, 126, 131
conservatism 3, 5, 11, 39, 46, 54, 67, 70, 108, 126, 190
constitution 79, 80, 84, 85, 86
corporate state 26, 32, 97, 99, 125, 128, 131
cooperatives 72, 119, 127

Deakin 40, 42, 69, 102, 105, 106, 138, 182
democracy 6, 8, 12, 79, 82, 97, 167
democratic centralism 166, 184
dependency 68, 96, 105, 108, 137, 139, 182
dialectical materialism 155, 158
dictatorship 5
Divine Right 83, 84
dualism 2
dual labour 71, 99, 126, 207
ecology 3, 116, 133, 134, 206, 234

élite 16, 21, 47, 50, 55, 127, 131, 177, 196, 223
empiricism 50, 119
enabling state 113, 137, 177, 202
Engels, F. 158, 159, 230
enlightenment 4, 116, 133, 206, 234
environment 7, 100
equality (egalitarianism) 83, 102, 126, 136, 180

Fabianism 117, 123, 125, 131, 185
Fascism 3, 16, 18, 23, 57, 59, 82, 108, 186
feminism 3, 12, 100, 229
free trade 70, 126, 132, 140, 145, 210, 224
feudalism 9, 10, 155
Fuehrer 19, 32

general will 87
geopolitics 36, 219, 220
Green movement 7, 13, 133, 184, 206, 234
growth 2, 7, 12, 177, 234

Hegel, G. 19, 32, 35, 40, 158
historical materialism 161
Hitler, A. 29
humanism 11, 34, 49, 61, 81, 84, 126, 157, 199, 216

ideologies 2, 6, 8, 11, 20, 36, 48, 127, 154, 177, 234
imperialism 31, 37, 58, 99, 101, 106, 121, 142, 179, 187, 214
individualism 2, 81, 83, 138, 197
industrialism 1, 7, 48, 99, 116, 119, 134, 181, 189, 196, 234

Jacobinism 87, 90, 114, 115, 118, 164, 165

Keynesianism 37, 56, 59, 94, 98, 101, 108, 117, 125, 143, 172, 187, 207
Kondratieff cycle 146, 171
Kropotkin 202

labour 8, 38, 41, 94, 116, 119, 123, 132, 134, 142, 146, 183, 208
Leninism 88, 114, 121, 153, 165, 166, 169, 174, 184, 206, 222, 224

liberalism 3, 11, 12, 56, 59, 78, 231
libertarianism 57, 59, 62, 69, 70, 81,
    100, 197, 204
Locke, J. 4, 11, 84, 87

Hobhouse 109

Maoism 156, 169, 181
Marx, K. 4, 19, 26, 36, 69, 90, 96, 98,
    108, 117, 157, 158, 196
Master race 30, 31
Mensheviks 165, 174
mercantilism 58, 87, 93, 214, 217, 220
meritocracy 6
militarism 8, 142
multiculturalism 38, 139

nationalism 12, 17, 23, 29, 101, 117,
    123, 214
National Civic Council 74
National Front 36, 38
National Security State 34, 172
natural law 10, 11, 86, 199
Nazism 16, 23, 27, 29
nihilism 30
neo-Fascism 33
neo-imperialism 224
New Left 75, 99, 132, 146, 187, 206,
    210, 230, 232
New Middle Class 72, 91, 100
New Right 33, 49, 56, 67, 91, 109, 128,
    131, 146, 189, 210

oligarchy 6, 131, 167, 174

Pacific Basin 109, 138, 139, 145, 183,
    189, 210
pacifism 25, 204, 209
patriarchy 61, 75, 99, 108, 229, 233
patriotism 23
physiocrat 102
pluralism 132
political spectrum 1, 3, 134, 196, 234
populism 34, 141
Post modernism 173
pragmatism 80, 116, 119, 209
privatisation 71, 74, 98, 129
progress 8, 49, 53, 57, 141, 168
proletariat 120, 121, 122, 156, 162, 164
protectionism 69, 94, 98, 106, 131, 138,
    139

racism 4, 22, 27, 34, 38, 106, 170, 204,
    222, 225
radicalism 5, 60, 79, 86, 105, 130, 165,
    188, 190

radical Right 33, 34, 35, 42
Rainbow Coalition 133
rationalism 19, 48, 50, 79
republicanism 9, 140
Revolution (American) 85–88 (French)
    1, 10, 30, 49, 51, 73, 78, 87, 156, 200
    (Russian) 91
romanticism 17, 21, 23, 29, 55

sexism 232
social contract 32, 37, 40, 50, 54, 57, 69,
    85, 87, 98
socialism 3, 11, 61, 74, 89, 101, 114,
    156, 167, 207
Social Darwinism 17, 20, 31, 32, 37, 62
    126, 162, 196, 216, 217
Social Democracy 56, 74, 91, 93, 114,
    115, 141, 165, 170, 196
Sorelian myth 21, 31, 102, 104, 105,
    118, 120, 138, 154
Soviet Union 23, 63, 167, 206
Stalinism 167, 169, 180, 187, 188, 206
state liberalism 87, 96, 102

technocracy 2, 6, 13, 37, 79, 81, 90, 96,
    99, 115, 118, 123, 133, 166, 176, 180,
    197, 234
theocracy 6
Tory 47, 68
totalitarianism 24, 116, 166
transnational capitalism 100, 126, 127,
    142, 207, 229
trauma theory 107, 141, 185, 188, 209
tripartite state 26, 27, 36, 124, 141

utilitarianism 40, 68, 80, 86, 89, 96,
    123, 209
utopia 49, 80, 115, 117, 120, 125, 130,
    135, 157, 200

vanguard 166, 183

Welfare State 37, 56–57, 61, 69, 71, 81,
    88–91, 115, 124, 131
Whig 47, 51, 56, 81
White Australia 106, 139, 188, 208
workers' control 71, 90, 127, 133, 197,
    202, 204, 209, 234
world systems 175, 221